NH

EUROPE'S MONEY

Problems of European Monetary Co-ordination and Integration

EUROPE'S MONEY

Problems of European Monetary Co-ordination and Integration

Edited by

RAINER S. MASERA
and
ROBERT TRIFFIN

CLARENDON PRESS · OXFORD
1984

Oxford University Press, Walton Street, Oxford OX2 6DP

London New York Toronto
Delhi Bombay Calcutta Madras Karachi
Kuala Lumpur Singapore Hong Kong Tokyo
Nairobi Dar es Salaam Cape Town
Melbourne Auckland

and associated companies in
Beirut Berlin Ibadan Mexico City Nicosia

Oxford is a trade mark of Oxford University Press

Published in the United States
by Oxford University Press, New York

© Centre for European Policy Studies 1984

British Library Cataloguing in Publication Data
Europe's money.
1. Money—European Economic Community
countries
I. Masera, Rainer   II. Triffin, Robert
332.4'566'094   HG930.5
ISBN 0-19-828483-7

Library of Congress Cataloging in Publication Data
Main entry under title:
Europe's money.
Rev. papers from a conference held in Brussels, Dec.
1982, sponsored by Centre for European Policy Studies.
Bibliography: p.
1. Money—European Economic Community countries—
Congresses.   2. Monetary policy—European Economic
Community countries—Congresses.   I. Masera, R. S.
II. Triffin, Robert.   III. Centre for European Policy
Studies. (Louvain-la-Neuve, Belgium)
HG930.5.E8694   1984   332.4'566'094   84-16575
ISBN 0-19-828483-7

Typeset by Joshua Associates, Oxford
Printed in Great Britain by
The Alden Press, Oxford

Preface

The present book has its origins in a conference entitled 'Western European Priorities', which the Centre for European Policy Studies organized in Brussels as its inaugural event in December 1982. Oxford University Press are also publishing two other books based on the conference: M. Emerson (ed.), *Europe's Stagflation* and A. Jacquemin (ed.), *European Industry: Public Policy and Corporate Strategy*. We hope that together these books will constitute a significant contribution to the discussion of central questions of public policy at a European level, complementing and reinforcing the contributions that the Centre has already begun to make through the *CEPS Papers*.

Although based on the conference, essays in the present book have been updated to take account of more recent events, and in one or two cases heavily revised. Rainer Masera has also contributed an introduction which explains the scope and purpose of the volume. The end-product is, therefore, more than just a collection of contributions to a conference, I should like to take this opportunity to acknowledge the work that Rainer Masera and Robert Triffin have done in moulding the present volume.

Neither the contributions of the authors nor the efforts of the editors would have materialized at all, however, had it not been for a grant from the Ford Foundation, which in this way, as in others, provided support to a new centre when it was most needed. It is therefore, finally, a particular pleasure to thank the President of the Ford Foundation and his staff for their help.

Centre for European Policy Studies,   PETER LUDLOW
Brussels, 1984.

Contents

List of Figures

List of Tables

Notes on Contributors

Willem H. Buiter is Cassel Professor of Economics (with special reference to money and banking) at the London School of Economics, a member of the Macroeconomic Policy Group of the Centre for European Policy Studies, a research associate of the National Bureau of Economic Research (Cambridge, Mass.), and Director of the programme in international macroeconomics at the Centre for Economic Policy Research, London.

Herman-Josef Dudler is director of the Money, Credit, and Capital Market Division of the Research Department of the Deutsche Bundesbank. His past positions include head of the Monetary and Fiscal Policy Division in the Economics and Statistics Department of the Organization for Economic Co-operation and Development, visiting economist with the International Monetary Fund, economist in the Money and Credit Department of the Federal Republic of Germany's Economics Ministry and assistant professor of money and banking at Cologne University.

Charles Goodhart is Chief Adviser at the Bank of England, where he has worked since 1969. His former positions include lecturer in monetary economics at the London School of Economics, economic adviser in the UK Department of Economic Affairs, and assistant lecturer at Cambridge University.

Rainer S. Masera heads the Research Department of the Banca D'Italia, which he joined in 1975, and is a member of the Group of Deputies of the Group of Ten. From 1977 to 1981 he was an alternate member of the Monetary Committee of the European Communities. He was an economist at the Bank for International Settlements from 1971 to 1975, and has also taught finance at the Istituto Universitario di Bergamo, and monetary economics at the University of Rome.

Tommaso Padoa-Schioppa is Deputy Director General of the Banca d'Italia, a member of the Group of Thirty, and a member of the Executive Committee and the Council for the Centre for European Policy Studies. From 1979 to 1983 he was Director-General for Economic and Financial Affairs at the Commission of the European Communities.

Francesco Papadia is head of the Financial Flows Division of the Research Department of the Banca d'Italia, where he previously worked as an economist. Between 1980 and 1983 he held the post of Economic Adviser in the Directorate-General for Economic and Financial Affairs of the Commission of the European Communities.

Niels Thygesen has been Professor of Economics at the University of Copenhagen since 1971 and has served as adviser to Denmark's National Bank since 1972. He is also a senior fellow of the Centre for European Policy Studies and a member of its Council. His previous positions include head of the Monetary Division of the Organization for Economic Co-operation and Development, and consultant to the Commission of the European Communities.

Robert Triffin is Professor Emeritus at Yale University, guest professor at the University of Louvain-la-Neuve, a senior fellow and a Council member of the Centre for European Policy Studies, and a consultant to the European Communities. He is also best known for his proposals for world monetary reform and regional monetary integration in Europe (where he was the main architect and negotiator of the European Payments Union), but he has also served on the United Nations Economic Commissions for Latin America, Asia and the Far East, and Africa. His monetary reforms in Latin America were widely imitated, and he continues to be consulted in this field by governments and central banks throughout the world. Author of numerous titles, Professor Triffin's noteworthy academic reputation began with his first book, *Monopolistic Competition and General Equilibrium Theory*.

Unless otherwise indicated, the views expressed in these chapters are attributable only to the authors in a personal capacity and not to any institution.

Introduction

RAINER S. MASERA AND ROBERT TRIFFIN

The chapters in this book are updated versions of the papers presented to the Monetary Affairs Group at the opening conference of the Centre for European Policy Studies (CEPS) in December 1982, on the 'Problems of European Monetary Co-ordination and Integration'.[1]

The economic and political difficulties hindering progress towards the institutional phase of the European Monetary System (EMS) suggested taking a fresh look at some fundamental issues related to the process of European monetary and exchange rate co-ordination, rather than concentrating directly on specific topics of the European monetary agenda. Thus some leading European monetary experts, from the academic world as well as from official institutions, were asked to look into what they regarded as the constraints on, and the prospects for, monetary policy and monetary co-operation in the 1980s. As it turned out, all the chapters draw attention to the monetary and fiscal policy mix as a key explanatory factor in the context of high and variable inflation.

This introduction highlights the common thread running through the different arguments and analytic presentations, by reviewing the chapters and then by drawing some general conclusions.

Part I: Global and regional perspectives: the case for the EMS

The book is opened by Robert Triffin's critical analysis of the internationally uncontrolled, flexible exchange-rate regime in force since 1971, and advocacy of the second-best virtues of the EMS.

Triffin's perceptions of the weakness of the Bretton Woods system and of the potential of European currency unification has contributed very significantly to both academic analysis and official recognition of the issues involved. A major theme in his chapter is that European monetary integration can only be assessed as part of the evolution of the international monetary system. In the 1960s there were no special European monetary arrangements because the existing international monetary system—despite incipient signs of strain—was considered adequate for the internal needs of the Communities. The gradual dissolution of the global framework, initially through wider margins of fluctuation and subsequently through the individual floating of most of the major currencies, prompted the European responses of joint floating in 1972 and the more elaborate framework of the EMS in 1978/9.

Triffin's chapter starts by showing how the 'managed' floating regime has led to an unparalleled inflation of world monetary aggregates, considered to be the primary cause of the world recession of the late 1970s and early 1980s. The lack of international co-operation by national governments has meant, moreover, that international investment patterns have been seriously distorted, with the private commercial system providing the main source of finance, and flowing at times in misguided directions. Resources should in principle be transferred from the richer and more capitalized to the poorer and less capitalized countries of the world. The chapter strongly denounces the inflationary proclivities of the system and the economic absurdity of net capital flows from poorer and less adequately capitalized countries to richer and more highly capitalized countries, especially the United States.

The volatility of exchange rates is documented and shown to have been a powerful brake on investment and GNP. The weakening of the US dollar from 1967 to 1979 is explained by the huge capital outflows from the United States, made possible and financed by the use of paper dollars as the international reserves for central and commercial banks. Since 1979, higher returns on dollar assets have been associated with net inflows and appreciation of the dollar.

Triffin cannot see the dollar standard having a rosy future in the long run for two main reasons. One is the dangerous level of US gross liabilities, which imply an inflationary threat because they act as high-powered reserves for foreign central and commercial banks. On the other hand, their counterpart consists largely of gross claims by private US banks on high-risk sovereign debtors. The second reason is the tendency for the US current account to develop enormous deficits in consequence of the dollar's overvaluation. The short-run strength of the dollar is due to reversible capital inflows resulting from high interest rates and political fears, both of which should not, it is hoped, persist in the future.

The case is therefore made for resuming negotiations for the development of a world monetary system filling the vacuum created by the Second Amendment to the International Monetary Fund (IMF) Articles of Agreement. The role of the Special Drawing Right (SDR) should be increased radically, while extra resources from the world institutions should be directed towards investments that break inflationary bottle-necks and help countries adjust to their balance-of-payments constraints. But Triffin remains pessimistic on this score because of the alleged short-sightedness of the present US administration. He therefore recommends regional reforms along the lines of the EMS. The hope is that the success of regional co-operation will stimulate the US to imitate it. However, Triffin ascribes part of the success of the EMS to date to fortuitous external circumstances (a strong dollar), rather than to the inherent merits of the system. Recurring tensions in exchange rates between stronger (such as the Deutschmark) and weaker (such as the Italian lira and the French franc) currencies demonstrate the shortcomings of the EMS.

The chapter ends with suggestions for a number of reforms: in particular the promotion of the European Currency Unit (ECU) as an alternative to Eurocurrencies by reducing the costs of its usage. The strengthening of the EMS is considered to be both an essential safeguard for Europe against the vagaries of today's unreformed *world* monetary system (or non-system?) and a demonstration of the feasibility and advantages of its fundamental reform, long advocated by the IMF, the Group of Ten, the Committee of Twenty, etc.

Triffin concludes that the ultimate aim should remain the restoration of a world monetary system. But this should be a decentralized one that would exploit the opportunities for mutually advantageous policies and negotiable commitments that can be ironed out at the regional level, reserving for the IMF the looser co-operation and agreements necessary and feasible at the world level.

Part II: Financial innovations and structural changes

The general perspective on the indissoluble links between the EMS and the international monetary system provided by Triffin is followed by two chapters which address the broad question of financial innovation, structural change, and the attendant impact on monetary policies. The first—by T. Padoa Schioppa and F. Papadia—looks at this question from an international point of view and ties in with Triffin's contribution. Its principal aim is to provide a theoretical analysis and empirical description of the issue of currency substitution in a world with high and variable inflation.

The chapter begins with a presentation of cross-sectional evidence on the relationship between levels of inflation and the quality of currencies, using rank-correlation techniques. The authors argue that inflation is a suitable proxy for quality (measured either as the variability of actual or unexpected inflation, interest rates, or exchange rates). Similar evidence is presented for currency use for trade, private portfolios, and international reserves. They conclude that currency use depends on quality (excepting the behaviour of the central banks of the industrial countries). The stability of real variables (real exchange rates, price

4EUROPE'S MONEY

dispersion, real interest rates) is also correlated with the level of inflation (and therefore monetary variables), implying scope for policy. To
interpret their evidence, the authors survey and develop the literature
on seigniorage, the inflation tax, and the real costs of inflation in the
context of currency substitution. They show, in particular, that
increases in the price (interest rates) of a currency and a lowering of its
quality will cause substitution towards other currencies.

On the supply side, they consider an oligopolistic paradigm describing central banks as producers of currency, engaged in quality and
price competition. An important policy conclusion reached is that
'unstable' monetary policies cause currency substitution away from
a currency, thus eroding the basis for necessary counter-cyclical policy.
With direct capital controls, this process will take longer. The potential
instability of oligopoly with regard to central banks suggests a need for
international co-operation and the allocation of sufficient resources
to, say, the IMF, to achieve stability. The authors conclude that
resources now available are not adequate to fulfil this task.

The issue of financial innovations and structural changes in banking
systems and the determination of the stock of money can also be
addressed from a different and essentially domestic point of view. This
is the line taken by Charles Goodhart in his chapter. He shows how the
monetary system process has been subject to extensive structural
change over the last ten years of high inflation. This is attributed to
the synergy of three main interrelated factors: (i) high, variable, and
unpredictable inflation and nominal interest rates; (ii) pressures for
deregulation; and (iii) rapid technological progress, notably facilitating
the flow, retrieval, and analysis of information.

These three changes have increased the degree of 'endogeneity' of
the private financial system and correspondingly reduced the extent to
which the monetary authorities can *directly* control monetary aggregates.

So long as the liabilities of the central bank continue to form the
monetary base of the system, the authorities can still, however, maintain their influence over short-term interest rates, with subsequent
effects on exchange rates, inflation, output, and therefore the demand
for and supply of bank deposits and credit, which provides an indirect
channel of control. The LM curve becomes steeper and more variable.

These changes have occurred most notably in the countries which
experienced relatively high inflation and which felt the tensions arising
from the coexistence of regulated interest rates and fluctuating free
market rates, in the context of a move towards financial deregulation,
e.g. the US and UK.

Goodhart's chapter also touches on the implications of these changes
for international banking and discusses the risk of imprudence as the
wholesale banking business spreads into the international area. Increased

international liquidity was accompanied by increased 'exposure' of bank capital. International co-operation is therefore essential. Banks subject to laxer regulations are able to capture a large share of the market because they are more 'competitive'. A 'house-of-cards' collapse can then be initiated by the bankruptcy of such less prudent banks from these countries, which can also involve those countries that have more prudently required their banks to maintain greater capital 'adequacy'.

Part III: Fiscal constraints on monetary co-ordination

The need for co-ordination in macroeconomic policy management and the constraints on the pursuit of effective monetary policies are also the main themes of the two following chapters by Buiter and Masera. But the emphasis in these chapters is on the interactions between fiscal and monetary policy, given the budgetary constraints. Both chapters argue that fiscal deficits and their impact on the real economy must be assessed with great attention in periods of high inflation.

The importance of Buiter's chapter lies in its careful setting out of the prerequisites of a coherent stabilization policy—which comprises fiscal, financial, and monetary policy. Without a proper analytical, and empirical understanding of these issues, the preliminary question of policy co-ordination among EMS countries would obviously remain unsolved.

The chapter addresses the theoretical shortcomings of accounting analysis for the government sector. The conventional method of measuring the public sector deficit does not correctly reflect the change in a government's net wealth. As a consequence, government policy that pursues a target deficit unwittingly misconstrues the net effect on the private and overseas sectors, and therefore causes their consumption paths to deviate from the optimal ones. The most important inadequacies arise because of the failure to account for capital gains/losses on nominal debt due to inflation and exchange rate changes, and for the effects of cyclical fluctuations in output. These are automatic de-stabilizers which will exacerbate the cycle. By properly measuring the deficit, the government will realize its true effect on net wealth and will be able to design its policy to try to achieve the permanent (optimal) consumption path. However, conventional accounting measures are also necessary because they reflect constraints, such as capital-market imperfections, that prevent the private sector from obtaining its optimal consumption. Taxes and transfers should be designed as automatic stabilizers to smooth out consumption.

Masera's chapter also focuses on some key features which are often neglected in traditional presentations of both Keynesian and monetarist models: i.e. the public sector's budget constraint—in nominal as well as in real terms—and the need to consider the wealth effects connected with the changes in stocks of assets at constant prices. However, while Buiter concentrates on the analysis of public and private sector accounts, Masera takes the general evolution of economic theory as a basis for re-examination of some of the simplifying hypotheses implicitly introduced in both Keynesian and monetarist models. Moreover the author draws attention to the rigidities which hamper adjustment in the various markets summarizing the economy. This constitutes an attempt to combine the lessons to be drawn from economic theory with 'practical' policy constraints.

Data are presented showing the importance of the inflation tax in Italy in the 1970s. This tax on financial wealth acted as a means of reducing real disposable income and ultimately the total real wage bill at a time of wage push and a very high degree of indexation of nominal wages to prices. Attention is drawn to the implications for the effectiveness—or rather ineffectiveness—of exchange-rate depreciation. It is also shown that as inflation has gradually come to be anticipated, the yield from the inflation tax has fallen drastically because of the rise in interest rates required by the household sector.

Significant links do exist between monetary and fiscal action. However, the chapter warns against some extreme views advanced in the literature, namely that bond financing of the deficit is more expansionary than monetary-base financing and that fiscal parameters determine the long-term growth rate of the monetary base. These arguments crucially depend on the assumption that outlays for interest are not matched by any form of revenue, in contrast with other forms of expenditure. This hypothesis is implicitly made when interest-rate payments are singled out as an expenditure item in the budget restraint.

Finally, the chapter contends that if the determination of prices and real variables cannot in reality be dichotomized, restrictive policy measures to eradicate inflation should not be based exclusively on the control of monetary aggregates and credit to the private sector. The real costs of monetary adjustment would be minimized if coherent policy actions were taken in other fields, notably in the procedures of budget deficit formation and in wage-indexation mechanisms.

Part IV: The EMS in practice

The final part of the book is devoted to a more direct and specific analysis of the practical problems encountered in the process of European monetary integration. Dudler's and Thygesen's chapters focus on the workings of the EMS and provide a descriptive and analytical assessment of the process of monetary and exchange-rate co-ordination in Europe.

Dudler's chapter discusses the long-standing issues of European monetary integration by juxtaposing individual countries' national preferences and the basic attitudes of their monetary authorities against Community initiatives and concerns. This 'political economy' approach starts from an historical description of the evolution of the idea of European monetary integration. A distinction is drawn between two lines of thought; the first is that monetary co-operation and stable exchange rates are *necessary* for the healthy development of the EC; the second is that monetary and exchange-rate stability are natural *outcomes* of the development of the customs union. A brief account is given of individual member countries' preferences in this debate, with differences of opinion seeming to depend on the relative size of the particular country. Dudler then explains the roles and responsibilities of various EC committees with regard to monetary policy co-ordination and concludes that while the apparatus is adequate, the will to co-ordinate is lacking. The choice of instruments and intermediate objectives is shown to be wide and varied. This is due to the specificity of financial infrastructures and to differences of opinion about the monetary transmission mechanism. Again, the relative size of countries seems to matter.

Dudler's view is that mechanisms for symmetric monetary response will only become a reality when a sufficient degree of financial integration is reached and when inflation targets become uniform. Until then, the concept of an 'EC money stock' will be irrelevant. In addition he stresses, as did Masera, that the viability of the EMS depends on a degree of consistency in budgetary and income policies. The author soberly concludes that the EMS has provided the benefits of temporarily 'fixed' exchange rates, but has not taken the EC much closer to full monetary union.

In the last chapter of the book, Thygesen takes a more optimistic line in assessing the EMS experience and its prospects. The chapter reviews the constraining impact of the EMS under three headings: (1) the use of exchange-rate adjustments, (2) co-ordination of domestic monetary policies and the changing role of monetary targets, and (3) the contribution of monetary and exchange-rate policy to economic convergence. Thygesen argues that the yardstick for assessing the performance of the EMS is not full monetary union but rather the likely scenario of events had the EMS not existed, leaving member countries to manage their currencies individually. In this respect he feels that the influence has been of far more importance than usually suggested.

The performance of the EMS economies has been significantly affected by the additional constraint of the greater stability of intra-

EMS exchange rates compared with the volatility of exchange-rate relationships with major third currencies (the US dollar, sterling, and the yen). The element of joint decision-making in this important area is not in doubt. It appears to have been a factor in reducing the real-wage rigidity that was a firmly entrenched feature of a number of European economies in the pre-EMS period.

In some respects the external environment has been more conducive to cohesiveness among the EMS economies than was anticipated at the launching of the system in 1979. The most important factor has been the unanticipated strength of the US dollar; after all, the EMS was conceived as a response to the expectation of a persistently weak dollar. The participating countries badly needed an improvement in their competitiveness *vis-à-vis* the United States after the large dollar depreciation of 1977-8. It was not expected that a main task would be to defend the EMS currencies against the reverse problem of an excessive dollar appreciation, and that the currency of the strongest EMS economy, the Federal Republic, would become cyclically so weak at times as to be sustained by the EMS commitments. Seen in this light, the relative cohesiveness of the EMS should not lead to complacency and a refusal to reinforce the structure by a combination of institutional steps and tighter policy co-ordination. In this respect Thygesen stresses that, while monetary policies have been reasonably co-ordinated, fiscal and other demand-management policies have continued to diverge. However, strong doubts can be entertained about the possibility of controlling inflation solely through monetary action at times of rapid growth of government debt and given today's high debt/income ratios.

In Thygesen's view, the EMS experience up to late 1982 indicates that the external constraint has not made national monetary or credit aggregates more difficult to achieve. He therefore attributes the *de facto* suspension of targeting in the EMS countries in 1983 to two inter-related reasons: the failure of real interest rates to come down in conditions of low activity and some countries' perception of the potential risks involved in insisting on strict money control at a time of rapidly expanding public-sector deficits. The high proportion of bond financing can be maintained only through rising interest rates, which would add to the deficit. On balance he argues that there would be no advantage in the EMS countries moving towards nominal income targeting and concludes by warning against the risks of the large monetary expansion of 1983. On the other hand, he argues that instability of velocity due to financial innovation—while important in the United States and the United Kingdom—is not found in the countries taking part in the European exchange-rate agreements on a scale that would disqualify monetary targeting as a viable medium-term monetary strategy.

General conclusions

We come finally to our general and personal conclusions, based on the various arguments presented in the essays contained in this book. It is our conviction that progress towards exchange-rate stability and monetary discipline among European countries requires *concurrent action in three main areas.*

To start with, reaffirmation of the political and economic will to move towards European monetary integration must be made through *the creation of an independent European monetary institution,* entrusted with the task of issuing high-powered ECUs. Fundamental changes in present policies and institutional frameworks would be required. The *European Monetary Fund*—which might be rechristened the *European Federal Bank*—would be based on the issue of ECUs. This would imply that the ECU would no longer be defined as a basket of currencies, but would acquire an independent status. Guarantees should obviously be introduced to guard against inflationary abuses of its issue. Specifically, this would imply: (i) cutting the automatic link (under current rules of operation) between gold prices and ECU creation; and (ii) setting a presumptive quantitative (percentage) ceiling on the overall growth of ECUs, which might indeed represent a reference point for the setting of nominal monetary growth aggregates in the EC.

This change in the nature and operation of the ECU would, in our view, be consistent with the move towards overall reform of the international monetary system. Here, along analogous lines, the IMF would be fully based on the SDR, rather than on present quota arrangements. The IMF would also be entrusted with more direct powers in the surveillance of exchange rates among major currencies (the ECU, the yen, and, of course, the dollar) and of the process of international liquidity creation in the Euro-markets.

The operation of this central European monetary institution would have to be accompanied by control of European monetary and/or credit targets, due account being taken of the impact of financial innovation. A uniform approach to financial supervision and regulation would also be highly desirable.

The second, and equally crucial, area of action is that of *structural adjustments in budgets.* This specifically implies co-ordination of fiscal parameters with a view to each EC country achieving budgetary equilibrium at low rates of inflation and at sustainable or 'natural' rates of unemployment. Here it should be observed that budgetary equilibrium need not require balanced budgets. In a growing economy small deficits can be sustained and are indeed consistent with the economy's need for growing real financial balances. In particular, countries should aim at reducing the direct and indirect inflationary taxation of government debt to a low (in principle, zero) common denominator. This gradual effort, which would require very different adjustments in the various EC countries, might be supplemented by the creation of a central fiscal authority at EC level, which would ensure the provision of certain services/transfers. These would be taken away from the national domain, as suggested for instance in the well-known McDougall Report.[2]

The third and final point is that these efforts towards monetary and fiscal harmonization should be supplemented by *the reform in some EC countries of certain institutional arrangements* which impinge on the nature of the trade-off between output and inflation stabilization. Indexation mechanisms, both for wages and financial assets are a primary example.

This overall blueprint for action and for further research and analysis may appear ambitious and far-fetched. The very fact that we argue that the EMS experiment cannot be written off as a failure, but instead must be viewed as a partial success, might induce a certain complacency. This, we believe, would be a fatal mistake. The process of European monetary integration is now at a crossroads and is unstable. Either sufficient determination and long-term wisdom manifest themselves in the near future, implying progress along the lines suggested above, or the whole concept of European integration, not only in the monetary field, might suffer serious setbacks.

Notes and sources

[1] This conference followed from previous international seminars on 'European Economic and Monetary Union' organized by Robert Triffin, under a grant from the Ford Foundation, at Louvain-la-Neuve, Geneva, and Copenhagen, 1979–81. The proceedings of these seminars were published under his editorship as:

(i) *EMS: The Emerging European Monetary System*, National Bank of Belgium, Brussels, April 1979;
(ii) 'The European Monetary Fund: Internal Planning and External Relations', with an introduction by Alexander K. Swoboda, *Banca Nazionale del Lavoro Quarterly Review*, Rome, September 1980;
(iii) *The Private Use of the ECU*, with André A. L. Swings as co-editor, Kredietbank, Brussels, 1980;
(iv) 'The European Monetary System: The First Two Years', with an introduction by Neils Thygesen, *Banca Nazionale del Lavoro Quarterly Review*, Rome, September 1981.

[2] Donald McDougall *et al.*, *Report of the Study Group on the Role of Public Finance in European Integration*, Commission of the European Communities, Brussels, 1977.

PART I

GLOBAL AND REGIONAL PERSPECTIVES: THE CASE FOR THE EMS

/3 - 76

4313
4320
US,, global

I

How to End the World 'Infession': Crisis Management or Fundamental Reforms?

ROBERT TRIFFIN*

Synopsis

The economic and political consequences of the acceptance of any 'national' reserve currency as a parallel 'world' currency nearly inevitably lead, sooner or later, to the collapse of such a system. In September 1931, they led to the collapse of the inter-war gold-exchange standard, anchored mostly on the pound, and to the long depression of the 1930s. Similarly, forty years later they led to the collapse of the post-war gold-exchange standard, anchored overwhelmingly on the dollar, and to the unholy combination of inflation and recession better described as 'infession' (i.e. inflation followed by recession rather than 'stagflation', which calls to mind a mere stagnation followed by inflation).

The present world inflation—as distinct from national inflations—has its roots outside the monetary field. But it could not have reached such fantastic proportions if world reserves—measured at constant gold prices and exchange rates—had not been *more than quadrupled since 1969* by the acceptance of paper claims on the United States, financing at first huge and persistent US losses of net reserves by the major reserve-centre country of what has become primarily a *'paper-dollar standard'*. This flooding of the official world reserve pool has made possible, and has been compounded by, so-called Euro-bank and Euro-bond credits, which eased—through further inflation—the re-cycling of petro-dollar balance-of-payments disequilibria following two successive oil shocks.

The floating of gold prices and exchange rates has imparted further instability to world reserves measured in dollars at market prices: *a multiplication by twelve* from December 1969 to September 1980, followed by a *33% decline* over the short span of 2¼ years to December 1982.

* Yale University, the University of Louvain-la-Neuve, and the Centre for European Policy Studies.

Net US capital exports by non-banks, averaging nearly $8 billion*
per year over the period 1970-8, explain the huge depreciation of the
dollar *vis-à-vis* the strongest currencies—such as the Deutschmark and
the Swiss franc—over this period, but were overfinanced by a huge
accumulation of foreign dollar debt by the US money market. This
accumulation enabled foreign countries to moderate, in the following
years, through market interventions, a steep recovery of the dollar
exchange rate prompted by reverse capital flows (from non-banks)
towards the US, averaging $38 billion a year in 1979-82, and peaking
at $68 billion a year in 1982.

This is untenable both for the rest of the world—faced with
illiquidity, if not insolvency for several countries—and for the US
itself, where the overvaluation of the dollar is leading to unprecedented
merchandise deficits. They reached $36 billion in 1982 and were offi-
cially expected to reach or exceed $100 billion in 1984.

These economic consequences of such a world monetary 'system'(?),
as well as political disagreements regarding the foreign policies that
it finances, make its long-run survival undesirable and—let us hope!
—unlikely. Fundamental reforms are as indispensable today to *end*
the world 'infession' as they were more than two decades ago, when
I vainly argued before the Joint Economic Committee of the US
Congress that they were indispensable to *avoid* it.

Yet a world-wide agreement on such reforms is still generally deemed
unnegotiable today. Its negotiability might be accelerated by regional
agreements negotiable among various groups of like-minded countries
to palliate, as far as possible, the consequences of the present world
disorder. Any early strengthening of the ECU-based EMS should be
accepted by its members as necessary to meet forthcoming exchange
crises of the dollar *vis-à-vis* the D-mark, and to make European interest
rates less dependent on the wide fluctuations of US interest rates.
A successful ECU might attract into its orbit other countries in Western
Europe, the Middle East, Africa, and even the Communist world, whose
trade relations are primarily Europe-oriented. Other countries in Asia
and the Western hemisphere will have to pay heed to their trade relations with Japan and the United States as well as with Western Europe.

The ultimate aim should remain the restoration of a world monetary
system, but a highly decentralized one, exploiting to the fullest the
opportunities for mutually advantageous policies and negotiable commitments that can be ironed out at the regional level, and reserving
for the IMF only the looser co-operation and agreements necessary and
feasible at the world level.

---

* 1 billion = 1,000 million throughout the book.

TABLE 1.A
World monetary reserve assets, by sources: 1969-82

	End of					
	1969	1972	1979	1980	1981	1982
At stable official rates (SDR billions)	79	147	274	319	347	336
Foreign exchange	34	96	213	254	273	257
SDR and IMF transactions	4	10	21	25	34	40
World gold	41	41	40	40	40	40
Impact of fluctuations in gold prices and exchange rates	–	40	570	657	453	470
Total ($ billions)	79	188	844	976	800	807

Yearly growth rates: %	1972/ 1969	1979/ 1972	1980	1981	1982
At stable prices	17	9	16	9	-4
At market prices	34	24	16	-12	1

TABLE 1.B
Regional distribution of net reserves at the end of 1982,
at market prices and exchange rates ($ billions)

| | World | US | Rest of the world | | | |
			Total	Industrial countries	Oil exporting-countries	Other LDCs*
Assets	806	143	663	419	103	141
Liabilities	−328	−199	−129	−100	−2	−27
Net reserves	478	−56	534	319	101	114
Credit reserves	−3	−176	179	38	82	59
Foreign exchange	x	−184	184	27	74	83
SDR and IMF transactions	3	7	−5	11	8	−24
Gold at market price	476	121	355	282	19	55
Gold at $35 per ounce	36	9	27	22	1	4
Revaluation	440	111	328	260	18	51

* Less developed countries.

TABLE 1.C
*Official reserves (excluding gold) and deposit banks' foreign assets
and liabilities, December 1982 ($ billions)*

	Assets	Liabilities	Net assets
I. *Official reserves*[1]	<u>331</u>	<u>328</u>	<u>+3</u>
United States	22	194	−172
Other industrial countries	138	105	+33
Oil exporting countries	84	2	+82
Other countries	86	27	+59
II. *Deposit banks*[2]	<u>2237</u>	<u>2244</u>	<u>−7</u>
United States	412	301	+111
Other industrial countries	1304	1344	−40
Oil exporting countries	46	26	+20
Other countries	475	573	−98
III. *Total*	2568	2572	−4
United States	434	495	−61
Other industrial countries	1442	1449	−7
Oil exporting countries	130	28	+102
Other countries	561	600	−39
Components of International Reserves	<u>331</u>	<u>328</u>	<u>+3</u>
SDRs	20	24	−4
IMF accounts	28	21	+7
Foreign exchange	283	283	x

[1] Excluding gold deposits with the European Monetary Co-operation Fund (FECOM) and including discrepancy in regional totals under 'other countries'.

[2] The totals shown are the sums of IFS regional estimates, which differ only very slightly ($4 billion) from its world estimates.

Source: *International Financial Statistics*, April 1983.

TABLE 1.D

International capital position and balance of payments of the United States: 1969–82 ($ billions)

	End of year capital position			Average yearly flows			Total flows
	1969	1978	1982	1970–8	1979–82	1982	1970–1982
I. Liabilities (–)	–103	–387	–804	–32	–104	–146	–701
A. *Money market*	–49	–263	–450	–24	–47	–80	–401
1. Foreign official	–19	–176	–195	–17	–5	–8	–175
2. Other	–30	–87	–255	–6	–42	–72	–255
B. *Other*	–54	–124	–354	–8	–57	–67	–300
II. Assets (other than IV)	128	394	–760	30	92	112	633
A. *Money market*	30	150	436	13	72	113	406
1. Official reserves	17	19	34	–	4	4	17
2. Bank claims	13	131	402	13	68	109	389
B. *Other*[1]	98	244	324	16	20	–1	226
III. *Net capital position*[1]	+25	+7	–44	–2	–13	–34	–68

A. Money market	−19	−113	−14	+6	+34	+25	−10
1. Official reserves	−2	−157	−161	−159	−4	−1	−17
2. Other	−17	+44	+147	+164	+38	+26	+7
B. Other	+44	+120	−30	−74	−68	−38	+8
IV. Foreign aid grants and loans	31	54	74	108	12	10	8
A. Grants				65	6	5	5
1. Military				21	1	1	2
2. Other				44	5	5	3
B. Assets	31	54	74	43	6	5	3
V. Income accounts[2]	56	61	30	54	−5	3	4
A. Net investment earnings				238	27	30	13
B. Current transactions				−184	−33	−27	−9
1. Merchandise				−194	−36	−29	−9
2. Military				4	1	1	1
3. Services				31	6	5	1
4. Pensions and remittances				−25	−3	−2	−2

[1] Excluding 'Foreign Aid Assets' mostly akin to grants and unusable to defend the exchange rate on the exchange market.

[2] Equal to III and IV except for valuation and coverage adjustments.

Source: *Survey of Current Business*, US Department of Commerce.

Introduction

I no longer believe that *bis repetita placent*. They irritate instead when
they relentlessly denounce and incriminate the major shortcomings of
analysis and policy which are primarily responsible for the so-called
'stagflation' in which our world has now been plunged for more than
a decade.

Yet, what else can I say? I shall, like Jean Monnet, accept to be
regarded as unduly pessimistic by some, and naïvely optimistic by
others, but fight persistently for fundamental reforms of the international monetary scandal which short-term palliatives or 'crisis
management' will not cure tomorrow any more than yesterday.

The first section of this chapter will summarize the major shortcomings of the prevalent diagnosis and the ineffective prescriptions
flowing from it. It may be skipped by all those who are already too
aware of those errors of analysis and policy.

The second section will outline and document the major trends in
the evolution of the world monetary system and its disastrous consequences on inflation, exchange rates, interest rates, and international
economic and political relations.

The third and final section will reassess the long-term prescription
derived from these facts: a resumption of aborted attempts to construct
a more rational and decentralized monetary order stressing feasible
co-operation at the world level, but also the more ambitious co-
operation—and even integration—feasible only at the regional level.

I. Prevalent shortcomings of analysis and policy

The very word 'stagflation' suggests that our world inflation followed
(and was caused by?) a world economic stagnation. The truth is exactly
the reverse: world inflation preceded world stagnation—or rather
recession—and is primarily responsible for it. The situation's re-
christening as 'infession' would better describe the actual sequence
and causation of events in the 1970s.

Most of the academic writings of the last decade blame the fixed
—but adjustable rather than stable—exchange rates of the Bretton
Woods era for both inflation and deflation:

(i) *Overvalued exchange rates* caused balance-of-payments deficits
    on current account and bearish speculative capital movements.
    The consequent reduction of exports, flooding of imports, and
    switches of domestic investments from the domestic to foreign
    markets brought a decline of economic activity and employment
    and an exhaustion of international monetary reserves, triggering

restrictive policies which further aggravated recession and unemployment.

(ii) Conversely, *undervalued exchange rates* caused balance-of-payments
surpluses on current account and bullish capital imports. The
consequent purchase of foreign exchange by the banking system
increased the domestic monetary issues financing increased economic activity and overemployment, but resulting in domestic
inflationary pressures and inducing the authorities to adopt restrictive monetary policies and higher interest rates. These policies, in
turn, aggravated both the deflationary pressures and speculative
capital movements of the overvalued currency countries.

The prescriptive panacea flowing from this analysis was the generalized adoption of flexible rates, necessary to eliminate at the root all
balance-of-payments disequilibria, destabilizing capital movements,
and the transmission of inflationary and deflationary pressures beyond
national borders. The partial acceptance of this prescription has in fact
been followed by a multiplication of balance-of-payments disequilibria
on current account, disruptive capital speculation, inflation, and
unemployment throughout the world for more than a decade already.
Milton Friedman's followers may still argue, however, that this is due in
part to continued—and indeed larger—official exchange-rate interventions and destabilizing monetary policies.

The other favourite scapegoat of the bulk of our economic analysis
of infession is the explosion of oil prices, which has indeed enormously
aggravated balance-of-payments disequilibria, contributing undoubtedly
to contagious price increases world-wide, and to monetary inflation in
the oil-exporting countries. For the oil-importing countries, however,
the economic impact could be very different from country to country.
While the transfer of purchasing power to the oil-exporting countries
exercised a deflationary monetary contraction on all of the oil-importers,
this could be far more than offset for some of them.

The oil-exporting countries sterilized only a minimal fraction of
their hugely increased export earnings through gold purchases. These
are estimated by *International Financial Statistics* to have risen in
volume (measured uniformly at SDR 35 per ounce) from only SDR
1.2 billion at the end of 1972 to SDR 1.5 billion at the end of 1981.
Even recalculated at current gold prices, this SDR 300 million increase
remains insignificant compared to cash surplus investments abroad,
estimated to have totalled $475 billion over the years 1974-81.[1] Bank
deposits in industrial countries account for $160 billion of this total
and would normally lead, under a fractional system of cash reserves, to
a multiple monetary expansion in the recipient countries.

The overall impact of the oil-exporting countries' surpluses on the major countries undoubtedly aggravated balance-of-payments deficits, but over-financed them for some countries, at the cost of a growing foreign indebtedness in their capital accounts.

In any case, the oil-price explosion can hardly be blamed—as it so often is!—for the world inflation and the collapse of the Bretton Woods system. The first oil shock took place only at the end of 1973 —several years after the inception of world inflation around 1970 and partly in response to it. World monetary reserves had already doubled from 1969 to 1972; the dollar had long been inconvertible in practice through 'gentlemen's agreement' and *de jure* since August 1971 (more than two years before the first increase in oil prices); and the gradual adoption of flexible exchange rates had already been generalized in March 1973.

II. Factual record and interpretation

Breakdown of the world monetary system

Interesting and valid in part as it undoubtedly is, this prevalent analysis bizarrely pays little or no attention to the major cause of the world infession. *World-wide recessions as well as inflations have always been linked to the breakdown of the monetary system.* The August 1971 collapse of the gold-exchange standard based on the dollar, just as the September 1931 collapse of the gold-exchange standard based on the pound sterling, had long been predicted by others as well as by myself.[2] Both of these major collapses could be traced to the same root: what President de Gaulle called the 'extravagant privilege' of the reserve-currency countries to finance nearly unlimited deficits through their own IOUs.[3]

Such a privilege can hardly fail to encourage the reserve-currency centre to indulge in the politically attractive laxist policies which foreign countries show themselves willing to finance. Its resulting balance-of-payments deficits are not constrained—as they are for other countries—by the limited international reserves at its disposal. They can be financed by a persistent build-up of external liabilities well beyond the gold—or other foreign assets—in which they are legally redeemable at any time; and this financing continues as long as redemption rights are not used by the foreign creditors.

This gave Britain only a relatively short respite when it restored in 1926 the pre-1914 parity of the pound. Gold convertibility had to be suspended in 1931 when its creditors called for payment in gold or dollars, and the straight gold standard replaced the gold-exchange standard.

The respite was much longer for the mighty dollar after the Second World War. Even when gold convertibility was officially suspended for the dollar in 1971, foreign money markets continued to accumulate huge dollar claims for their surpluses: about $450 billion by the end of 1982 as against $50 billion at the end of 1970.[4]

Inflationary impact of US deficits upon the world

This huge financing of US deficits had an enormous inflationary impact on world monetary reserves throughout the years 1970-81.

Measured in SDR, at constant gold prices and exchange rates (see Table 1.1), world reserves increased at the very modest pace of 2.8% yearly over 1950-69, but at an explosive pace of 13% yearly over 1970-81, bringing them by 1981 to 14¼ times their 1969 amount.

Measured in dollars at current gold prices and exchange rates, world reserves nearly decupled from 1970 to 1981—as I will not cease to repeat, increased nearly nine times as much over the short span of eleven years as over all previous years and centuries. They had risen even more, to a peak of more than $1040 billion in September 1980, when gold reached the record end-month price of $666.75 per ounce, i.e. more than nineteen times its latest official valuation. The steep decline of gold prices to $397.50 per ounce at the end of 1981 was the main factor in the 26% overall decline in world reserves over the following year and a quarter.

The fantastic mushrooming of the international private capital market has added a further dimension to the financing facilities available to settle balance-of-payments disequilibria. Gross external bank claims are estimated by the Bank for International Settlements (BIS) to have risen from about $95 billion in 1969 to $1542 billion in 1981, and net bank lending (after deduction of redepositing among banks) from $50 billion to $940 billion. In twelve years they were multiplied respectively 14½ and 9 times, at a pace of 26% and 28% a year.[5] The BIS estimates that Eurobond and foreign bond issues provided additional financing of $254 billion gross and $202 billion net over the years 1975-81, of which $49 billion gross and $36½ billion net fell in 1984 (about double their 1975 amount).

Failure of official policies

These two incredible explosions of financing facilities obviously reflect a total failure of official policies. As for private financing, some feeble efforts were made belatedly to check its excesses, but with only minimal results at first.

Regarding the official creation of international reserves, it took the authorities four years to heed my 1959 warnings. Close and continuous meetings were finally initiated in October 1963 by the International Monetary Fund (IMF) and the Group of Ten and were pursued for more than ten years, culminating in the June 1974 report of the

TABLE 1.1

The inflationary explosion of world reserves[1]

Measured in	End of year	Amounts (billions)	Ratio		Period increase (billions)		Yearly growth rate %
			1949 = 1	1969 = 1			
SDR = $	1949	46	1.00		*20 years*		
	1969	79	1.73	1.00	1950–69	33	2.8
SDR	1981	347	7.54	4.39	*12 years* 1970–81	268	13.0
$	1981	777	16.89	9.48	1970–81	698	21.0

[1] In this as in other tables, small apparent addition or subtraction discrepancies are due to rounding estimates to the nearest billion.

Source: Except when otherwise noted, all tables in this chapter are calculated from the international reserve tables of *International Financial Statistics*, Yearbooks 1979 and 1982, and September 1982, International Monetary Fund.

Committee of Twenty.[6] Their recommendations for fundamental reforms of the world monetary system endorsed most of my 1959 recommendations to the US Congress. But this was the 'swan song' of the official reformers, summarily dismissed at Jamaica and in the Second Amendment to the IMF Articles of Agreement.

Table 1.2 contrasts the fantastic fluctuations of world reserves from December 1949 to June 1982 with their orderly growth under the defunct Bretton Woods regime. Measured in SDRs (at constant gold prices and $-SDR exchange rates), they rose by 224 billion from the end of 1969 to the end of September 1980, and then by 36 billion to the end of June 1982, at an annual rate of about 21 billion throughout (line I). This means that world reserves increased more than three times as much over those 12½ years as in all preceding years and centuries since Adam and Eve. Measured in dollars (at market gold prices and $-SDR exchange rates), their rise from 1969 to September 1980 amounted to $967 billion (12 times as much as since Adam and Eve), and their subsequent decline amounted to $384 billion, or nearly 37% over 1¾ years (line III).

Measured at constant prices (in ounces, or in SDRs), gold played no role in these fluctuations (line I). The increases of reserves measured in SDRs were entirely due to 'credit reserves', i.e. SDR allocations, IMF transactions, and mostly foreign exchange holdings.

The enormous fluctuations of reserves, measured in dollars at market prices and exchange rates (line III), were due entirely to the impact of fluctuations in gold prices and exchange rates (line II). They obviously reflected the total loss of control of the monetary and political authorities. It would be unkind to recall that when they belatedly accepted, in 1963, the need to examine the functioning of a world monetary system obviously threatened with collapse, the ministers of finance and governors of central banks proclaimed repeatedly and emphatically that they would explore all the aspects of the system that might call for reform except two, which, they all agreed, should remain the unshakeable pillars of any future system: stable exchange rates and stable gold prices at $35 an ounce. The only two major reforms of the Bretton Woods regime have, in fact, been the very opposite: the generalized adoption of floating exchange rates and the wide fluctuations in gold prices. The latter reached a peak of $850 (more than 24 times the 'unshakeable' $35 price) on 21 January 1980, plunged later by nearly two-thirds to less than $300 an ounce, and have continued to fluctuate erratically up and down.

The adoption of the 1969 IMF Amendment proclaimed that Special Drawing Rights would become the centre of the system, replacing foreign exchange as an adjunct to insufficient gold supplies. This was rightly deemed necessary to curb the inflationary flooding of world

Table 1.2
Sources of reserve creation

	SDRs or dollars (billions)[1]					Period changes		
	End of					20 years 1949/ end 1969	10¾ years Jan. 1970/ Dec. 1983	1¾ years Oct. 1980/ June 1982
	1949	1959	1969	Sept. 1980	June 1982			
I. *Measured in SDRs*	46	57	79	303	339	33	224	36
A. World gold	34	40	41	40	40	6	−1	–
B. Credit reserves	11	17	38	263	299	27	225	36
1. Concerted: SDRs and IMF	–	1	4	25	36	4	21	11
2. Foreign exchange	11	16	34	238	263	23	204	25
II. *Impact of fluctuations in gold prices and exchange rates*	x	x	x	743	323	x	743	−420
A. World gold	x	x	x	725	325	x	725	−400
B. Credit reserves	x	x	x	18	−1	x	18	−19
1. Concerted: SDRs and IMF	x	x	x	−56	−26	x	−56	31
2. Foreign exchange	x	x	x	74	24	x	74	−50
III. *Measured in dollars, at market gold prices and exchange rates (I + II)*	46	57	79	1046	662	33	967	−384
A. World gold	34	40	41	765	365	6	724	−400
B. Credit reserves	11	17	38	281	297	27	243	17
1. Concerted: SDRs and IMF		1	4	31	11			

	% of gross reserves measured in dollars							
I. Measured in SDRs	100	100	100	29	51	100	23	9
A. World gold	76	70	52	4	6	19	—	—
B. Credit reserves	24	30	48	25	45	81	23	9
1. Concerted: SDRs and IMF	—	1	6	2	5	13	2	3
2. Foreign exchange	24	28	43	23	40	68	21	6
II. Impact of fluctuations in gold prices and exchange rates	x	x	x	71	49	x	77	−109
A. World gold	x	x	x	69	49	x	75	−104
B. Credit reserves	x	x	x	2	—	x	2	−5
1. Concerted: SDRs and IMF	x	x	x	−5	−4	x	−6	8
2. Foreign exchange	x	x	x	7	4	x	8	−13
III. Measured in dollars at market gold prices and exchange rates	100	100	100	100	100	100	100	−100
A. World gold	76	70	52	73	55	19	75	−104
B. Credit reserves	24	30	48	27	45	81	25	4
1. Concerted: SDRs and IMF	—	1	6	−3	2	13	−4	11
2. Foreign exchange	24	28	43	30	43	68	29	−7

Notes and sources to Table 1.2 at foot of p. 28.

reserves by national reserve currencies threatened with inconvertibility. In fact, however, foreign exchange reserves grew at a faster pace than ever over the following years: by about 20 billion yearly, as against little more than 1 billion (line I B2 or III B2), while SDR allocations and other IMF transactions, taken together, increased by only about half a billion dollars yearly, and totalled less than 2% of world reserves at the end of June 1982 (line III B1, in %).

Volatility of exchange rates

The volatility of exchange rates under the present system is briefly documented in Table 1.3. The dollar depreciated sharply *vis-à-vis* the other four major currencies, except sterling, from 1969 to 1976. It then depreciated further by 30% to 41% over the following three years, but appreciated by 18% to 42% over 1979–81. These major fluctuations reflect only the peaks of continuous and increasing see-saw movements. For instance, fluctuations exceeded ½% a day in 54% of the 1981 trading days, compared with 33% of the trading days in 1973.

Such volatility can hardly be regarded as beneficial to economic

TABLE 1.3

Exchange rates of the dollar vis-à-vis *major currencies*[1]

	Deutsch-mark	Swiss franc	Pound sterling	Japanese yen
1969 par value per $[2]	4.00	4.3728	2.40	360.00
% change	−35	−41	+49	−16
Highest 1976 rate	2.5945	2.6000	1.6060	302.25
% change	−33	−41	−30	−33
Lowest 1979 rate	1.7300	1.5335	1.8005	202.20
% change	+42	+34	+27	+18
Highest 1981 rate	2.4645	2.1382	1.7263	239.45

[1] End of month inter-bank exchange rates (excluding service charges): foreign currency amounts per dollar, except for the pound sterling, which shows dollar amounts per pound.
[2] Par value of the Deutschmark until September 29. Parity equivalent of the Swiss franc until 9 May 1969.

Notes and sources to Table 1.2, pp. 26 and 27.

[1] SDR estimates are uniformly calculated at SDR 35 per ounce of gold, with the $ equal to the SDR, while $ estimates are uniformly calculated at market gold prices and $-SDR exchange rates, the differences showing the impact of fluctuations in gold prices and exchange rates upon the $ estimates. (This entails a number of corrections in the IFS estimates, which include FECOM and BS gold at market price under foreign exchange holdings measured in SDRs.)
Source: International Financial Statistics, Yearbooks 1979 and 1982, and September 1982.

activity, employment, or internal monetary stability. Firms engaged in foreign trade or exposed to import competition are deterred from long-term investments, at home as well as abroad, since such investments risk becoming highly unprofitable as a result of unpredictable changes in exchange rates. This acts as a powerful brake on GNP and employment.

Advocates of floating rates argue that the system avoids the transmission of inflationary impulses from the more to the less inflationary countries. This is true, but (as I pointed out in my 1960 book, *Gold and the Dollar Crisis*) it also has the disadvantage of 'bottling up' within each country the inflationary or deflationary impact of its own policy mistakes.

Under fixed exchange rates, an excessive rate of credit expansion tends to spill out into balance-of-payments deficits rather than in substantial price rises, which are held down by import competition. Floating rates may avoid or reduce external deficits, but they do so at the cost of increases in import prices, which are quickly transmitted to general levels of prices, costs, and wages. Speculation accelerates and amplifies these disequilibrating movements without, by itself, correcting the internal financial policies causing them.

At some point restrictive monetary policies will become indispensable to avoid a currency collapse, but intervening price and wage rises are likely to be irreversible also and to make depreciation of the currency irreversible. Thus floating rates are nearly inevitably marred by an inflationary bias and a devaluation bias that cannot fail to make private exchange-rate speculation far less 'stabilizing' than envisaged by the proponents of exchange-rate flexibility.

Deflationary policy mistakes, on the other hand, will result in currency appreciation, similarly accelerated by bullish speculation. This may reduce or eliminate balance-of-payments surpluses on current account, but is unlikely to reduce sticky wages. It will tend instead to reduce the over-valuation of the currency, economic activity, and employment.

Volatility of interest rates

The volatility of exchange rates was matched and influenced by the volatility of interest rates.

As Table 1.4 shows, short-term market rates in the United States (Federal Funds rate monthly averages) rose from a low of 3.29% in February 1972 to a high of 19.10% in June 1981. Recurrent intervening fluctuations cut them at times by nearly 2/3, quadrupling them at other times, over periods of 2½ to 4 years, and reaching up to 3.06% upwards and 6.63% downwards in a single month. This, of course, had a deep impact on international capital movements and interest rates throughout the world, adding to other national sources of instability and deterring long-term investment and borrowing commitments.

TABLE 1.4

Major fluctuations of United States money market rates: 1970–81

Month	Monthly Averages (% year)	Decreases		Increases	
		in %	over	in %	over
January 1970	8.98				
February 1972	3.29	−5.69	25 months		
July 1974	12.92	– – – – – – – – – →		+9.61	29 months
January 1977	4.61	−8.31	30 months		
January 1981	19.08	– – – – – – – – – →		+14.47	48 months
December 1981	12.37	−6.71	11 months		
Totals	+3.39	−20.71	66 months	+24.10	77 months

Capital flows

Another feature of the functioning of the world monetary system is also at the very opposite of proclaimed official intentions and plain common sense. Economic logic, as well as humane concerns, should lead the richer and more capitalized countries of the industrial world to help economic development in the poorer and less capitalized countries of the Third World through capital exports. This goal is indeed repeatedly endorsed in pious United Nations resolutions. But in the area that should be the most amenable to official control, i.e. the creation of international reserves, the present system of reserve creation overwhelmingly benefits a few of the richest and most heavily capitalized countries rather than the poorer countries most in need of capital. This is brought out in Table 1.5, which shows how the main groups of countries shared in the major sources of financing of world reserves, as of the end of 1982.[7]

(i) Credit reserves account for nearly 90% of world assets measured in SDRs, at constant gold prices and SDR-$ exchange rates (300 billion out of a 336 billion total), but only for 41% of gross reserve assets measured in dollars, at current gold prices and SDR-$ exchange rates (330 billion out of 807 billion). Leaving aside an insignificant amount of net claims on the IMF (3 billion), they are invested overwhelmingly in the industrial countries: 299 billion, i.e. 91%. Only a minor fraction is invested in the non-industrial countries: 29 billion, i.e. 9% (see 'Credit Reserves' in fifth column).

This is mainly due to the fact that foreign exchange holdings constitute the bulk (86%) of credit reserves and are, of course, held practically entirely in a handful of so-called 'reserve-centre' countries, but not in any of the Third World countries or currencies.

When the SDR amendment to the IMF Articles of Agreement was adopted in 1969, the authorities proclaimed that SDRs would become the major instrument of the international reserve system. Yet total SDR allocations still constitute only about 6% of world reserves measured in SDRs, and 3% of world reserves measured in dollars at current gold prices and exchange rates. Two-thirds of them have been allotted to the industrial countries. IMF lending, on the other hand, is directed almost entirely towards the non-oil countries of the Third World. But, taken together with SDR allocations, this represents only 12% of world reserves measured in SDRs, and less than 6% of world reserves measured in dollars.

Fluctuations in gold prices, anathema to the authorities until they could no longer prevent them, account for 58% of world reserve assets, measured in dollars. Of their $440 billion total, 84% went to the industrial countries: 25% to the United States and 59% to the others. Only 16% went to the non-industrial countries, which hold most of their reserves in foreign exchange rather than in gold: 4% to the oil-exporting countries and 12% to the others.

(ii) The geographical distribution of net reserves (deducting reserve liabilities from reserve assets) is as, or even more, ludicrous. It shows the United States—still one of the richest and most capitalized countries of the world—as a net debtor of 149 billion of the net world reserves measured in SDRs (39 billion) and of 54 billion of the net world reserves measured in dollars (479 billion), this net debt being reduced by 95 billion by the increase in gold prices. Leaving gold aside, the United States emerges with a net reserve debt of SDR 160 billion or $175 billion, and the other countries with equivalent net credit claims (plus an insignificant amount— 3 billion—of net claims on the IMF). The countries of the Third World are the major lenders (79% of the total), the OPEC countries accounting for 46% and the others for 33%. The industrial countries other than the United States account for the remaining— and smallest—fraction of 21%.

(iii) Attractive as it may seem to the reserve-currency centres benefiting from it, this pattern of reserve investments made, of course, unviable the gold-exchange standard which gave rise to it, as brought out in Table 1.6. It was responsible for the breakdown of the sterling gold-exchange standard in September 1931, and for the collapse of the dollar gold-exchange standard in August 1971.

I predicted this collapse in 1959, after seeing the sharp decline of US net reserves from $23 billion to $11 billion over ten years. This decline continued at about the same pace over the following

TABLE 1.5

Sources and regional distribution of reserve assets, reserve liabilities, and net reserves
as of the end of 1982 (billions)

	Measured in SDRs			Measured in dollars			Impact of fluctuations in gold prices and exchange rates on		
	Assets	Liabilities	Net	Assets	Liabilities	Net	Assets	Liabilities	Net
I. Credit reserves	300	297	+2	330	328	+3	+31	+31	—
Industrial countries	146	271	−125	161	299	−138	+15	+28	−13
United States	21	179	−159	23	198	−175	+2	+18	−16
Other	125	91	+34	138	101	+37	+13	+9	−3
Non-industrial countries	154	26	+128	170	29	+140	+16	+3	+13
Oil exporting	76	1	+74	83	2	+82	+8	+1	+8
Other	78	25	+54	86	27	+59	+8	+2	+5
IA. Foreign exchange	256	256	x	283	283	x	+26	+26	x
Industrial countries	115	256	−141	127	283	−156	+12	+26	−15
United States	9	174	−165	10	192	−182	+1	+18	−17
Other	105	82	+24	116	90	+26	+11	+8	+2
Non-industrial countries	141	—	+141	156	—	+156	+14	—	+15
Oil exporting	67	—	+67	74	—	+74	+7	—	+7
Other	75	—	+75	82	—	+83	+8	—	+8

	43	41	+2	48	45	+3	+4	+4	—
IB. SDR and IMF accounts									
Industrial countries	31	15	+17	34	16	+18	+3	+2	+2
United States	11	5	+7	13	5	+7	+1	+1	+1
Other	20	10	+10	22	11	+11	+2	+1	+1
Non-industrial countries	12	26	−14	13	29	−16	+1	+3	+1
Oil exporting	9	1	+7	10	2	+8	+1	—	+1
Other	3	25	−21	.4	27	−24	—	+3	−2
II. Gold reserves	36	—	+36	476	—	+476	+440	—	+440
Industrial countries	31	—	+31	402	—	+402	+321	—	+371
United States	9	—	+9	121	—	+121	+112	—	+112
Other	22	—	+22	282	—	+282	+260	—	+260
Non-industrial countries	6	—	+6	74	—	+74	+68	—	+68
Oil exporting	1	—	+1	19	—	+19	+18	—	+18
Other	4	—	+4	55	—	+55	+51	—	+51
III. Total reserves (I + II)	336	297	+39	805	328	+479	+471	+31	+439
Industrial countries	177	270	−94	563	299	+264	+386	+28	+359
United States	30	179	−149	143	198	−54	+114	+18	+95
Other	147	91	+55	420	101	+319	+273	+9	+263
Non-industrial countries	159	26	133	244	29	+215	+84	+3	+81
Oil exporting	77	1	+76	103	2	+101	+26	+1	+25
Other	82	25	+57	141	27	+114	+59	+2	+55

Source: International Financial Statistics, 1983 Yearbook.

TABLE 1.6

Regional evolution of net reserves: 1949–82

	World	United States	Rest of world			
			Total	Industrial countries	Oil exporting countries	Other countries
I. *Measured in SDRs (billions) at 35 per ounce of gold and $ = SDR*						
End of: 1949	34	23	12	2	1	8
1959	40	11	29	19	3	8
1969	40	−2	42	23	4	15
1972	41	−55	95	62	10	24
1978	40	−137	177	76	46	54
Sept. 1980	39	−131	170	37	71	62
1981	40	−148	187	44	80	63
June 1982	39	−154	194	55	78	61
Dec. 1982	39	−151	190	56	76	58
II. *Measured in dollars (billions) at market gold prices and exchange rates*						
End of: 1972	72	−52	123	83	11	29

1978	241	−128	369	211	66	92
Sept. 1980	700	−7	707	431	117	158
1981	419	−77	497	271	108	118
June 1982	335	−95	430	232	96	101
Dec. 1982	479	−56	535	320	101	114
III. In % of world reserves:						
SDR estimates						
End of: 1949	100	66	34	6	3	24
1959	100	27	73	47	6	19
1969	100	−5	105	58	10	36
1972	100	−135	235	152	24	59
1978	100	−341	441	191	115	136
Sept. 1980	100	−332	432	94	180	158
1981	100	−373	473	110	202	160
June 1982	100	−391	491	140	197	154
Dec. 1982	100	−387	487	143	195	149
$ estimates						
End of: 1972	100	−72	172	116	16	40
1978	100	−53	153	88	27	38
Sept. 1980	100	−1	101	62	17	23
1981	100	−18	118	65	26	28
June 1982	100	−28	128	69	29	30
Dec. 1982	100	−12	112	67	21	24

Source: Appendix Table 1.IIC.

ten years, bringing down US net reserves by 13 billion (from
+11 billion to −2 billion) and accelerated considerably in later
years (by SDR 53 billion over 1970-2 and SDR 96 billion over
1973-82). The 1981 decline of 11 billion is about equal to the
yearly average of the preceding eight years. The percentages in the
bottom half of Table 1.6 record the evolution of the regional
distribution of world reserves. They show how the system of
reserve creation has made the non-industrial countries (even the
non-oil-exporting ones) the major reserve creditors, and the United
States the major reserve debtor, both under the gold-exchange
standard of yester-years and under the paper-exchange standard
of today.

      This does not mean, however, that the non-industrial countries
are the main creditors and the United States the main debtor on
capital account in general. We must now turn to the more complex
relationship between balances of payments on current and capital
account and the accumulation of reserve claims and debts. This
has enormous political as well as economic implications, which
are bound to affect deeply the future of international relations
between the United States and other countries, and the survival
of present monetary policies and institutional arrangements.

Regional pattern of balances of payments and of reserve investments

A sensible international monetary system should prompt the richer
and more capitalized countries to accumulate current-account surpluses
for economic as well as humane reasons, enabling them to provide to
the poorer and less capitalized countries the financing of balance-of-
payments deficits justified by the investments necessary to their
economic growth and to the maintenance of consumption levels
indispensable to the very survival of their people.

      But what is happening in fact? Table 1.7 summarizes, in the form
which I find most meaningful, the mountain of estimates collected by
the International Monetary Fund and dispersed in its Balance of
Payments Yearbooks and Supplements from 1977 to 1981.[8]

(i) *The less capitalized countries*—i.e. the countries of the Third
    World other than those exporting oil—indeed experience external
    deficits, probably excessive but over-financed by capital imports,
    therefore enabling them to increase each year their international
    monetary reserves.
(ii) *The oil-exporting countries* are today the only ones accumulating
    current-account surpluses, of which they devote about half to
    capital exports—partly towards the industrial countries—and the
    other half to reserve accumulation.

TABLE 1.7

Changes in international monetary reserves and balances of payments: 1970–80 (SDR billions)

	Industrial countries			Non-industrial countries			World
	United States (a)	Other countries (b)	Total (c = a + b)	Total (d = e + f)	Oil exporting countries (e)	Other countries (f)	Total (g = c + d)
I. Net reserves: (A – B)	−134	+66	−69	+105	+80	+25	+37
A. Assets	+3	+143	+146	+136	+82	+54	+282
B. Liabilities (−) constituting reserves:	−138	−77	−215	−31	−2	−29	−245
1. Constituting foreign authorities' reserves	−129	−29	−157	−2	–	−2	−159
2. Exceptional financing	−5	−40	−45	−24	−1	−23	−69
3. SDR allocations	−4	−8	−12	−5	−1	−4	−17
II. Gold demonetization and valuation adjustments	+4	+1	+6	+6	+3	+3	+11
III. Transactions: (I + II = A − B)	−129	+67	−63	+111	+83	+27	+49
A. Current account balances	+3	−78	−75	−61	+166	−227	−135
B. Capital exports and errors and omissions	+133	−145	−12	−172	+83	−254	−184
1. Recorded capital exports	+185	−85	+100	−197	+68	−265	−98
2. Errors and omissions	−52	−60	−112	+25	+15	+11	−86

(iii) *The industrialized countries other than the United States* incur enormous current-account deficits, largely over-financed by huge capital imports, thus leaving them also with considerable increases of their reserves.

(iv) *This is the crux of the inflationary explosion of world monetary reserves* denounced above, *and of their excessive absorption by the industrialized countries.* These reserves, indeed, are not invested in the countries most in need of capital, but only in a few rich countries whose currency is deemed 'strong', primarily the United States. These growing 'reserve borrowings'—indebtedness —of the United States enable it to be by far the largest capital exporter, although its current-account surpluses are negligible and grossly inadequate for one of the richest and most capitalized countries of our planet: less than 0.02% of its GNP over the years 1970-80.

Table 1.D (pp. 18-19) brings out the elements of strength and of weakness imparted to the dollar by its crucial role as 'parallel world currency' in the creation and investment of world monetary reserves. For this purpose it recasts in a highly novel fashion the standard presentation of the US international capital position and of the balance-of-payments flows which explain most of the changes in this position.[9]

The first two columns summarize the *year-end capital* position for 1969 and 1981, far more important, to my mind, than the current balance-of-payments flows habitually used by most analysts to explain the exchange-rate fluctuations of the dollar. Indeed, the sharpest exchange-rate fluctuations may be prompted more by political crises (such as, recently, the fears of a world war unleashed by events in Iran, Afghanistan, the Middle East in general, Poland, etc.) than recent balance-of-payments flows. When such a crisis erupts in fact, the vulnerability of the dollar, or of other major currencies, on the exchange markets of the world is influenced by the *stock* portfolio positions in these currencies much more than by mere balance-of-payments *flow* accretions over recent months.

The stock estimates—or rather 'guesstimates'—in the first two columns of my table differ fundamentally from the last official estimates of this sort presented in August 1982 by the *Survey of Current Business.* The *Survey*, for instance, records the US net capital position at the end of 1981 at the huge figure of $160 billion, while my table hazards a guesstimate of *minus* $6 billion. There are two main reasons for this.

The first is that I exclude from total assets (reported as $717 billion) 'foreign aid' loans and other assets held overwhelmingly 'long term' in rupees, cruzeiros, etc., which are more akin to grants than to normal credit claims and could hardly be mobilized to strengthen the rate of the dollar against other major currencies, such as the Deutschmark.

The second is that I include in my liabilities estimates contingent SDR liabilities,[10] but mostly huge errors and omissions—recently relabelled 'statistical discrepancy'—which most commentators, including the authors of the *Survey* article, attribute mostly to unrecorded capital inflows.[11]

What is significant, in these estimates, is *not* the net capital position, but the enormous size (about $784 billion in 1982 compared to $103 billion in 1969) of the gross foreign assets and liabilities which reflect the crucial intermediary role of the United States as the major world banker. Foreigners have invested about $784 billion in the United States, and the United States has reinvested about the same amount of capital abroad ($761 billion).

My tables break down these huge investments and reinvestments into three broad categories.

Lines I.A, II.A, and III.A of Table 1.D—'money market'—reflect the role of the dollar as a so-called 'parallel' world currency. They include as US liabilities the Treasury securities and other liabilities reported by US banks, in which foreign central banks and commercial banks hold most—and until recently nearly all—of their foreign-exchange assets. These liabilities have been the overwhelming source of the huge, inflationary increases of foreign official reserves and of commercial banks' foreign assets since the end of 1969: foreign official assets in the United States have risen nearly 10 times, and other Treasury and bank-reported liabilities (mostly to banks) 8½ times over this brief span of thirteen years (see fifth column).

Only a handful of other currencies (the pound, the French franc, and particularly the Deutschmark, the Swiss franc, and the yen) share with the dollar this awesome privilege and responsibility, and only to a very minor extent.

As far as the United States is concerned, the role of 'world bank' is played mostly by the commercial banks. Only $34 billion of the $195 billion of foreign official reserves invested in the United States are reinvested abroad by the monetary authorities.[12] Commercial banks, on the other hand, have accumulated $402 billion of foreign claims, i.e. $147 billion more than the investments received by them from abroad (see third column).

Other foreign investments in the United States are 'guesstimated' at about $354 billion, and foreign investments by the United States at $324 billion, leaving a net foreign-investment position of minus $30 billion which is the very opposite indeed of what should be expected, economically as well as humanely, from one of the richest and most capitalized countries in the world.

It is made up primarily of direct investments, totalling $221 billion gross and $119 billion net, and of unrecorded liabilities ('errors and omissions') totalling $134 billion, the bulk of which ($121 billion) was accumulated over the last four years.

This breakdown of capital movements between money-market transactions and other capital transactions helps, I hope, explain the heavy depreciation of the dollar in relation to the other major currencies, such as the Deutschmark, from 1969 to 1979 (minus 53%) and its substantial recovery since then. My comments in this respect will be based, however, on the balance-of-payments 'flow' statistics summarized in the last four columns of Table 1.D.

The main explanation of the dollar's weakness and recovery seems to me to lie in the contrasting evolution of net money-market investments (line III.A) and other net investments (line III.B) over the periods 1970–8 and 1979–82. Net money-market borrowings of $10 billion a year were followed by net repayments of $25 billion a year, while other net investments switched from outflows of $8 billion to inflows of $38 billion (and even $68 billion in 1982). This meant in fact that the net official reserves of foreign countries increased only very slightly in the last four years (by $1 billion per year), compared with increases of nearly $17 billion a year over the previous nine years. From 1970 to 1978, practically all foreign countries—even the most inflationary ones—experienced huge increases of reserves, removing for them normal balance-of-payments constraints. In the following four years, on the contrary, market investments channelled outside banks increased the demand for the dollar and prompted a spectacular recovery in its exchange rates, which foreign monetary authorities tried to slow down by strengthening anit-inflationary policies, particularly through high interest rates. Dollar transactions ceased to be a powerful engine of domestic inflation abroad, contributing instead to anti-inflationary, recessive pressures on foreign economies.

Let me now turn briefly to the topic most often stressed by my academic colleagues, i.e. the impact of current-account transactions on the capital movements summarized above.

The most striking observation to be made in this respect is that fluctuations in the current-account balance, as usually measured, have been practically insignificant on the average. They moved merely from a yearly deficit rate of $1.8 billion over the years 1970–8 to an average deficit of $0.6 billion over the years 1979–82. Table 1.D recasts these estimates in a way which seems to me far more significant as an explanation of the capital movements summarized above.

Income accounts, excluding all capital movements, left throughout (except in 1982) a positive surplus, over-absorbed however by capital outflows which I have grouped together as weakening—rather than strengthening—the net asset balance of significance to the future strength of the dollar on the exchange market: straight grants and foreign aid assets, largely akin to them. (I include among these grants 'military' as well as 'economic' grants, and under 'income accounts' the military transfers of goods and services financed by them.)

Having been a good prophet—alas!—in my 1960 book *Gold and the Dollar Crisis*, I have no wish to look again into the crystal ball and to spoil the optimism that still prevails today about the future of the dollar on the exchange markets. This optimism may, or may not be justified as far as the short run is concerned, but I cannot avoid raising two anguished questions about the longer-run, or even medium-run future. (The updating of my 1981 estimates to 1982 shows a continued aggravation of the prospects which worried me when I wrote the initial version of this chapter.)

The first of these questions has also begun to worry most analysts. Turning back to column 3, I see that money-market liabilities (estimated at $450 billion at the end of 1982) are $14 billion larger than money-market assets ($436 billion), but also that this net figure reflects a variety of assets and liabilities whose real significance is by no means the same: net official reserve liabilities of $161 billion,[13] largely off-set by net bank assets of $147 billion. This net assets estimate is made up, however, of $255 billion gross liabilities which banks must be able to honour, and $402 billion gross assets, of which a substantial fraction might not be easy to mobilize in case of need. Nearly half of them are held in Western Hemisphere countries, mostly Mexico, Brazil, and Argentina, whose foreign debt problems have been making headlines in our newspapers for some time and will continue to do so in the foreseeable future.[14]

My second worry is about the evolution of the net income accounts. Their $3 billion average net surplus over the four years 1979–82 was made up of a huge surplus of net income on past investments ($30 billion, sharply up from only $5 billion in the 1960s, and $13 billion over the years 1970–8). This was increasingly absorbed, however, by a huge deficit on other current transactions, increasing sharply from $9 billion in 1970–8 to $27 billion in 1979–82, and including a deficit on merchandise account of $29 billion, more than triple the $9 billion average deficit of the previous nine years, and officially forecast to reach, or exceed, $100 billion in 1984.

Will it be possible to sustain for long what is widely regarded as an over-valued dollar rate, reminiscent of the late 1960s? What is obvious is that the recent strength of the dollar is not due to any substantial improvement of current-income transactions, but to an enormous inflow of foreign capital attracted to the United States by the fears of a third world war, untenably high interest rates, and confidence in the anti-inflationary programme of the Reagan Administration.

Equally obvious is the fact that the strength of the dollar should not, and cannot, remain indefinitely dependent, as is the case today, on such continued capital inflows into one of the richest and most capitalized countries of the world. We must certainly face the possibility of a decrease, cessation, or even reversal of such inflows, in the event— deeply to be hoped—of an abatement of the fears of war and of a decline in interest rates. Although successful price-wise, the Administration programme has also so far vastly increased the fiscal deficits whose correction was previously deemed imperative. Finally, the persistence of such capital movements would be bound to raise increasing objections abroad, and to prompt the adoption of policies distasteful to all: domestic deflationary measures, and/or protectionism and exchange controls.

More and more people have become convinced that it is high time to reverse the dismantlement of the international co-operation policies and institutions which had assured, until the 1970s, an unprecedented degree of prosperity to the world, rather than the undreamed-of combination of inflation and recession that has flowed from the policies and institutions initiated with the total breakdown, rather than needed reform, of the Bretton Woods system.

Political implications

Economists cannot claim any special competence on the political implications of the factual record presented above. Yet the persistence of such an aberrant and disastrous institutional framework for the world monetary system is largely due to political factors, and its collapse or reform will also be determined by political as well as by economic considerations.

I shall hazard, therefore, a few comments which may be skipped as inappropriate for an *economist*, but which no *citizen* responsible for the political decisions of his government can afford to ignore.

The method (?) of world-monetary-reserve creation and investments described above obviously contributes to strengthening enormously the financial, economic, political, and military hegemony inevitably exercised in world affairs by the United States. This hegemony was used after the last world war with rare wisdom and generosity to accelerate the reconstruction of a war-devastated world, and is still welcomed today by a fearful world as a necessary counterpart to the Soviet military power. Economically, it makes it possible in fact, if not in law, to insert a certain degree of highly desirable coherence in a world of countries which remain attached to their illusory legal sovereignty, but are in fact inextricably interdependent on one another.

The recycling of petro-dollars by the United States contributed, for instance, to meet the two oil-price explosions of the early 1970s and 1980s with a speed which might not have been feasible for a reformed IMF, especially if its reform had been adopted too late to give it sufficient time to develop the more efficient machinery needed to shoulder its responsibilities.

To this valid explanation of the persistence of a world monetary system anchored on the dollar, must be added, however, a number of other, less acceptable, motivations.

One of these is the routine-bound attitude of politicians and bureaucrats reluctant to change entrenched habits of thought and operation. Central bankers, for instance, have in general been the main opponents of monetary reform for that reason and for others. It was easier to continue using the dollar as a world parallel currency—even after its role in this respect became widely abused by the United States to finance its military expenditures in Vietnam and elsewhere—than to launch any composite IMF, or European monetary unit to replace it. To the attraction of huge interest earnings on US investments was added the fact that any international substitute for the dollar would entail the participation of the political authorities in decisions which central bankers understandably prefer to keep to themselves. They are as concerned with their own independence from politicians as with a national sovereignty which they, at least, know to be an illusion.

The continued accumulation of huge dollar holdings after the dollar's proximate devaluation became unavoidable and widely expected, and even after it became inconvertible and depreciated in fact for years on the exchange markets, was due to other, equally obvious, motivations. The refusal by any central bank to support the dollar on its exchange market would entail an appreciation of the country's currency, i.e. the loss of the competitive advantage conferred on its firms by the overvaluation of the dollar. Even if the undervalued currency countries could have acted promptly and simultaneously, their decisions would have had to meet strong opposition from all the firms— and their workers—producing for exports or for the domestic market in competition with imports from the United States. This made simultaneous action highly improbable. President de Gaulle, for instance, might have been tempted to stop intervening in the dollar market, or to cash for gold the dollars bought by the Bank of France (which he did indeed for a time, when the dollar was still convertible into gold) even at the risk of losing France's competitive advantage over the United States in the automobile market. But he could hardly do so if the Federal Republic of Germany and Italy did not follow suit, thus forcing the French automobile industry to face increased competition from Volkswagen, Fiat, etc., as well as from Ford, Chrysler, and General Motors.

The United States should not be blamed, therefore, for imposing upon foreign central banks the acceptance of a gold-convertible dollar at first, and later of an inconvertible paper dollar, as a main instrument of international monetary reserves. It did not initially seek that dangerous position for its currency, at the cost of increasing its overvaluation, and entailing balance-of-payments deficits and unemployment for important sectors of its economy.

The factors which have preserved the role of the dollar until now as an anchor for the world monetary system may not be counted upon to preserve it indefinitely in the future. The financial resources derived from it by the United States have been used, since the late 1960s and particularly today, for purposes increasingly questioned by a large fraction of public opinion, in the United States and elsewhere, even though the figures quoted in Table 1.D above show that they were not used to increase domestic consumptions and investments in the United States, but were essentially spent or invested abroad.

The first objection is the wild inflationary trend and skewed investment pattern imparted thereby to the world monetary system and abundantly discussed above.

The second is that the fiscal and monetary policies now pursued by the Reagan Administration are deemed to aggravate the world recession, notably through their incidence on interest rates.

The third—too rarely mentioned by economists—is that the resources that should be earmarked for collectively agreed high-priority goals of the international community are used instead for other objectives which may be distasteful to those who ultimately finance them.

One of these is the over-financing by commercial banks of lax policies of all sorts, unduly postponing anti-inflationary readjustments in a large number of countries. Together with US military—and often so-called 'economic'—aid, these have made possible an absurd level of military expenditure, often devoted to keeping in power corrupt and political dictatorships abhorred by public opinion, as well as warring ventures, fortunately kept localized so far, but which might spread into broader conflicts.

Domestic opponents of the Batistas, Trujillos, Somozas, etc. are thus led to seek the support of the USSR and to put in place regimes which are then dubbed 'Marxist–Leninist' and therefore deemed dangerous and unacceptable to the United States and its allies.

The world inflation cannot possibly be brought under control, nor the danger of nuclear suicide removed, as long as our political leaders —in the Atlantic world, as well as in the Communist world and in the 'non-aligned' countries—do not succeed in drastically curtailing the $750 billion or more now wasted each year on rearmament by a world already vastly over-armed, contrary to the deepest aspirations of their statesmen and of their people.

Finally, the inflationary financing of the United States hegemony by the world monetary system is threatened by a host of other policy conflicts—such as those about agricultural subsidies, steel prices, East–West trade, etc.—which threaten the cohesion of the Atlantic Alliance as well as the economic co-operation indispensable to world peace and prosperity.

III. Policy conclusion: the indispensable re-ordering of the world monetary system

Resuming world-wide negotiations

The policy conclusion flowing from this factual record seems to me inescapable. A fundamental re-ordering of the world monetary system remains as indispensable today to end the world infession as when I vainly argued, more than two decades ago,[15] that it was indispensable to avoid it.

The reforms that I advocated at that time were at long last substantially endorsed by responsible officials in the early 1970s, after ten years of continuous debates and negotiations at the IMF, the Group of Ten, the Committee of Twenty, etc.,[16] but this near-consensus was cavalierly brushed aside in the Jamaica Agreement and in the Second Amendment to the IMF Articles of Agreement. This Second Amendment is, to my mind, a sinister joke, whose only merit was to legalize belatedly the illegal repudiation of members' Bretton Woods commitments, without substituting any significant commitments in their place.

The keystone of the reforms on which a near-consensus had been reached was that SDRs (which I would rebaptize ICU, for International Currency Unit, or preferably IRM, for International Reserve Money) should be substituted as rapidly as possible for gold and national reserve currencies, permitting the IMF to adjust the bulk of reserve creation to the optimal non-inflationary potential of world trade and production. A presumptive rate of growth—à la Milton Friedman —averaging 3 to 5% a year should be inscribed in the Treaty, and any significant departure from it should require special weighted majorities of 2/3, 3/4, 4/5, or even more of members'—revised—voting power. All countries should notify the par value of their national currency to the IMF in this common denominator,[17] and surplus countries should retain their credit claims exclusively in this form, the new ICU or IRM being used in all market interventions and settlements, and for the accumulation of private as well as official working balances.

The IMF should use its expanded lending potential for its traditional operations, and—within the limits specified above—for longer-term loans for development financing of the least capitalized countries of the Third World through the intermediary of the World Bank, its affiliate institutions, regional development banks, etc., and even for other high-priority world purposes such as those of the World Health Organization, the fight against international pollution, etc.[18]

The transition from the present monetary disorder to a new world monetary order would, of course, have to deal with the huge 'overhang' of gold and national reserve currencies (particularly dollars) inherited from the past.

The latter should be exchanged for IRMs, with the 'maintenance of value' clause traditional in IMF transactions. This could be made more acceptable to the reserve-currency debtors if their resulting debt to the Fund were expressed in the most appropriate form, i.e. 'consols' (*rentes perpétuelles* in French) without any imperative maturity date, but repayable at the initiative of the debtors and accepted by them in settlement of any subsequent surpluses in their balance-of-payments. This would have the further merit of expressing operationally an obvious and inescapable truth, i.e. that *real* repayment of international credits can only be effected through the recovery of a surplus position by the debtor. All that financial arrangements can do otherwise is to reshuffle among the creditors the claims on a deficit country, but it is equally true that these creditors can receive *real* repayment for their claims only by running deficits. The 'consol' denomination would help dispel the financial fog clouding these transactions—and often misleading the transactors themselves into unfortunate and ineffective policy decisions—and adjust international lending practices to the facts of life.

Note also that the 'consols' accumulated by a reformed IMF should be negotiable in the market, under agreed conditions, whenever advisable to mop up excessive, inflationary, levels of liquidity.

Gold should similarly be exchanged from IRMs and gradually disposed of by the Fund in the market, as silver was in the past by member countries. If, however, this proved unnegotiable, for well-entrenched psychological and political reasons, it could be left to the present holders with the option of selling it themselves on the market, using it as collateral for loans, or selling it to other countries or to the Fund at any price acceptable to both parties.

The most urgent measure on which agreement should be sought, however, would be a fundamental reform of the absurd legal tradition under which book-keeping profits on gold—or foreign exchange—revaluation are passed on, sooner or later, to countries' treasuries, facilitating the monetary financing of further budgetary deficits by the very countries whose currency has depreciated, most often as a result of higher rates of inflationary financing than those of other countries. This is the most absurd of vicious circles, which central banks postpone as long as they can, but which is rarely—if ever—eluded indefinitely. These profits—or 'losses' for the less inflationary countries whose currency appreciates—should be sterilized in book-keeping 'revaluation accounts', to be drawn upon only in cases of *force majeure*, and only—if negotiable (?)—with the assent of the Fund.

The present time would be particularly propitious for such a reform. Gold holdings are now valued in central banks' balance sheets at a wide variety of arbitrary prices, ranging from the defunct official price to close to market prices, but gold profits, even when registered under these arrangements, have not yet been actually monetized. They already influence, nevertheless, the ability of governments and central banks to delay balance-of-payments adjustments, either by drawing on their reserves without showing any decline in their book-keeping amounts, or by obtaining, more easily, foreign loans backed by gold collateral.

Ministers of Finance, moreover, might be more receptive to sterilization proposals, now that the decline in gold market prices entails huge losses, rather than profits, on the world's gold reserves. Table 1.2 shows a decline of $400 billion from peak estimates of $765 billion in September 1980 to $365 billion at the end of June 1982. Such a sterilization might help restore badly shaken confidence in countries' national currencies.

In order not to lengthen this chapter further, I shall spare you a host of qualifications and suggestions regarding the actual negotiation of these proposed reforms and of other measures now called for by the fantastic mushrooming of Xeno-currency and Xeno-bond markets over the last decade. These have undoubtedly provided the oil-importing countries with the financing facilities indispensable in the short run to avoid the unsustainable reserve losses and deflationary impact entailed by drastic increases of oil prices, and which an unreformed IMF could not possibly have provided in time.

Inflationary reserve creation—well beyond the presumptive guidelines mentioned above—was unavoidable under these circumstances, but called imperatively for an institutional framework ensuring that:

(i) the financing facilities should not be excessive and delay unduly the policy adjustments required to restore a sustainable equilibrium as rapidly as possible; and that

(ii) they be earmarked for the investments most necessary to break inflationary bottlenecks, rather than for luxury consumption and armament expenditures in the poorer, as well as in the richer, countries.

Such an institutional framework is still missing today, and cannot be provided as long as the official authorities remain constricted by national borders which the private sectors have learned to by-pass by adjusting not only their policies, but their institutions ('multinational' firms), to the factual interdependence of all countries in the world economy.

It should be welcomed by the private sectors themselves, enabling them to conduct their own transactions in such a way as to serve the common good, in accordance with Adam Smith's 'invisible hand' so obviously missing today. It has become particularly necessary to enable the monetary authorities, national and international, to perform the role of 'lender of last resort' that might prove indispensable tomorrow to ward off renewed crises on the Xeno-currency market.

World-wide agreement on such reforms remains, nevertheless, distant at best.

The figures quoted above concerning the sources of the wildly inflationary reserve increases of the last decade and the distribution of reserve investments between the industrial and the less capitalized countries have not yet succeeded in laying to rest the initial objections raised against my reform proposals. Influential policy makers remain more concerned about the danger of inflationary financing of development in the Third World than about the continued flooding of world reserves by national currencies under the fixed—but adjustable—exchange rates and gold-convertible currency standard of yesterday, and under the floating exchange rates and inconvertible paper-currency standard of today.

The economic 'experts' to whom they listen must share some of the blame for this abdication of the negotiators of world monetary reform. Their 'realistic' appraisal of political obstacles deemed 'insuperable' inclines them to explain—and thus justify and 'whitewash'—the worst policy mishaps rather than to avoid them in the future.

No world reform is conceivable, of course, without the participation of the United States, and little can be hoped for in this respect in the immediate future from the present US Administration and its experts.

This brings me to the role of regional agreements in world-wide monetary reform.

Regional agreements

I have long pleaded for regional agreements as complementary rather than as alternative to world-wide monetary reforms.[19] Such agreements should be part and parcel of a world-wide, but decentralized monetary system exploiting to the full the very different degrees of policy co-operation and mutual commitments actually negotiable at any point of time between legally sovereign countries. Regional agreements and organizations have demonstrated their ability to achieve a growing co-ordination of policies and even institutions among countries highly interdependent on one another, keenly conscious of this interdependence, and amenable to such co-ordination because of similar national viewpoints inherited from a common geographical and historical background and a relatively homogeneous stage of economic development. Only looser co-operation and commitments are both feasible and necessary as a framework for national or regional decisions and policies giving rise to conflicts of interest, real or imagined, which cannot be arbitrated at the regional level.

What is true in the long run is even more relevant today. In the absence of universal agreement on essential world monetary reforms, the countries acutely aware of the disastrous impact of the world monetary disorder upon their economies should seek to reduce this impact, as far as feasible, by intra-regional and inter-regional agreements among all those willing to accept them. Their success in such undertakings offers the best chance to prompt others—including the mighty United States[20]—to imitate and join them.

The most hopeful sign of possible progress along these lines since the *breakdown* of Bretton Woods, in August 1971, is undoubtedly the modest *breakthrough* achieved at long last in March 1979 with the initiation of the *European Monetary System (EMS)*. The countries of the European Community have recognized that it is obviously impossible for each of them to use its national currency in the denomination and settlement of trade, services, and capital transactions carried out beyond national borders. Some of the countries involved in such transactions will, perforce, have to accept the use of one of their partners' currencies, or of a third currency. The prestige of the once mighty gold-convertible pound sterling and, later, of the mightier gold-convertible US dollar assured for a time the widespread acceptance of these currencies, in preference even to national currencies, as so-called 'parallel currencies' accepted nearly everywhere in the world as the best means for international settlements and for the accumulation of private working balances as well as of official reserves.

This was, however, for the reasons mentioned above, unviable in the long run. The switch from the gold-convertible dollar to a wildly fluctuating paper-dollar has made it less and less desirable as a world parallel currency. But the absence of any generally accepted alternative has retained for it a major role in the 'oligocentric' monetary system under which it now shares this role with the Deutschmark, the Swiss franc, the Japanese yen, etc. Every other country tries to relate its exchange rates and reserve accumulation to a major currency or to various baskets of major currencies reflecting their relative importance in its own external trade and payments pattern.

The countries of the European Community have tried to reduce the disadvantages of such a system by agreeing on the ECU as a common keystone for their efforts to reduce—and eventually eliminate—unnecessary fluctuations in intra-European exchange rates, which dominate by far their external trade, services, and capital transactions.

Table 1.8 clearly indicates that the ECU might also become a main pole of attraction for a similarly simplified system among a much wider group of countries including Western Europe, the Middle East, Africa, Australia, New Zealand, and the Communist countries. Many of these countries might welcome some form of *de jure* or *de facto* association with the ECU and the EMS. The ECU might become, in particular, a currency of denomination, and even settlements, for the oil trade of the OPEC countries, although they might prefer an ACU (Arab Currency Unit) made up—let us say—of matching shares of 40 or 45% each of ECUs and SDRs, and 10 or 20% of the major and stronger currencies of the Persian Gulf Area.[21] Some arrangement of this sort might possibly emerge from the recent formation of the 'Gulf Co-operation Council'.

Table 1.8 also shows, however, that the other countries—in Asia and in the Western Hemisphere—could not stabilize their own foreign trade sufficiently through such a close association with Western Europe alone. They are bound to seek an uneasy compromise between a Europe-oriented area, encompassing for most of them about 40% rather than 75% of their trade, and other countries or areas—particularly the United States and Japan—also accounting for a major portion of their foreign trade.

The undenied success of the EMS over its first years of operations should elicit interest for similar regional integration progress in other parts of the world. It should, most of all, encourage further progress by the Community itself towards the second stage of EMS, i.e. the EMF (European Monetary Fund), initially promised for the end of March 1981, but postponed—temporarily, I hope—for a number of good and bad reasons.

The worst argument for postponement is that of the initial opponents of EMS. They admit that its success surprised them, but argue that since it has worked so well, there is no urgency to improve it: it can continue *as is* until greater success and harmonization of national policies—and particularly of still widely disparate inflation rates—makes its proposed strengthening more acceptable to all participants.

The EMS success, however, has been due far more to favourable external circumstances than to transactions of the FECOM (Fonds Européen de Cooperation Monetaire).[22] The weakening of the Deutschmark, particularly, *vis-à-vis* the dollar has reduced tensions between EMS currencies, making recourse to the EMS intervention and credit mechanisms relatively minor in practice. Reverse developments in the Deutschmark–dollar rate have already begun and it would be sanguine to affirm that their amplification in the foreseeable future is inconceivable. The present EMS will face, in this event, immense difficulties which it is poorly equipped to handle, but which would make its successful operation more indispensable than in the 'fair weather' in which it has functioned so far.

I have submitted to the Community in this respect seven suggestions that I need not restate here. Some of you are familiar with them already, and others may read them.[23]

Some of these suggestions merely recommend an early implementation by EMS of the world-wide suggestions made above[24] (particularly with respect to the gold and dollar assets of the FECOM and of its members) and apply them to the issue of ECUs. They should lift one of the main objections to the ECU as a potential engine of inflation. A second objection to the acceptability of ECU settlements should also disappear if it were clarified that ECU reserve accounts are already fully usable for settlements within the Community and fully convertible, if needed, for outside settlements. When a member country incurs external deficits not financed by credits, it settles them by drawing *pari passu* on its ECU reserves with the FECOM (20%) and on those held outside the FECOM (80%), and may legally continue to do so until its reserves are fully exhausted.

If the deficits financed by ECU withdrawals are with other Community members, the global gold and dollar assets of the FECOM remain unchanged, its liabilities being merely redistributed between payers and payees. Convertibility would become a problem for the FECOM only if the global deficits of the Community as a whole towards the outside world threatened to exhaust its gold and dollar holdings. Such a danger is hardly to be feared: in spite of the exceptionally huge deficits incurred in 1981 and 1982, owing to new price rises for oil—whose prices are now declining—and of the sharp drop in gold prices, the gold and dollar assets of the FECOM still totalled more than $45 billion at the end of 1982. And if this were not deemed sufficient —which is practically inconceivable—Community countries could still mobilize in addition part of the $16 billion available under their 'swap agreements' with the United States.

These swaps should also, according to the brilliant suggestion of Jacques Van Ypersele, be multilateralized in the form of swaps with the European Monetary Fund and denominated in ECU. This would permit a more appropriate distribution of drawings and repayments between Community currencies than the near-exclusive use today of the Deutschmark in such transactions (which often needlessly aggravates the tensions on the intra-Community exchange rates). The reserve losses of some countries will undoubtedly force them, if they persist at the current pace, to change their policies or readjust their exchange rates *vis-à-vis* the ECU. This could entail some depreciation of the ECU itself *vis-à-vis* the dollar if these readjustments take place primarily through depreciation of weak currencies rather than, alternatively, through upward revaluation of

TABLE 1.8

Regional constellation of world trade in 1979

(Exports plus imports, in % of their world total for each region or country)[1]

Regions with regions →	1. European Community	2. Other Western European countries	*Western Europe* (1 + 2)	3. Africa[2] and Middle East	4. South Africa, Australia, and New Zealand	5. Communist countries[3]	*ECU Area*[?] (1 to 5)	6. United States	7. Canada	8. Latin America	*Western hemisphere* (6 to 8)	9. Japan	10. Other Asian countries	*Asia* (9 + 10)	*World*
1. European Community	52	15	67	11	2	5	84	7	1	3	11	2	3	5	100
2. Other Western European countries	47	16	63	10	1	10	84	7	1	3	11	2	3	5	100
Western Europe (1 +2)	51	15	66	11	2	5	84	7	1	3	11	2	3	5	100
3. Africa[2] and Middle East	39	11	49	7	1	2	60	15	1	5	21	12	7	19	100
4. South Africa, Australia, and New Zealand	29	6	35	6	5	4	50	17	2	2	20	17	13	30	100
5. Communist countries[3]	29	20	49	14	2	?	65	8	2	2	12	13	10	23	100

ECU Area? (1 to 5)	47	14	61	10	2	4	78	9	1	3	13	5	4	9	100
6. United States	20	5	26	13	3	2	44	x	18	15	33	11	11	23	100
7. Canada	10	2	12	3	1	2	18	69	x	4	73	5	4	9	100
8. Latin America	20	6	27	10	1	2	39	31	3	19	53	6	2	8	100
Western hemisphere (6 to 8)	19	5	24	11	2	2	38	19	11	14	45	9	8	17	100
9. Japan	10	3	13	20	6	6	45	22	3	5	30	x	25	25	100
10. Other Asian countries	16	3	19	11	4	4	38	19	1	2	22	22	18	40	100
Asia (9 + 10)	13	3	16	16	5	5	41	20	2	3	26	12	21	33	100
World	36	11	47	11	2	4	64	13	3	6	22	7	7	14	100

[1] The two diagonal lines frame the percentage of *mutual trade* of each regional group or country.
[2] Excluding South Africa.
[3] For the communist countries only trade with the non-communist countries, their mutual trade not being reported in *Direction of Trade*.
Source: Calculated from *Direction of Trade Yearbook 1973–9*, International Monetary Fund, 1980.

others in the ECU basket,[25] but it should not, in any case, lead to the inconvertibility of the ECU.

Advantage should also be taken of member countries' gold and dollar deposits to streamline and rationalize the absurdly complex and unco-ordinated credit arrangements inherited by the FECOM from a host of successive decisions taken before the liquidity and solvency guarantees derived from such deposits. This should entail the merging of present—and very different—provisions regarding 'marginal' and 'intramarginal' interventions on the exchange market and their settlement through ECU transfers in the books of the FECOM, rather than partly in dollars and partly through bilateral claims and debts in national currencies as is still the case today.

Finally, the acceptance of the ECU by the private market progresses today at a pace that should reassure the most sceptical central bankers, and encourage them to lift the administrative obstacles that are still met today by the private sectors wishing to make use of ECUs in their transactions.

The merging of national currencies into a single Community currency (now dubbed ECU), envisaged for the ultimate stage of full *Economic and Monetary Union* in several summit conferences of the EC heads of state and government, is certainly not for tomorrow. But the use of the ECU as an alternative to Euro-currencies might progress in a spectacular way within the course of 1984.

On the purely political plane, it presents the rare advantage of being able to rally the support of the most backward nationalists as well as of the enthusiasts of a United Europe. To cite only one name, a man like Michel Debré, whose intellectual integrity and strength of conviction force our admiration, would oppose strenuously the replacement of the French franc by the ECU, but he could have no objection—far to the contrary—to the use of the ECU in lieu of the Euro-dollars, Euro-marks, Euro-Swiss francs, etc. in which about $900 billion of European banks' assets and liabilities are currently denominated.

On the economic plane, the use of the ECU in intra-European contracts offers to the creditors as well as to the debtors a unit of account and settlements whose stability is—by its very definition —superior to that of the national currencies of the ECU basket, and the closest possible to exchange-rate stability for their external transactions. Indeed, intra-Community transactions constitute more than half of those transactions for most of the Community countries (about 75% for Belgium), while on average their transactions with the United States hardly reach 7% of this total.

Surely, the creditors who have full confidence in their forecasts— or those of their advisers—as to the future evolution of exchange rates will continue to invest their funds preferably in the currencies they deem to be the 'strongest'. But the enormous losses incurred in the past, at times on dollar holdings, and at other times on Deutschmarks, Swiss francs, etc., cannot fail to incite the many company treasurers to prefer the ECU, for their board of directors and their shareholders are certain to lavish far more blame on them for the exchange losses that they may incur, in case of forecasting errors, on the positions taken by them in a national currency, than for having failed to maximize the exchange profits that one or the other of these would have offered in comparison with ECU investments. Moreover, lenders must find borrowers, and the insistence of the former on using the hardest currencies will inevitably deter the latter—understandably allergic to them—or have to be off-set by lower interest rates. The ECU may prove a more acceptable compromise for all concerned.

Whatever one may think of these arguments, it is a fact that the private sectors are amply demonstrating today their interest for the ECU alternative to Euro-currencies. A round-table which I was privileged to organize at the University of Louvain-la-Neuve in June 1980, between a few academics and central bankers, but mostly a score of major European commercial banks,[27] was followed in short order by multiple and much larger meetings of hundreds of bankers and by a number of concrete initiatives, on which documentation is provided and updated periodically in the *ECU Newsletter* of the Istituto Bancario San Paolo of Turin. More than forty big banks in the Community countries, Switzerland, the United States, and Japan already accept ECU deposits and deposit certificates, lend in ECU, participate in the floating of ECU bonds, or exchange ECUs for national currencies, on sight and forward. In little more than two years, bonds have been issued or guaranteed in ECU for a total of nearly 6 billion and several thousand bank deposits and saving accounts have been opened in ECU.

Community officials are now examining with bank representatives a series of measures susceptible of lifting administrative obstacles and reducing the costs on ECU transactions, and the European Council has launched a first study of the official reforms deemed desirable and negotiable in the near future.

The administrative obstacles are due to the fact that the ECU basket includes both the national currency and other currencies, and is therefore subject to a double series of regulations and controls. The first reform called for, and already in effect in Belgium, France, and Italy, is to eliminate this handicap by assimilating the ECU to foreign currencies. This should be only a first step. Later reforms should aim at giving the ECU a preferential status, such as the availability of loans of last resort, requiring of course a minimum of prudential regulations, badly lacking today for most Euro-market transactions.

The excessive costs of transactions denominated in ECU are due to the fact that payments between customers of different banks used to entail a double set of foreign-exchange operations, the ECU having to be converted first into a national currency by the payer and then re-converted into ECU by the payee. Moreover, each bank had to cover itself against exchange risks by investing in national currencies, *pro rata* of their shares in the basket, any difference between its ECU loans and its ECU deposits. Banks are now studying various alternative formulas, some more ambitious than others, reducing these unneces-sary costs through the organization of one or several clearing houses, with or without the participation of national central banks and/or the Bank for International Settlements.

Two other possibilities under active discussion are the minting of ECU coins and the denomination of travellers' cheques in ECU to familiarize the public with an instrument too little known by it so far.

The success of these various initiatives could pave the way to two other developments.

The first would be the use of the ECU outside the Community, notably in financial transactions by other countries of Europe, the Middle East, and Africa, whose trade with one another and with the countries of the Community is more important by far than with other monetary areas.

The second possibility is a redefinition of the ECU, revolutionary and premature at this stage, but imperative in the long, or even medium term.

The ECU is, like the dollar, a reference currency and should *not* be defined by the currencies referring themselves to it. Each member country must already notify the exchange rate at which it stands ready to sell and to redeem its national currency against the ECU, and occasionally the changes of this rate which might still be deemed necessary, after mutual consultation, pending the ultimate, but still distant, completion of the planned *Economic and Monetary Union* of the Community.

But the ECU itself should remain unchanged, as was formerly the case for the IMF unit account. The ECU should be merely an ECU, as the dollar is a dollar, and—according to Gertrude Stein—'a rose is a rose, is a rose . . .'.

IV. Conclusions

The conclusions of this over-long chapter can be brief:

(i) The negotiation of the world-wide monetary reforms largely agreed upon in 1974 should be immediately resumed and incorporate additional provisions regarding the rôle of gold in the system and the financing of international disequilibria by the private market.

(ii) Pending the success of such negotiation, regional monetary agreements should provide whatever shelter is feasible against the present world monetary disorder. They should, in the longer run, become part and parcel of a more decentralized world monetary system.

(iii) The immediate strengthening of the EMS, in particular, should demonstrate the advantages and feasibility of the reforms advocated on a world level, accelerate their negotiation, and increase their effectiveness. It could, in the meantime, become an example and a pole of attraction for international monetary policy and arrangements in a wide 'Europe-oriented Area' encompassing all Western Europe, the Middle East, Africa, New Zealand, and Australia.

(iv) Responsible officials should view this line of action as politically beneficial to themselves and to their citizens rather than as involving unacceptable surrenders of national sovereignties which have become illusory and deceptive to all concerned and would indeed regain more effectiveness in the decentralized world monetary order proposed above.

Appendix

The reserve tables in the text are all calculated from the working tables below, which will be of interest only to the experts wishing to check—and improve—my own procedures and calculations.

(i) *Tables 1.I.A, B and C* show the *sources* of international monetary reserves. *Table I.A* differs from the IFS reserve tables in two respects:

    (a) The breakdown of reserves by *sources*, rather than by *composition*, entails the replacement of 'SDR *holdings*' by the full amount of 'SDR *allocations*', and of 'Reserve Positions in the Fund' only by 'IMF net credit'. The portions of 'Reserve Positions in the Fund' resulting from transfers of countries' gold and SDRs to the Fund are not, indeed, a source of reserve increases, and are credited in my tables to gold and to SDR allocations. The reserve-creating impact of IMF transactions is confined to 'IMF net credits', rather than to the full amount of 'Reserve Positions in the Fund'.

    (b) Gold holdings of the Bank for International Settlements, of the European Payments Union, of the European Fund, and particularly of the FECOM are—misleadingly—included by IFS under 'Foreign exchange' rather than under 'Gold', and *at market prices*. They are shown in Table I.A under 'Gold' at SDR 35 per ounce.

Tables 1.I.B and 1.I.C recalculate at market prices the estimates of Table 1.I.A, first in SDRs (Table 1.I.B), and secondly in US dollars (Table 1.I.C).

(ii) *Tables 1.II.A, B, and C* show the *geographical distribution* of Table I.A estimates between two major regions (the industrial and the non-industrial countries) and four sub-regions: (a) the United States (because of its importance and of the predominant role of dollar holdings in reserve creation); (b) other industrial countries; (c) the oil-exporting countries; and (d) the other non-industrial countries.

    They also show separately:

    (a) Gross reserve assets: Table 1.II.A

    (b) Reserve liabilities: Table 1.II.B

    (c) Net reserve claims or liabilities: Table 1.II.C

On the advice of the IMF staff, discrepancies between the IFS world totals and the sum of its regional totals are ascribed to the non-oil exporting developing (non-industrial) countries.

(iii) *Table 1.III* summarizes both the sources and the regional distribution of reserve assets, reserve liabilities, and net reserves, measured in SDRs and in dollars. The last four columns show the impact of fluctuations in gold prices and exchange rates upon the dollar estimates.

(iv) *Table 1.IV* calculates the IMF assets, liabilities, and net reserves at the end of 1981, broken down between gold, SDR and credit transactions, and measured both in SDRs and in dollars, the difference showing the impact of gold-price and exchange-rate fluctuations upon the dollar estimates.

(v) As noted at the bottom of page 73, these estimates are calculated from *International Financial Statistics*, April 1983, and *Yearbook 1982*, rather than from the revised estimates of *Yearbook 1983* used in Tables 1.5 and 1.6 in the text.

TABLE 1.1.A

Sources of international monetary reserves: 1949–82

A. Measured in billions of SDRs, at SDR 35 per ounce of gold and $ = SDR

End of	1949	1959	1969	1972	Sept. 1980	1980	1981	1982
I. *World gold of:*	34.4	40.1	40.8	41.3	40.2	40.2	40.2	40.0
A. *IMF*	1.5	2.4	2.3	5.4	3.6	3.6	3.6	3.6
B. *Countries*	33.0	37.7	38.5	35.9	36.5	36.6	36.6	36.4
1. Reported in IFS	32.9	37.8	39.0	35.7	33.3	33.3	33.3	33.1
2. *Plus* European institutions	0.1	−0.4	−0.4	0.2	3.3	3.3	3.3	3.3
(a) BIS	0.1	−0.5	−0.5	0.2	0.3	0.3	0.3	0.3
(b) EPU–EF–FECOM	x	–	0.1	–	3.0	3.0	3.0	3.0
II. *Credit reserves*	11.1	17.0	37.9	105.9	262.9	278.6	307.0	296.1
A. *Reported in IFS*	12.6	19.4	39.8	111.7	313.7	325.4	342.5	338.3
B. *Minus gold of:*	−1.5	−2.3	−1.9	−5.8	−50.8	−46.7	−35.5	−42.1
1. International Monetary Fund	−1.5	−2.4	−2.3	−5.4	−3.6	−3.6	−3.6	−3.6
2. European institutions at market prices	−0.1	0.1	0.4	−0.4	−47.2	−43.1	−31.9	−38.5
(a) at 35 per ounce	−0.1	0.1	0.4	−0.2	−3.3	−3.3	−3.3	−3.3
(b) Revaluation:	x	x	x	−0.2	−43.9	−39.8	−28.6	−35.3
(1) BIS–EPU–EF	x	x	x	−0.2	−3.4	−3.2	−2.3	−2.8
(2) FECOM	x	x	x	x	−40.5	−36.6	−26.3	−32.5

A. *Concerted internationally*	0.2	0.8	4.4	9.6	25.2	25.0	34.1	39.6
1. SDR allocations	x	x	x	9.3	17.4	17.4	21.4	21.4
2. IMF net credit	0.2	0.8	4.4	0.3	7.8	7.6	12.7	18.1
(a) Reserve position in IMF	1.7	3.3	6.7	6.3	12.6	16.8	21.3	25.5
(b) *Minus* from transfers of:	−1.5	−2.4	−2.3	−6.0	−4.8	−9.2	−8.6	−7.3
(1) Gold	−1.5	−2.4	−2.3	−5.4	−3.6	−3.6	−3.6	−3.6
(2) SDRs	x	x	x	−0.6	−1.2	−5.6	−5.0	−3.7
(a) Gross use of IMF credit	0.2	0.9	5.1	1.1	8.6	8.5	13.4	19.3
(b) *Minus* IMF profits	–	−0.1	−0.7	−0.8	−0.8	−0.8	−0.7	−1.2
B. *Foreign exchange*	10.9	16.2	33.5	96.3	237.7	253.7	272.9	256.6
1. Reported in IFS	11.0	16.1	33.0	96.7	284.9	296.7	304.8	295.1
2. *Minus* European institutions' gold at market price	−0.1	0.1	0.4	−0.4	−47.2	−43.1	−31.9	−38.5
1. Identified US debt	3.2	10.1	17.9	64.4	144.8	154.5	168.1	175.7
(a) Direct	3.2	10.1	16.0	56.7	119.5	129.0	145.8	156.6
(b) US banks branches abroad	...	...	1.9	7.7	25.2	25.5	22.3	19.1
2. Unidentified	7.7	6.1	15.6	31.9	93.0	99.2	104.8	80.9
III. *Total reserve assets:* I + II	45.5	57.1	78.7	147.2	303.1	318.9	347.2	336.2
1. Reported in IFS	45.5	57.1	78.7	147.4	347.0	358.7	375.8	371.5
2. *Minus* revaluation of European institutions' gold	x	x	x	−0.2	−43.9	−39.8	−28.6	−35.3
1. Countries' gold	33.0	37.7	38.5	35.9	36.5	36.6	36.6	36.4
2. Gold transferred to IMF	1.5	2.4	2.3	5.4	3.6	3.6	3.6	3.6
3. Credit reserves	11.1	17.0	37.9	105.9	262.9	278.7	307.0	296.1

TABLE 1.I.B.

Sources of international monetary reserves: 1949–82

B. Measured in billions of SDRs, at market gold prices and $/SDR exchange rates

End of	1949	1959	1969	1972	Sept. 1980	1980	1981	1982
I. *World gold*	34.4	40.1	40.8	70.5	583.0	531.1	392.2	474.3
A. *IMF*	1.5	2.4	2.3	9.2	52.6	47.8	35.3	42.8
B. *Countries' gold:*	33.0	37.7	38.5	61.4	530.4	483.3	356.8	431.5
1. Reported in IFS	32.9	37.8	39.0	61.0	483.3	440.2	325.0	392.9
2. *Plus* European institutions	0.1	−0.1	−0.4	0.4	47.2	43.1	31.9	38.5
(a) BIS	0.1	−0.1	−0.5	0.3	3.7	3.5	2.6	3.0
(b) EPU–EF–FECOM	x	–	0.1	0.1	43.5	39.6	29.3	35.5
II. *Credit reserves*	11.1	17.0	37.9	102.1	214.0	234.5	295.3	256.9
A. *Concerted internationally*	0.2	0.8	4.4	5.8	−23.7	−19.2	2.4	0.4
1. SDR allocations	x	x	x	9.3	17.4	17.4	21.4	21.4

2. IMF net credit	0.2	0.8	4.4	−3.5	−41.1	−36.5	−19.0	−21.1
(a) Reserve position in IMF	1.7	3.3	6.7	6.3	12.6	16.8	21.3	25.5
(b) *Minus* from-transfers of:	−1.5	−2.4	−2.3	−9.8	−53.7	−53.4	−40.3	−46.5
(1) Gold	−1.5	−2.4	−2.3	−9.2	−52.6	−47.8	−35.3	−42.8
(2) SDRs	x	x	x	−0.6	−1.2	−5.6	−5.0	−3.7
(a) Gross use of IMF credit	0.2	0.9	5.1	1.1	8.6	8.5	13.4	19.3
(b) *Minus* IMF profits:	–	−0.1	−0.7	−4.6	−49.7	−45.0	−32.4	−40.4
(1) on use of IMF credit	–	−0.1	−0.7	−0.8	−0.8	−0.8	−0.7	−1.2
(2) on gold holdings	x	x	x	−3.8	−48.5	−44.2	−31.7	−39.2
B. *Foreign exchange*	10.9	16.2	33.5	96.3	237.7	253.6	272.8	256.6
1. Identified US debt	3.2	10.1	17.9	64.4	144.8	154.5	168.1	175.7
(a) Direct	3.2	10.1	16.0	56.7	119.5	129.0	145.8	156.6
(b) US banks branches abroad	...	...	1.9	7.7	25.2	25.5	22.3	19.1
2. Unidentified	7.7	6.1	15.6	31.9	93.0	99.1	104.7	80.9
III. *Total reserve assets*: I + II	45.5	57.1	78.7	172.7	797.0	765.7	687.5	731.2
1. Countries gold	33.0	37.7	38.5	61.4	530.4	483.3	356.8	431.5
2. Gold transferred to IMF	1.5	2.4	2.3	9.2	52.6	47.8	35.3	42.8
3. Credit reserves	11.1	17.0	37.9	102.1	214.0	234.5	295.3	256.9
Memo: SDRs per ounce of gold	35.00	35.00	35.00	59.78	508.02	462.20	341.51	414.19
US dollars per SDR	1.0000	1.0000	1.0000	1.0857	1.3124	1.2754	1.1640	1.1031

TABLE 1.1.C

Sources of international monetary reserves: 1949–82

C. Measured in billions of US dollars, at market gold prices and $/SDR exchange rates

End of	1949	1959	1969	1972	Sept. 1980	1980	1981	1982
I. World gold	34.4	40.1	40.8	76.6	765.0	677.3	456.5	523.2
A. IMF	1.5	2.4	2.3	10.0	69.0	61.0	41.1	47.3
B. Countries' gold	33.0	37.7	38.5	66.6	696.2	616.4	415.4	475.9
1. Held directly	32.9	37.8	39.0	66.2	634.2	561.4	378.3	433.5
2. Held through European institutions	0.1	−0.1	−0.4	0.4	61.9	54.9	37.1	42.5
(a) BIS	0.1	−0.1	−0.5	0.4	4.8	4.4	3.0	3.3
(b) EPU–EF–FECOM	x	–	0.1	0.1	57.1	50.5	34.1	39.2
II. Credit reserves	11.1	17.0	37.9	110.9	280.8	299.1	343.7	283.4
A. Concerted internationally	0.2	0.8	4.4	6.3	−31.1	−24.4	2.8	0.4
1. SDR allocations	x	x	x	10.1	22.8	22.2	24.9	23.6

2. IMF net credit	0.2	0.8	4.4	−3.8	−53.9	−46.6	22.1	−23.2
(a) Reserve position in IMF	1.7	3.3	6.7	6.9	16.6	21.5	24.8	28.1
(b) *Minus* from transfers of:	−1.5	−2.4	−2.3	−10.6	−70.5	−68.1	−47.0	−51.3
(1) Gold	−1.5	−2.4	−2.3	−10.0	−69.0	−61.0	−41.1	−47.3
(2) SDRs	x	x	x	−0.7	−1.6	−7.1	−5.8	−4.1
(a) Gross use of IMF credit	0.2	0.9	5.1	1.2	11.3	10.8	15.6	21.3
(b) *Minus* IMF profits:	–	−0.1	−0.7	−4.9	−65.3	−57.4	−37.7	−44.5
(1) on use of IMF credit	–			−0.8	−1.0	−1.1	−0.8	−1.3
(2) on gold holdings	x	x	x	−4.1	−64.2	−56.4	−36.9	−43.3
valued at market price (−)	−1.5	−2.4	−2.3	−10.0	−69.0	−61.0	−41.1	−47.3
valued at $35 per ounce	1.5	2.4	2.3	5.8	4.8	4.6	4.2	3.6
B. *Foreign exchange*	10.9	16.2	33.5	104.6	312.0	323.5	317.7	283.0
1. Identified US debt	3.2	10.1	17.9	69.9	190.0	197.1	195.7	193.8
(a) *Direct*	3.2	10.1	16.0	61.5	156.9	164.6	169.7	172.7
(b) *US banks' branches abroad*	...	...	1.9	8.4	33.1	32.5	26.0	21.1
2. Unidentified	7.7	6.1	15.6	34.7	122.0	126.5	122.0	89.2
III. *Total reserve assets*: I + II	45.5	57.1	78.7	187.5	1046.0	976.4	800.2	806.6
A. Countries' gold	33.0	37.7	38.5	66.6	696.2	616.4	415.4	475.9
B. Gold transferred to IMF	1.5	2.4	2.3	10.0	69.0	61.0	41.1	47.3
C. Credit reserves	11.1	17.0	37.9	110.9	280.8	299.1	343.7	283.4

Notes and Sources: See Table 1.III.

TABLE 1.II.A

Regional distribution of international monetary reserves: 1949–82
A. Reserve assets (SDR billions)

End of →	1949	1959	1969	1972	Sept. 1980	1980	1981	1982
I. *Credit claims*	12.6	19.5	40.2	111.3	266.5	282.3	310.6	299.8
Industrial countries	6.1	12.5	26.0	79.4	129.7	140.8	153.3	145.9
United States	1.5	2.0	5.1	2.5	9.0	12.2	16.3	20.7
Other	4.6	10.5	20.9	77.0	120.7	128.6	137.0	125.2
Non-industrial countries	6.5	6.9	14.2	32.0	140.2	141.5	157.3	153.9
Oil exporting	0.5	1.6	2.8	8.9	70.8	72.2	80.0	75.6
Other	6.0	5.3	11.4	23.2	69.5	69.3	77.4	78.3
A. *SDR holdings*	x	x	x	8.7	16.2	11.8	16.4	17.7
Industrial countries	x	x	x	7.1	12.0	8.9	11.9	14.1
United States	x	x	x	1.8	3.1	2.0	3.5	4.8
Other	x	x	x	5.3	8.9	6.8	8.4	9.3
Non-industrial countries	x	x	x	1.6	4.2	2.9	4.5	3.7
Oil exporting	x	x	x	0.3	1.6	1.2	1.8	2.1
Other	x	x	x	1.3	2.6	1.7	2.7	1.6
B. *Reserve position in IMF*	1.7	3.3	6.7	6.3	12.6	16.8	21.3	25.5
Industrial countries	1.6	3.1	5.9	5.2	8.1	10.7	13.5	17.1
United States	1.5	2.0	2.3	0.4	1.3	2.2	4.3	6.7
Other	0.1	1.1	3.6	4.8	6.8	8.5	9.2	10.4
Non-industrial countries	0.1	0.2	0.8	1.1	4.5	6.1	7.8	8.4
Oil exporting	–	–	0.2	0.3	3.1	4.1	5.8	6.7
Other	0.1	0.2	0.6	0.8	1.4	2.1	2.0	1.7

C Foreign exchange	10.9	16.2	33.5	96.3	237.7	253.7	272.9	256.6
Industrial countries	4.5	9.4	20.1	66.9	106.2	121.3	127.8	114.7
United States	–	–	2.8	0.2	4.7	7.9	8.4	9.3
Other	4.5	9.4	17.3	66.7	101.5	113.3	119.4	105.5
Non-industrial countries	6.4	6.8	13.4	29.4	131.5	132.4	145.1	141.8
Oil exporting	0.5	1.6	2.6	8.3	66.1	66.9	72.4	66.8
Other	5.9	5.2	10.8	21.1	65.4	65.5	72.7	75.1
II. Gold	33.0	37.7	38.5	35.9	36.5	36.6	36.6	36.5
Industrial countries	30.0	33.9	32.9	30.8	30.8	30.8	30.8	30.8
United States	24.6	19.5	11.9	9.7	9.3	9.3	9.2	9.2
Other	5.4	14.4	21.0	21.2	21.6	21.6	21.6	21.6
Non-industrial countries	3.0	3.8	5.7	5.1	5.7	5.8	5.7	5.6
Oil exporting	0.7	0.9	1.3	1.2	1.4	1.4	1.5	1.5
Other	2.3	2.8	4.4	3.9	4.3	4.4	4.3	4.2
III. Total	45.5	57.1	78.7	147.2	303.1	318.9	347.2	336.2
Industrial countries	36.0	46.4	58.8	110.1	157.1	171.7	184.1	176.7
United States	26.0	21.5	17.0	12.1	18.3	21.5	25.5	29.9
Other	10.0	24.9	41.9	98.0	138.9	150.2	158.6	146.8
Non-industrial countries	9.5	10.7	19.9	37.1	146.0	147.2	163.0	159.5
Oil exporting	1.2	2.5	4.1	10.0	72.2	73.6	81.4	77.0
Other	8.3	8.2	15.8	27.1	73.8	73.6	81.6	82.5

TABLE 1.II.B

Regional distribution of international monetary reserves: 1949–82

B. Reserve liabilities (SDR billions)

End of →	1949	1959	1969	1972	Sept. 1980	1980	1981	1982
A. *SDR allocations*	x	x	x	9.3	17.4	17.4	21.4	21.4
Industrial countries	x	x	x	6.7	11.9	11.9	14.4	14.4
United States	x	x	x	2.3	4.0	4.0	4.9	4.9
Other	x	x	x	4.4	7.9	7.9	9.5	9.5
Non-industrial countries	x	x	x	2.6	5.5	5.5	7.0	7.0
Oil exporting	x	x	x	0.4	1.1	1.1	1.5	1.5
Other	x	x	x	2.2	4.4	4.4	5.5	5.5
B. *Gross IMF credits*	0.2	0.9	5.1	1.1	8.6	8.5	13.4	19.3
Industrial countries	0.1	0.5	3.8	–	1.2	1.0	0.5	0.1
United States	–	0.5	1.0	–	–	–	–	–
Other	0.1	–	2.8	–	1.2	1.0	0.5	0.1

Non-industrial countries	0.1	0.4	1.3	1.1	7.4	7.4	12.8	19.2
Oil-exporting	–	–	0.1	0.1	–	–	–	–
Other	0.1	0.4	1.1	1.0	7.4	7.4	12.8	19.2
C. *Foreign exchange*	10.9	16.2	33.5	96.3	237.7	253.6	272.8	256.6
Industrial countries	10.9	16.2	33.5	96.3	237.7	253.6	272.8	256.6
United States	3.2	10.1	17.9	64.4	144.8	154.5	168.1	175.7
Other	7.7	6.1	15.6	31.9	93.0	99.1	104.7	80.9
Non-industrial countries	–	–	–	–	–	–	–	–
Oil exporting	–	–	–	–	–	–	–	–
Other	–	–	–	–	–	–	–	–
Total	11.1	17.1	38.5	106.7	263.6	279.4	307.6	297.3
Industrial countries	11.0	16.7	37.3	103.0	250.8	266.5	287.8	271.1
United States	3.2	10.6	18.9	66.7	148.8	158.5	173.0	180.6
Other	7.8	6.1	18.4	36.4	102.0	108.0	114.7	90.6
Non-industrial countries	0.1	0.4	1.3	3.7	12.9	12.9	19.8	26.2
Oil exporting	–	–	0.1	0.5	1.1	1.1	1.5	1.5
Other	0.1	0.4	1.1	3.2	11.8	11.8	18.3	24.7

TABLE 1.II.C
Regional distribution of international monetary reserves: 1949–82
C. Net reserve claims or liabilities (SDR billions)

End of ⟶	1949	1959	1969	1972	Sept. 1980	1980	1981	1982
I. Net credit claims	+1.5	+2.3	+1.7	+4.6	+2.8	+2.8	+2.9	+2.5
Industrial countries	−5.0	−4.2	−11.3	−23.7	−124.5	−125.8	−134.6	−125.2
United States	−1.7	−8.6	−13.8	−64.2	−139.8	−146.3	−156.8	−159.9
Other	−3.2	4.4	2.4	40.5	15.3	20.6	22.2	34.6
Non-industrial countries	6.4	6.6	13.0	28.4	127.3	128.5	137.5	127.7
Oil exporting	0.5	1.6	2.7	8.4	69.7	71.1	78.5	74.1
Other	5.9	5.0	10.3	20.0	57.7	57.4	59.0	53.6
A. SDR: holdings minus allocations	x	x	x	−0.6	−1.2	−5.6	−5.0	−3.7
Industrial countries	x	x	x	+0.4	+0.1	−3.0	−2.5	−0.3
United States	x	x	x	−0.5	−1.0	−2.0	−1.4	−0.1
Other	x	x	x	+0.9	+1.1	−1.0	−1.1	−0.2
Non-industrial countries	x	x	x	−1.0	−1.3	−2.6	−2.5	−3.3
Oil exporting	x	x	x	−0.1	+0.5	+0.1	+0.3	+0.6
Other	x	x	x	−1.0	−1.7	−2.7	−2.8	−3.9
B. To or from (−) IMF	+1.5	+2.3	x	+0.6	+1.2	+5.6	+5.0	+3.7
1. Net credits	+1.5	+2.3	+1.7	+5.2	+4.0	+8.3	+8.0	+6.1
Industrial countries	+1.4	+2.5	+2.0	+5.2	+6.9	+9.7	+13.0	+16.9
United States	+1.5	+1.5	+1.3	+0.4	+1.3	+2.2	+4.3	+6.7
Other	–	+1.0	+0.8	+4.8	+5.6	+7.4	+8.7	+10.3
Non-industrial countries	–	−0.2	−0.4	–	−2.9	−1.3	−5.0	−10.8
Oil exporting	–	–	+0.1	+0.2	+3.1	+4.1	+5.8	+6.7
Other	–	−0.2	−0.5	−0.1	−5.8	−5.4	−10.8	−17.5

2. *Minus unallocated IMF net reserves*

reserves	−1.5	−2.3	−1.7	−4.6	−2.8	−2.8	−2.9	−2.5
(a) Gold holdings (−)	−1.5	−2.4	−2.3	−5.4	−3.6	−3.6	−3.6	−3.6
(b) Profits (+)	−	+0.1	+0.7	+0.8	+0.8	+0.8	+0.7	+1.2
C. *Foreign exchange*	x	x	x	x	x	x	x	x
Industrial countries	−6.4	−6.8	−13.4	−29.4	−131.5	−132.4	−145.1	−141.8
United States	−3.2	−10.1	−15.1	−64.1	−140.1	−146.6	−159.7	−156.4
Other	−3.2	+3.4	+1.7	+34.8	+8.6	+14.1	+14.6	+24.6
Non-industrial countries	+6.4	+6.8	+13.4	+29.4	+131.5	+132.4	+145.1	+141.8
Oil exporting	+0.5	+1.6	+2.6	+8.3	+66.1	+66.9	+72.4	+66.8
Other	+5.9	+5.2	+10.8	+21.1	+65.4	+65.5	+72.7	+75.1
II. *Gold*	33.0	37.7	38.5	35.9	36.5	36.6	36.6	36.5
Industrial countries	30.0	33.9	32.9	30.8	30.8	30.8	30.8	30.8
United States	24.6	19.5	11.9	9.7	9.3	9.3	9.2	9.2
Other	5.4	14.4	21.0	21.2	21.6	21.6	21.6	21.6
Non-industrial countries	3.0	3.8	5.7	5.1	5.7	5.8	5.7	5.6
Oil exporting	0.7	0.9	1.3	1.2	1.4	1.4	1.5	1.5
Other	2.3	2.8	4.4	3.9	4.3	4.4	4.3	4.2
III. *Total*	+34.4	+40.0	+40.1	+40.5	+39.4	+39.4	+39.5	+38.9
Industrial countries	+25.0	+29.7	+21.5	+7.1	−93.7	−94.9	−103.8	−94.4
United States	+22.8	+10.9	−1.9	−54.5	−130.5	−137.1	−147.5	−150.7
Other	+2.2	+18.8	+23.4	+61.6	+36.8	+42.1	+43.8	+56.2
Non-industrial countries	+9.4	+10.3	+18.6	+33.4	+133.1	+134.2	+143.3	+133.4
Oil exporting	+1.2	+2.5	+4.0	+9.6	+71.0	+72.5	+79.9	+75.5
Other	+8.2	+7.8	+14.7	+23.9	+62.0	+61.8	+63.3	+57.8

Notes and Sources: See Table 1.III.

TABLE 1.III

Sources and regional distribution of reserve assets, reserve liabilities, and net reserves: 1949–82
(SDR or dollars, billions)

	Measured in SDRs — End of				Measured in dollars — End of		Period changes — in SDRs			in $		Impact of fluctuations in gold prices and SDR-$ exchange rates — at end of		on period changes	
	1949	1969	1978	1982	1978	1982	1950–69	1970–8	1979–82	1970–8	1979–82	1978	1982	1970–8	1979–82
I. Reserve assets	46	79	282	336	556	807	33	203	54	477	251	274	471	274	197
United States	<u>26</u>	<u>17</u>	<u>15</u>	<u>30</u>	<u>69</u>	<u>143</u>	<u>−9</u>	<u>−2</u>	<u>15</u>	<u>52</u>	<u>74</u>	<u>54</u>	<u>113</u>	<u>54</u>	<u>59</u>
Rest of world	<u>20</u>	<u>62</u>	<u>267</u>	<u>306</u>	<u>486</u>	<u>663</u>	<u>42</u>	<u>205</u>	<u>39</u>	<u>424</u>	<u>177</u>	<u>219</u>	<u>357</u>	<u>220</u>	<u>138</u>
Industrial countries	10	42	158	147	317	419	32	116	−11	275	102	159	272	159	113
Oil exporting	1	4	46	77	67	103	2	42	31	63	36	21	26	21	5
Other countries	8	16	63	82	103	141	8	47	19	87	38	40	59	40	19
II. Reserve liabilities	11	39	242	297	315	328	28	203	55	276	13	73	31	73	−42
United States	<u>3</u>	<u>19</u>	<u>152</u>	<u>181</u>	<u>197</u>	<u>199</u>	<u>16</u>	<u>133</u>	<u>29</u>	<u>179</u>	<u>2</u>	<u>45</u>	<u>18</u>	<u>45</u>	<u>−27</u>
Rest of world	<u>8</u>	<u>20</u>	<u>90</u>	<u>117</u>	<u>117</u>	<u>129</u>	<u>12</u>	<u>70</u>	<u>27</u>	<u>98</u>	<u>12</u>	<u>27</u>	<u>12</u>	<u>27</u>	<u>−15</u>
Industrial countries	8	18	81	91	106	100	11	62	10	88	−6	25	9	25	−16
Oil exporting	–	–	–	1	–	2	–	–	1	–	2	–	1	–	1
Other countries	–	1	8	25	11	27	1	7	17	10	16	3	2	3	−1

III. *Net reserves:*

I + II	34	40	40	39	241	479	6	—	—1	201	238	201	440	201	239
United States	23	—2	—137	—151	—128	—56	—25	—135	—14	—126	72	9	95	9	86
Rest of world	12	42	177	190	369	534	30	135	13	327	165	192	344	192	152
Industrial countries	2	23	76	56	211	320	21	53	—20	187	109	135	264	135	129
Oil exporting	1	4	46	76	66	101	3	42	30	62	35	20	25	20	5
Other countries	8	15	54	58	92	114	6	40	34	77	22	38	56	38	17

Notes: 1. SDR estimates are uniformly calculated at SDR 35 per ounce of gold, with the $ equal to the SDR, while $ estimates are uniformly calculated at market gold prices and $-SDR exchange rates, the differences showing the impact of fluctuations in gold prices and exchange rates upon the $ estimates. (This entails a number of corrections in the IFS estimates, which include FECOM and BIS gold at market price under foreign exchange holdings measured in SDRs.)

2. US liabilities are slightly understated, and other industrial countries' liabilities correspondingly overstated, because of the inclusion of unidentifiable foreign exchange liabilities under the latter.

3. For the world as a whole, net reserves are equal to world gold, *minus* IMF undistributed profits and; after 1980, minor accounting adjustments for members short-term borrowings under enlarged access policy and for borrowed reserves held in suspense.

Sources: *International Financial Statistics*, April 1983, and *Yearbooks* 1979 and 1982; except for estimated US foreign exchange liabilities, calculated from line 1 of Table 3.15 and line 60 of Table 3.14 of the *Federal Reserve Bulletin*.

TABLE 1.IV

Balance sheet of the International Monetary Fund at the end of 1981
(SDR or dollars, millions)

	Total	Gold holdings	SDR holdings	Use of Fund credit
I. *Measured in SDR[1]*				
1. Assets	22,006	3,620	5,019	13,367
2. Liabilities	21,323	3,620	5,019	12,684
3. Net reserves (1 — 2)	683	–	–	683[3]
II. *Measured in $[2]*				
1. Assets	62,519	41,118	5,842	15,559
2. Liabilities	24,820	4,214	5,842	14,764
3. Net reserves (1 — 2)	37,699	36,904	–	795[3]
III. *Impact of fluctuations in gold prices and exchange rates on*				
1. Assets $(II_1 - I_1)$	40,513	37,498	823	2,192
2. Liabilities $(II_2 - I_2)$	3,497	594	823	2,080
3. Net reserves $(II_3 - I_3)$	37,016	36,904	–	112

[1] Estimates measured in SDR (line I.1, 2, and 3) value gold at SDR 35 per ounce, and assets and liabilities in SDRs.

[2] Estimates measured in $ (lines II.1, 2, and 3) value gold at $397.50 per ounce (end of 1981 price), and other assets and liabilities in dollars, at $1.1640 per SDR.

[3] SDR 683 million and $795 million are the sum of:
   a. SDR 968 million (= $1,127 million) profits not credited to members;
   b. *plus* SDR 100 million (= $116 million) of member's short-term borrowings under enlarged access policy;
   c. *minus* SDR 385 million (= $448 million) of borrowed reserves held in suspense.
   (These last two items would not appear in calculations for earlier years.)

Notes and Sources

[1] *World Economic Outlook*, International Monetary Fund, Washington D.C., 1982, Table 24, p. 165.

[2] For the dollar, as early as 1957 in my *Europe and the Money Muddle*, more extensively in my October 1959 presentation to the US Congress Joint Economic Committee, and in my 1960 *Gold and the Dollar Crisis* (both books being published by Yale University Press, New Haven, Conn.). The latest of these warnings was entitled 'How to Arrest a Threatening Relapse into the 1930s', *Bulletin of the National Bank of Belgium*, November 1971.

[3] Historians might be interested to refer to the first condemnation of the gold-exchange standard, as early as 1795, by Emmanuel Kant in the fourth article of his *Eternal Peace, A Philosophical Essay*:

No objection can be taken to seeking assistance, either outside or within the State, on behalf of the economic administration of the country. . . . But a credit system under which debts go increasing indefinitely . . . is a dangerous money power. This arrangement—the ingenious invention of a commercial people in this century —constitutes in fact a treasure for war, exceeding the treasures of all other States taken together. It can only be exhausted by the ensuing deficit of the exchequer, which may be long postponed by trade prosperity and its impact upon production and profits.

This facility for waging war, combined with the inclination of rulers towards it (an inclination that seems implanted in human nature) is therefore a great obstacle to perpetual peace. Its prohibition must be made a preliminary article of it, all the more so as the inevitable bankruptcy would encompass many other States in the eventual ruin, without any fault on their part. The other States are therefore justified at least in allying themselves against a State acting with such arrogance.

(This slightly modernized version is my own, but based largely on the translation of Jean Darbellay in *Vers la Paix Perpétuelle*, 2nd edition, Presses Universitaires de France, Paris, 1974.)

[4] The sum of foreign official assets, treasury securities, and other claims on US banks, reported in Table B 105, page 281 of the *Economic Report of the President*, February 1983. This includes minor amounts of claims in the creditor countries' currencies.

[5] The table on page 116 of the June 1982 BIS *Annual Report* provides consolidated figures for the period 1978-81. I have used previous BIS reports and Morgan Guaranty's *World Financial Markets* to calculate my rough estimates for 1969. For those who would question the latter, or consider—justifiably—that the yearly gross rates of 26% and 28% are unduly blown up by the small size of these 1969 estimates, I note that the yearly growth rate for 1981 was still 21% for both gross and net bank lending.

[6] 'Report to Board of Governors by Committee of Twenty', *International Monetary Reform: Documents of the Committee of Twenty*, IMF, Washington D.C., 1974.

[7] Table 1.III in the Appendix analyses the contrasting evolution of world reserve increases over the periods 1950-69, 1970-8, and 1979-82. Note that the 'World' total in this table, as in others, does not include the Communist countries, for which complete estimates are not available to the IMF.

[8] For further details, and for a presentation of major changes between three sub-periods (1970-3, 1974-8, and 1979-80) see my paper on 'The Impact of Balance of Payments Transactions upon the 1970-80 Explosion of International Reserve Assets under the Present Monetary System', *Aussenwirtschaft*, June–September 1982.

[9] Changes in valuation—resulting in part from exchange-rate fluctuations —and in coverage account for other, but relatively minor changes, in the evolution of the international capital position. See 'The International Investment Position of the United States in 1982' in the August 1983 issue of the *Survey of Current Business*, pp. 42-8, and similar articles in the August or September issues of previous years.

[10] These might be disregarded, but their inclusion is necessary in order to permit my later reconciliation (in the last four columns of Table 1.D) of the year-end stock estimates with the balance-of-payment flows which explain their changes.

[11] Their 1969 year-end guesstimate of $5 billion is obviously worthless, but the $133 billion one for the end of 1982 is due nearly entirely to the more reliable estimates of 1970-82, which certainly should not be disregarded as they are in the *Survey* table.

[12] The remaining $11 billion being held in gold, valued at its last official price.

[13] A regional breakdown is, regrettably, impossible to calculate for net official reserves, liabilities being reported separately only for Western Europe, Canada, and the Western Hemisphere. Official assets can be broken down, but are relatively minor ($34 billion), although understated by the measurement of reported gold assets ($11 billion) at the last official rate of $42.22 per ounce.

[14] Gross bank lending to the non-OPEC developing countries and to Eastern Europe by all the banks reporting to the BIS was estimated to total about $291 billion at the end of 1981: $230 billion to the former, and $61 billion to the latter.

[15] In *Europe and the Money Muddle* (Yale University Press, 1957), and particularly in my 28 October 1959 statement to the Joint Economic Committee of the US Congress, reproduced in *Gold and the Dollar Crisis* (Yale University Press, 1960). I repeated this warning on the eve of the 1970s recession in the article, 'How to Arrest a Threatening Relapse into the 1930s' (November 1971).

[16] See particularly: (i) the Executive Directors' report on the *Reform of the International Monetary System*, IMF, August 1972, and (ii) the 14 June 1974 'Report to Board of Governors by Committee of Twenty' in *International Monetary Reform: Documents of the Committee of Twenty*, IMF, 1974.

[17] It is ludicrous to reflect that there is none at present in the revised IMF Articles of Agreement.

[18] See my article on 'The Use of SDR Finance for Collectively Agreed Purposes', *Banca Nazionale del Lavoro Quarterly Review*, March 1971.

[19] See Part Three of *The World Money Maze* (Yale University Press, 1966), pp. 375–543, particularly pp. 407–18 reproducing my first memorandum to the IMF, in September 1947, on this subject; and the most recent of many other articles in 'The Relationship Between the International Monetary System and Regional Monetary Systems', in *Arab Monetary-Integration*, edited by Khair El-Din Haseeb and Samir Makdisi for the Centre for Arab Unity Studies and the Arab Monetary Fund (Croom Helm, London and Canberra, 1982).

[20] Note that the European Monetary Co-operation Fund (FECOM) could supplement the IMF in the operations suggested on p. 46 to solve the 'dollar overhang' problem. It could offer ECU 'substitution accounts' to reluctant dollar holders more interested in ECU holdings than in SDR holdings. The dollars so acquired by it would also be exchanged for 'consols', cashable only to settle future deficits of the European Community.

[21] This would include in the ACU a reasonable proportion of yens and dollars, absent from the ECU, while avoiding the excessive proportion of US dollars in the SDR.

[22] I use this acronym because it is better known in Europe and easier to pronounce than the English acronym EMCF, for *European Monetary Co-operation Fund*.

[23] See 'Le système monétaire européen', *Banque*, Paris, May 1981, which reproduces a conference of 23 March 1981, for the Paul-Henri Spaak chair at the Université de Louvain-la-Neuve, and/or 'The first two years of FECOM transactions', *Economic Papers* (Commission of the EC, Brussels, July 1981). The latter so far has only been released as an internal paper, but should be released some day to other interested readers.

[24] Including the definition of member countries' exchange rates by reference to the ECU, rather than the reverse, as is now the case.

[25] But see my suggestion below for a redefinition of the ECU.

[26] See André L. Swings and Robert Triffin (eds.), *The Private Use of the ECU* (Kredietbank, Brussels, 1980).

PART II

FINANCIAL INNOVATIONS AND STRUCTURAL CHANGES

2

Competing Currencies and Monetary Stability

TOMMASO PADOA-SCHIOPPA AND FRANCESCO PAPADIA*

Introduction

When asked to give the explanation of the greater price stability of the Federal Republic of Germany and other European countries in recent years, economists often invoke the lasting shock effect of the great hyper-inflation of the early 1920s. The memory of currencies inflating until they virtually ceased to exist and were replaced by foreign currencies until a new domestic currency was created, acted, so the story goes, as a powerful brake on indulging again in excessive money creation.

In more recent years, there has been a great deal of talk about a 'dollarization' phenomenon, whereby a country's currency which has been subject to a very high rate of inflation is replaced by the dollar or some other foreign currency. It is not yet evident that the erosion of the national currency's role has produced, in the countries which have recently suffered high rates of inflation, the same immunizing effect which it is claimed to have produced in Germany sixty years ago. The basic phenomenon is, however, the same: substitution of the unstable national currency by a more stable foreign one.

With some complacency, currency-substitution is often said to affect only countries experiencing hyper-inflations, or small economies which have close relationships with large neighbours. This chapter sets out to show that the erosion of the role of a currency also occurs with more moderate rates of inflation and in medium-sized economies. By looking at the international use of the various currencies, one can find certain signs of this: what takes place at a frantic pace in hyper-inflations happens in slow motion in less extreme conditions. This is so because in the international economy, currencies are continuously competing with one another, very much like real goods in an oligopolistic market.

Section II sets out the facts supporting this contention, while Sections III and IV provide some interpretations. Some conclusions for national and international policy-making can be found in Section V. A brief summary of the argument as a whole is given in Section VI.

* Banca d'Italia.

I. Two stylized facts

Inflation and the quality of currencies

Until the beginning of the 1970s, the differences in monetary perform-ance of most market economies were relatively minor. A system of fixed exchange rates and US leadership assured that all Western countries, and especially industrial ones, broadly followed the same monetary policy.

Since the early 1970s, dramatic differences have developed. Some countries, such as Switzerland, the Federal Republic, and the Nether-lands, have chosen a 'strict' monetary course. Others, such as the US, Japan, and France have followed an 'intermediate' one. A last group of countries, including the UK, Italy, and some developing countries (two of which—Brazil and Mexico—are considered in our sample), have followed a 'generous' monetary path.

This characterization cannot of course be regarded as immutable. The UK, for example, has definitely shifted from the generous to the intermediate group, while Japan has arguably shifted from the inter-mediate to the strict one. One can express the same concept in more technical terms by saying that there is ground to believe that our purely cross-sectional empirical analysis is not entirely appropriate. There appears, however, no straightforward alternative.

In classifying countries one has in mind, of course, their inflationary records, or the growth rates of their monetary aggregates, or the strength of their currencies on the foreign exchange market, or perhaps some other variable. Indeed, there are many ways to assess the monetary performance of a country, although all have to do with either the value or the quantity of money. The value of money can be defined firstly, against real goods, through the aggregate price level; secondly, against other currencies, through exchange rates; and thirdly, against itself in a future period, through rates of interest. The quantity of money can in turn be defined in terms of increasingly wider aggregates from the money base to M1, M2, and so on.

This multiple definition of the price and quantity of money, each with its macro-economic significance, is in itself a source of difficulty in assessing the performance of a currency. A more basic problem is that the very concept of performance or quality, to use the term mentioned in the title of this paragraph, is somewhat vague. There is an old and convincing idea that, for all the functions of money, the more predictable a currency will be, the better it will fulfil its role. The book edited by L. Yeager,[1] where it is argued that a desirable monetary constitution should assure a predictable currency, gives a lucid exposition of this argument. Predictability can be defined, operationally, by some synthetic measure of the discrepancy between realized and expected values of the price of money. The concept of predictability is distinguished, in principle, from the one of stability. The first refers to the differences between expected and actual values, the second to the changes over time of the price of money. In practice, of course, given the difficulty of observing expectations, things are less straightforward.

Furthermore, at a more advanced level of sophistication, it could be argued that as we have learned (since Markowitz and Tobin[2]) that the risk of an asset does not consist in its variability *per se*, but in its contribution to the variability of a diversified portfolio, analogously in an open economy we should not consider the predictability (or the stability) of a currency *per se*, but as a component of a portfolio of currencies.

There has been much work in this direction, but even the more advanced research of which the authors are aware (e.g. the survey article by Adler and Dumas[3]) has not produced conclusive theoretical or empirical evidence. Perhaps this is the explanation for the fact that the great majority of models where variability of money is considered (including the one by B. Klein used in the appendix) do not include portfolio considerations. This explanation certainly applies to this chapter.

In practice, with the actual data to hand, some of the above problems appear to be more tractable than expected. In Table 2.1 about a decade of monetary history is summarized for ten countries—eight industrial and two developing ones: the US, Japan, FRG, France, UK, Italy, the Netherlands, Switzerland, Brazil, and Mexico. The following monetary variables have been considered (see columns in Table 2.1):

(i) rate of inflation: actual, expected, and unexpected;
(ii) interest rates: short, nominal, and real;
(iii) exchange rates: effective and real;
(iv) monetary aggregates: base, M1, and M2;
(v) non-aggregate variables: variance of relative prices, dispersion of inflationary expectations, and degree of integration of national and international financial markets.

Countries have then been classed from low to high. Thus for each variable, rank one will be assigned to the country with the lowest average or variability of the variable concerned. The ranking for each of the four variables indicated in the rows of Table 2.1 has been made in the same way. Finally, coefficients of rank correlation have been computed for each pair of variables and reported in the table. A few interesting facts emerge from these calculations.

The first conclusion to be drawn from Table 2.1 is that *predictability and stability, although distinguishable in principle, seem to coincide in practice*. This can be seen in the first two rows of the table, which show the rank correlation coefficients of the variability[4] of the

TABLE 2.1

Rank correlation coefficient of the average and the variability of some monetary variables for ten countries
(Quarterly Data, 1973–81)

(Rank correlation coefficients)

	Variability of: inflation			interest rates		exchange rates		monetary aggregates			Average of:		
	actual (2)(5)	expected (2)	unexpected (3)	short nominal (2)(5)	real (3)(5)	effective (1)(4)(5)	real (1)(4)(5)	base money (1)(2)	M1 (1)(2)	M2 (1)(2)	Relative inflation (5)	Dispersion of inflation (5)	Integration of financial markets (5)
Variability of:													
unexpected inflation	.927***	.879***	1.00	.429	1.00	.564*	.552	.503	.661***	.818***	.429	.600	.452
expected inflation	.952***	1.00	.879***	.333	.833***	.624	.539	.648**	.867***	.867***	.393	.829**	.571
Average of variable in column	.709**	.758**	—	.738***	-.786**	-.285	.697**	.552*	.539	.576*	—	—	—
Average of inflation	.709**	.685**	.818***	.762**	.643	.358	.139	.515	.491	.636**	.571	.829**	.571

Data were unavailable for some countries, while in other cases an estimate was required. The exact definitions and the description of the computations carried out are available on request from the authors.

(1) computed from rates of change of the variable

(2) variability defined as standard derivation of variable

(3) variability defined as $\sum \left[\dfrac{1}{n}(\text{expected}-\text{actual})^2\right]^{1/2}$

(4) variability defined as $\sum \left[\dfrac{1}{n}(\text{actual}_{t-1}-\text{actual}_t)^2\right]^{1/2}$

(5) observations not available for all countries.

$\left. \begin{array}{l} * \\ ** \\ *** \end{array} \right]$ significantly different from zero at $\left. \begin{array}{l} 10 \\ 5\ \% \\ 1 \end{array} \right]$

different variables listed above with the variability of unexpected and expected inflation. The first row shows, for example, that countries in which inflation is relatively more variable are also countries in which inflation is relatively more unpredictable (the correlation coefficient being .927). Similarly, the variability of unexpected inflation is associated positively with the variability of various monetary aggregates (with coefficients ranging from .503 to .818), exchange rates (.552 to .564) and the nominal interest rate (.429).

The first row in Table 2.1 also shows that some non-aggregate measures of variability are associated with the unpredictability of inflation. Thus the more difficult it is to predict inflation, the higher the variance of the prices of individual goods around aggregate inflation (.429), the more dispersed the inflationary expectations across individuals (.600), and the less integrated the national market in the international one (.452).[5]

The evidence of Table 2.1, however, goes further than this. The third row shows *a generally positive and often significant relationship between the average level and the variability of the variables considered.*[6] Thus if a country has a high actual and expected rate of inflation, it is also likely that inflation will be highly variable (coefficients of .709 and .758 respectively). Similarly, if a country has a relatively high average growth rate of monetary aggregates, these will tend to show greater variability. If the nominal interest rate is high, it is also likely to be unstable (.738). The relationship between average change and variability of the real rate of exchange is also significantly positive (.697), showing that countries which have lost in competitiveness have had a more variable real exchange rate than those which have gained in competitiveness.

The third row of the table shows an apparent exception. For the real interest rate, there is a strong negative rank correlation between the average level and the variability. In other words, countries in which the real interest rate has been generally high compared to others are also those in which the rate has been comparatively stable. This is an interesting point which does not contradict the other evidence, since for the real interest rate—contrary to the other monetary variables —a comparatively high value is a sign of monetary 'strictness' and stability.

A further finding which emerges from the last row in Table 2.1 is that *countries which have had a relatively low average inflation rate over the period have shown a tendency towards lesser volatility in all the variables examined.* Where the *average* rate of inflation was low, the *variability* of inflation (over time, over single goods, over individual expectations), of money aggregates, and of nominal and real interest rates has tended to be low. There is also evidence that the financial markets of countries where inflation was higher were less integrated with Euro-currency markets than those of countries with lower inflation. This is ascribed to the existence of capital controls. The relationship between average inflation and instability is, however, much weaker for the effective and real exchange rate, where the rank correlation coefficient is positive but quite low.

To sum up, the general message that comes through from the data in Table 2.1 is that *the average rate of inflation seems, for the countries and the period concerned, a good proxy for the overall 'quality' of the various currencies*, in the sense that low inflation currencies seem to be of high quality and vice versa. This conclusion can be reached by equating the quality of a currency to its predictability, and this in turn to its stability, since the evidence given in the table shows that empirically these two phenomena coincide. Stability in one aspect of money tends to be accompanied by stability in all other aspects, including real variables such as the real rate of interest and the real rate of exchange (with the qualifications relating to the exchange rate, as raised above).

Quality of a currency and its international use

The next question to be asked is whether the international use of a currency has any connection with its quality. This is new and difficult ground.

In order to carry out this exploration it is first of all necessary to define 'international use' in a way that is both conceptually satisfying and statistically measurable. For the latter, the difficulty lies in the lack of systematic evidence. For the former, problems arise because of the multiple functions of money and the somewhat undefined concept of 'international economy'. We have dealt with the first problem by trying to assemble evidence for the use of money not only as a means of payment and as a store of value, i.e. as a denomination of financial assets (deposits and official reserves), but also as a *numeraire* in trade contracts. As for the second problem, we have defined the 'international economy' as those operations which involve a 'non-resident', either as a creditor, a financial intermediary, or a trade partner.

We thus emerge with four different (but partly overlapping) types of international use for which some statistical evidence is available. They are the use of a currency as a denominator of:

(i) deposits held by non-residents with resident banks;[7]
(ii) deposits held with Eurobanks;[8]
(iii) international reserves held by central banks, distinguishing between industrial and developing countries;[9] and
(iv) invoices in international trade.[10]

For the various definitions of *financial* international use, the market shares of each currency have been computed. These shares are measured by converting the aggregates into a common currency (the SDR). This would be equivalent to measuring them from real values, i.e. deflating each currency aggregate by its price level, if Purchasing Power Parity held.[11] For international *trade*, the variable retained is the share of a country's imports or exports, which is denominated in national currency.

Obviously, the first determinant of the international *financial* role of a currency is the economic size of the issuing country. Economic size is by no means a concept free of ambiguity. There appear to be two main candidates: (1) the share of each country in the total 'world' GNP, and (2) the share in world trade. Foreign trade is an 'external' variable, thus likely to be more directly connected to money demand by foreigners. GNP, however, may be a better proxy for the overall 'size' of a country, in particular as far as *financial* size is concerned. Since there is no clearly superior definition in principle, some experiments were made. The result is that GNP gave better results. This is, however, nearly entirely due to the presence of Brazil and Mexico in the sample. Eliminating these two countries, the results do not change significantly whether one uses GNP or exports as a measure of size.

Having decided to use GNP as a measure of economic size, the difference has been calculated between the share of each country in world GNP and the share covered by its currency. The resulting figure has been called 'excess use', i.e., not justified by size.[12] The rank deriving from this 'excess use' has been compared with the quality rank, as measured by the indicators used in Table 2.1.

In Table 2.2, the rank correlation coefficients between various types of financial uses and various measures of quality have been computed. It can be seen that the positive association between the two is not limited to a particular definition of quality or use, although its strength does change, depending on what specific measurement is considered.[13] The general message emerging from the table, however, is in any event more important than the differences. This message is that, notwithstanding the simplicity of the method, a positive relationship appears between the financial use and the quality of the various currencies, over and above the one warranted by size alone.

This general message is reinforced if only industrial countries are considered and the currencies of Brazil and Mexico excluded. Then the rank correlation coefficients become generally higher. This is due to the fact that the cruzeiro and the peso are not really serious competitors for denominating financial liabilities held by international agents.

It is interesting to note that the currency composition of the reserves

TABLE 2.2

Rank correlation coefficients between 'excess financial use' of a currency and its quality

quality defined as: excess use use defined from:[1]	average inflation		variability of expected inflation		standard deviation of inflation	
	all countries in sample	excluding Brazil and Mexico	all countries in sample	excluding Brazil and Mexico	all countries in sample	excluding Brazil and Mexico
Eurobanks deposits	.527	.643*	.515	.595	.442	.452
Non-residents deposits	.527	.524	.576*	.619*	.479	.429
International reserves held by industrial countries	.127	.357	.103	.262	.030	.167
International reserves held by developing countries	.527	.524	.576*	.619*	.479	.429

[1] Excess use is defined as the difference between the share of a currency in a particular use and the share of the issuing country in total GNP. For the exact definitions of 'financial uses' see notes (3) to (6), p. 107 f.

* Significantly different from zero at 10%

of industrialized countries seems to have no correlation with quality. This suggests some interesting, though not altogether surprising, considerations. First, the central banks of industrialized countries are not profit-maximizers. Second, the role of the dollar in official uses remains more dominant than in private uses. The latter probably tends to have a leading function in the development of today's international monetary relationships.

To ascertain the existence of a relationship between the use of a currency for invoicing international trade and its quality, the share of each country's exports or imports, denominated in national currency has been regressed[14] against relative size (share of total GNP) and quality (average rate of inflation). The test is approximate because there is no particular reason to assume a linear specification, and even more particularly because there are many factors other than size and quality which influence trade denomination.[15] However, the phenomenon is strong enough and emerges clearly from Table 2.3. There one can see that, as expected, the larger a country, the larger the share of its international trade denominated in its own currency. What is more relevant, however, is that the higher the quality of a currency, the more it will be used to denominate exports and imports.[16]

TABLE 2.3

*Economic size, invoicing of international trade and
quality of currencies
(Regression of the share of exports/imports denominated in national
currency on the GNP share of the country and the 'quality' of its
currency).* *

dependent variable \ independent variable	constant	quality of currency	share of country in total GNP
Share of exports denominated in national currency	64.84	1.635 (2.534)	1.034 (1.500)
Share of imports denominated in national currency	25.40	.745 (1.557)	1.352 (2.645)

* *t*-statistics in parentheses. All variables refer to 1973–81 averages.

This seems to be a contradiction of Gresham's law, but in fact is not. Gresham's law applies only when there are fixed rates of exchange between two currencies (say gold and silver).

The general conclusion of this section is that the *international* use of a currency, both for financial and trade purposes, is not independent of its quality: *over and above the use implied by the size of the issuing country, high-quality currencies are over-used and low-quality ones are under-used.*

II. Interpreting the facts

Inflation and quality

The tendency for quality measures to be correlated among themselves and with the average rate of inflation is a complex phenomenon which requires a correspondingly complex explanation. Its components are not new to economists and will only be briefly sketched here.

The positive correlation between the variability of the rate of growth of monetary aggregates (base, M1, M2) on the one hand and the average level and variability of the rate of inflation on the other, can be interpreted as a weak restatement of the neutrality of money in the medium to long term. In addition to confirming the obvious (i.e. inflation is a monetary phenomenon in the long-run), it shows that the endless arguments about 'what is money' lose much of their virulence when one looks at them from a sufficiently long-term point of view. The different money measurements give very much the same message.

Equally unsurprising is the fact that the variability of nominal interest and exchange rates is connected to the level and variability of inflation. Interest and exchange rates are forward-looking asset prices, directly related to inflationary developments: if these latter are very unstable, the former will be so too.

What is less straightforward is the correlation between the variability of *real* exchange and interest rates on the one hand, and the level and variability of inflation on the other. In a world characterized by the neutrality of money, real variables should be separate from nominal variables. Since this is not the case, we have to invoke some short-term non-neutrality of money, with short-term dynamic effects superimposing themselves on the long-term tendency.

To explain the fact that the higher the average rate of inflation, the higher its variability, necessitates adding a further complication to the scheme and even using (a mortal sin for economists) a socio-political argument.[17] The idea is that if a monetary authority is capable of keeping the rate of inflation constant and is willing to do so, it is also capable of keeping it low, which it will tend to do to increase the welfare of its constituency. If, however, control of inflation is imperfect or half-hearted, this will be reflected both in the level and the variance of inflation.

Thus, the various facets of the overall relationship between inflation and other measures of monetary stability are not too difficult to rationalize. The general message can still be somewhat surprising, if one considers how often one hears and reads about the trade-off which should exist, for example, between the stability of money aggregates and that of exchange rates, or between the interest rate and inflation. There may well be a short-term trade-off. In the medium-to long-term perspective taken in this chapter, however, there is no evidence that stabilization in one sense entails instability in another. On the contrary, a *positive* relationship appears to exist between the stability of the various variables considered. And the message is even more striking since *real* variables also seem to be associated positively with the stability of monetary variables. This supports the hypothesis[18] that differences between countries do not depend on differences in 'tastes', with one country agreeing to 'trade-off' stability of one variable for stability in another variable, and another country making a different choice. Rather, these differences must depend on economic structure, such as the degree of indexation and sensitivity to terms-of-trade shocks, or on 'policy inefficiencies', i.e. faulty control of macro-economic policy levers.

The last three 'quality' aspects considered in Section II reflect micro, rather than aggregate, aspects.

The first (the fact that a high rate of aggregate inflation tends to go hand-in-hand with a high dispersion of relative prices around the general price increase) can be explained by assuming that the cost of adjusting prices is different in different industries, and/or that unexpected inflationary shocks are mistaken for changes in relative prices and that the elasticity of supply to the latter is different in different industries, or that due to downward price rigidity, any change in relative prices requires a differentiated change in absolute prices and hence a certain amount of aggregate inflation. The empirical evidence presented is insufficient to discriminate between these hypotheses.[19] The important fact remains that there are sound reasons to assume a positive relationship between aggregate and relative inflation.

The second fact (i.e. the correlation between the dispersion of inflationary expectations and the actual rate of inflation) has been explored analytically, and the conclusion is that the sign of the relationship is theoretically ambiguous.[20] We may therefore take the evidence given above as an empirical resolution of this theoretical ambiguity.

The third fact (i.e. the association between the average rate of inflation and the segmentation of national, with respect to international, financial markets) can be explained by the existence of capital controls set up to protect currencies of poor quality.

To sum up, the overall finding of a negative relationship between the rate of inflation and the 'quality' of a currency can be explained on

the basis of conceptual reasoning. Furthermore, various components of
this negative relationship have already been noted by economists.[21] The
evidence presented here is new only in that it shows the extent of the
phenomenon on a cross-sectional basis, and presents it as a whole,
rather than in its single aspects.

Quality and utilization

Constantino Bresciani-Turroni wrote, in 1925–6:[22]

During 1923, when in Germany every obstacle to the issue of paper
money had been removed, and the circulation was rising to increasingly
fantastic figures, eminent financiers and politicians maintained, and
endeavoured to show, that there was neither monetary nor credit
inflation in Germany. The argument on which the pretended demonstration was based is an example of an interesting economic sophism.
It admitted that the nominal value of the paper money issued was
certainly enormous, but the real value, that is the gold value based on
the exchange rate, of the mass of notes in circulation, was much lower
than that of money circulating in Germany before the war. How could
it be stated that there was inflation in Germany?

Bresciani-Turroni explained the reduction in real money balances in
hyper-inflations in terms of a negative relationship between the demand
for real balances and the 'expectation of an ultimate depreciation of
money'. He also noted:[23]

. . . at a certain stage in the depreciation of a paper currency, this ceases
to exercise the function of a store of value, and is replaced by foreign
exchange. At a further stage, when the depreciation is very rapid, the
depreciated paper is also replaced by foreign exchange as a means of
payment. This happened to the German mark, first in foreign trade,
then in internal wholesale trade, and later in retail trade. The practice
of making payments in foreign money spread rapidly.

More recently, S. Fischer[24] has studied the 'dollarization' phenomena,
whereby '. . . as a country's inflation rate increases, there is typically
a shift away from the domestic money towards a foreign money as a
store of value, as a unit of account, and as a medium of transaction'.
   The idea underlying both these explanations is that agents reduce
their demand for 'expensive' currencies in favour of cheap ones. Non-
interest-bearing money balances have an opportunity cost equal to the
nominal rate of interest which could be gained on interest-yielding
assets.[25] When price inflation in one currency is high and holding
money balances denominated in that currency becomes exceedingly
expensive, the rational response is to reduce holdings in that currency
and to increase those in currencies whose cost has remained lower.
   Agents' losses in holding money is the government's gain. The gain
accruing to the government from issuing money can be split into two

components: seigniorage and inflation tax. Seigniorage, normally positive even when inflation is zero, is equal to the real rate of interest times money balances. The inflation tax is the additional levy which the government extracts from money holders through the progressive decrease in the real value of their monetary liabilities. The argument put forward above can thus be reworded by saying that agents try to evade inflation tax and to substitute currencies with a low rate of inflation for those with a high rate. In so doing, they reduce the 'base' on which the tax is levied. There is a point at which the decrease in the base will more than offset the increase in the rate, whereupon the proceeds of the inflation tax will start to decrease.

This classical line of reasoning is normally applied to non-interest-bearing money. In Section II above, however, we saw that the quality of a given currency is correlated positively to a wide range of uses which include financial and trade contracts carrying a market-determined rate of interest.

The argument of Bresciani-Turroni still provides part of the explanation. In fact it is likely that, even if an interest rate is paid on monetary assets, this will be lower than the one paid on illiquid assets, and therefore the opportunity cost of holding a given money increases when interest rates rise due to inflation. Substitution effects due to price factors will therefore be at work in general on interest-bearing monetary assets as well.

There are, however, other arguments to explain the correlation between quality and utilization. They can best be illustrated by distinguishing different types of use.

Take trade contracts first. It is clear that there is a cost in changing prices:[26] a direct cost (changing labels, price listings, and the cost of making the decision), but also an indirect cost in terms of relationships with the customer. As it requires more frequent prices changes, denomination in a 'low quality' currency is less efficient. The use of high-quality currencies as a 'unit of account' will therefore increase. One further factor is that if a nominal contract, such as a delayed invoice, is denominated in an unpredictable currency, changes in its value will cause losses (gains) to the signing parties which, unless one assumes risk neutrality, will not offset each other and will therefore leave them worse off.

Take, then, bank deposits[27] held by non-residents, or international reserves held by central banks. A way to explain the large share of high-quality currencies is to consider these assets as arguments of the production of consumption function, in the sense that the efficiency of these processes is increased if the appropriate amount of money is used to 'grease' economic activity.[28] The effectiveness of the 'money grease', i.e. the contribution money gives to welfare, depends, in turn, on its quality.[29]

The idea of considering the quality, and not only the quantity, of money balances was expressed by B. Klein[30] in a closed economy context, where only one currency circulates. Under these conditions, he shows that an increase in the quality of a currency has in principle both a positive and a negative partial effect on its demand. On the one hand, improved quality, by making one unit of real money more effective in producing monetary services, will tend to reduce its demand. On the other hand, since the unit price of monetary services drops if the productivity of money goes up, the demand for them will increase correspondingly. Analytically the balance between these offsetting tendencies is uncertain. Empirically, Klein found that in the US, between 1880 and 1972, the first effect dominated the second.

When considering a multiplicity of currencies competing with one another to provide monetary services to their holders, an improvement in the relative quality of a currency will undoubtedly increase its *share* in total money balances (i.e. denominated in whatever currency).[31] A formal development of this argument is given in the Appendix to this chapter.

Of course, as mentioned above, price effects also influence the relative demand for the various currencies. The model presented in the Appendix preserves the usual result that as the cost of holding a given currency goes up (in terms of lost interest), the demand for it will go down. However, by establishing a positive, independent relationship between the share of a currency in total money balances and its quality, we offer an explanation for the reduced use of low-quality currency by international agents which does not depend on money paying a rate of interest lower than other assets.

We can summarize our interpretation as follows. Money is demanded for the contribution it gives to overall economic efficiency by lowering transaction costs and smoothing production and consumption activities. Its effectiveness in this role depends on its quality or predictability. International operators, who can substitute one currency for another, tend to use more high-quality than low-quality currencies. Price effects are also at work in the sense that 'cheap' currencies, i.e. those with a lower holding opportunity cost, tend to be used more, *ceteris paribus*, than 'expensive' ones. This effect, however, is likely to be minor for those monetary assets which carry a market rate of interest.

III. The money industry as an oligopolistic market

It is often said that the central banks (using the term loosely to stand for the wider and more exact term 'monetary authorities') resemble monopolistic firms, with the additional power to impose direct controls limiting the behaviour of private agents. Given the demand schedule, which by definition will have a very low cross-price elasticity with other goods, the central bank, like a monopolist, can fix either the price (exchange rate, rate of interest, price level) or the quantity of money it wants to supply. In such a scheme, the authority to impose direct controls can be seen as a further extension of monopolistic power: for instance, the possibility of increasing the quantity of money while keeping the rate of interest unchanged.

This familiar framework is at odds with the evidence presented above and, indeed, with the very reality of an open economy. Monies and their issuers compete with one another in the portfolio choices of private agents, and competition takes place along the two dimensions of price and quality.

Further, private financial intermediaries, and in particular international banks, compete on an increasing scale with central banks in providing monetary services.

If the paradigm of monopoly for the central bank is clearly inappropriate, there are several reasons to consider the opposite paradigm of perfect competition as equally inappropriate. The thorough rethinking which has taken place in the monetary approach to the balance of payments, with its hypothesis of perfect currency substitution, is significant in this respect. In the first place, there are very few currencies which can aspire to an international role: it is difficult to see the Bhutanese gultrum or the Maldivian rufiyaa offering any real competition against the US dollar. Furthermore, although there are significant cost and quality differences between the various currencies, the share of low-quality high-price currencies is still not zero and only in conditions of very severe hyper-inflation is the demand for national money balances driven close to zero. A way to visualize this is that although the Swiss franc is in all respects a 'cheaper' and a higher-quality currency than the Brazilian cruzeiro, it is still difficult to pay bus fares in São Paulo with Swiss francs. Last, and probably least, natural obstacles to free competition in the money industry (economies of scale, barriers to entry, minimum plant size, etc.) are often reinforced by direct controls and administrative measures which limit the freedom of residents to use foreign currencies. Direct controls come last, not because they are unimportant in practice but because, when working out the policy implications, which is our ultimate aim, one cannot invoke man-made interventions to explain the failure of perfect competition. As regards the competition of private financial intermediaries, even if it has greatly increased, their liabilities still are not a perfect substitute for central banks' liabilities.

If one excludes monopoly and perfect competition as models of

the money industry, then one has to deal with some form of oligopolistic market. This is intellectually and practically distressing. Intellectually, because the neat results of monopoly and perfect competition
lose much of their shining clarity when one deals with oligopolies.
Practically, because in oligopolistic markets the rule is the interdependence between firms—in our case the central banks—and we know
that potential instability is implicit in these game relationships.

In what follows we shall draw both on the evidence presented in
Section II and on the paradigm of oligopolistic competition to formulate
some propositions that are relevant from a policy point of view.

IV. Policy aspects

Having identified a phenomenon and having attempted to explain it,
it is natural to ask whether it matters and what should be done about
it. We shall try to answer these questions by formulating a few propositions that seem to be relevant to policy-makers and that follow
from the preceding analysis. For the sake of clarity, a distinction is
made between the national and the international economy. The former
is taken to mean not the domestic or the closed economy, but rather
the point of view of the interests of an individual country, as opposed
to that of a group of countries taken as a whole. This distinction,
however, should not blur the message that, in a certain way, domestic
and international aspects are one and the same thing: the two groups of
policy inferences, therefore, should be considered as a whole.

The national economy

From the point of view of economic policy as seen by an individual
country, the relevant implications of the above analysis can be summarized in the following three propositions:

(i) *The cost of monetary instability appears to be sufficiently strong
to induce operators who are not 'locked in' a national currency to
reduce significantly the use of low-quality currencies and to
increase the use of high-quality currencies.*

This first conclusion is based on the observation that agents who
practise a high degree of currency substitution prefer premium 'money
grease' to a low-grade one. Most operators, however, do not engage in
international transactions and therefore have only a very limited possibility for substitution. As a consequence, they have to bear the full
brunt of the use of 'lower grade' grease, and their production and consumption activities will suffer accordingly.

Efforts have been made to identify the costs of inflation and even to
measure them analytically.[32] Here, indirect evidence is given which

supports the view that these costs exist, are recognized, and are acted upon. This evidence is similar in nature and significance to that presented by those authors[33] who show a negative correlation between inflation and economic activity (not the traditional 'Phillips' positive one) and interpret this as meaning that inflation hinders economic functions and contributes to a decline in production. In offering such a theory, Milton Friedman[34] conjectured that inflation and economic activity are *negatively* related in the medium-term because of the disruptive effect of the former on the latter. This means an upward-sloping Phillips curve, in the sense that the higher the rate of inflation, the higher unemployment will be.

Note, however, that the evidence of Section II simply reveals preferences without giving any information about a short-term structural relationship between economic activity and inflation. Among other things, it is neutral with respect to the 'Keynesian v monetarist' controversy.

It is also worth adding that our indirect evidence is more general than that produced by ascertaining a negative effect of inflation on economic activity. This point should be clarified. National product is a very imperfect indicator of welfare, if anything, because it overlooks the fact that leisure is also an item of goods. As those authors who have studied hyper-inflation have demonstrated, the first negative effect of a very low-quality currency is on activities which are not considered in measures of national product: increasing amounts of time spent on transactions, increasing uncertainty on the price of goods, etc. Only later on is measured income affected.

The evidence given in this chapter, however, has nothing to do with measured income. It shows that agents tend to reduce the use of low-quality currencies, whatever the reason, and this is interpreted in the sense that they tend to use more efficient currencies—efficient in the sense that they permit the production of more goods and also more leisure. Thus even if inflation had no effect on measured income, the conclusion would still be that it is considered 'bad' by private agents.

(ii) *If the government sacrifices too often its long-term task of providing a stable currency in order to achieve short-term objectives, it erodes the very possibility of conducting an effective counter-cyclical policy.*

From the foregoing it is clear that a stable currency is an essential ingredient of production and consumption efficiency. It is also clear that stability and predictability are *long-term* features, i.e. qualities that—like durability—can only be ascertained and enjoyed over long periods of time. Since in our economic system the government is the ultimate issuer of the currency, it is the government's task to provide that particular public good which is monetary stability.

In modern societies, however, governments have also been assigned the task of providing another kind of stability—that of output and employment—or, put in another way, the task of stabilizing the cycle. In the interpretation that has been predominant in the post-war period among both economists and policy-makers, this task is regarded as one that sets *short-term* objectives.

One could say, with only slight over-simplification, that, whereas the relevant time-frame for the first type of stability (monetary stability) is the year, if not the decade, that for the second (output and employment stability) is the quarter, if not the month. Even if one accepts the evidence presented above, that in the long run no fundamental conflict exists between the two types of stability, one should be well aware of the fact that short-term conflicts and trade-offs do arise.

For a variety of reasons connected with the actual workings of the policy process, short-term perspective tends to prevail. This does not mean that the objective of monetary stability is absent from policy choices, but rather that it often tends to be formulated not in terms of ultimate price stability but in terms of a marginal reduction of the rate of inflation.

If, in the actual policy debate, insufficient importance is given to the need to maintain actively the long-term public good of a stable currency, almost inevitably the immediate benefit of a higher output will be regarded as more valuable than the immediate cost of a marginal —and often apparently negligible—increase in prices, just like the cost, in terms of security or clean air, of postponing marginal defence or anti-pollution expenditures may appear small compared to the benefit of not having to raise new taxes or to increase interest rates. Taking the view that we all die eventually, a short-sighted government tends to behave like a free rider.

The evidence presented above in this chapter suggests that, in so far as economic agents are able to move out of an unstable currency, a government that fails to achieve the long-term objective of supplying a stable currency also loses part of its ability to rely on monetary instruments for counter-cyclical purposes.

In the past, safeguards against short-sighted monetary management were provided by institutional arrangements such as the gold standard, the widely accepted principle of a balanced budget, or the lack of highly concentrated economic power in large corporations or labour unions. To offset the gradual weakening of these safeguards, different solutions have been proposed to restore the necessary role of long-term considerations in monetary policy.

Monetarists have suggested compelling the government to disregard short-term objectives and to stick to a rule, possibly with the help of appropriate legislation. This attitude completely excludes government discretion but recognizes, and in a sense reinforces, the institutional responsibility of the public sector to supply money.

Hayek,[35] like the monetarists, rejects discretion and shares the desire to assure the dominance of long-term considerations in the management of monetary policy; he proposes the virtually opposite solution of allowing free competition between public or, even better, private currencies. If only operators were free to demand and supply whatever currency they liked, monetary problems would disappear, wiped out by the 'magic of the market'. According to this view 'dollarization' phenomena are to be encouraged rather than resisted, and there is no particular need for any authority to provide a predictable money for its constituency. If a money supplier tried to supply a 'low quality' currency, the sanction would be an immediate loss of market share while no negative effect would accrue for private operators, who would switch to another money at no cost.

We tend to think that neither of these extreme solutions provides a satisfactory answer to the need for working out institutional arrangements which are conducive to monetary stability.

The monetarist solution, for its part, goes too far in suppressing discretion. Discretionary powers can be misused and appropriate safeguards against this danger have to be found. But they are nevertheless necessary to cope with both the need for speedy decisions and the fact that unforeseen shocks and events require diversified responses.

The Hayek solution, in its turn, does not seem feasible because if there is clearly competition between monies and 'quality' is one determinant of market share, it is also clear that the money industry is not, nor could it be, anywhere near to being a perfectly competitive one, as substitutability between currencies seems to be far from perfect and 'clientele' phenomena are observable.

By rejecting the radical monetarist or Hayekian solutions, we are left with an unglamorous middle road characterized by the grey area of discretion. That is not to say, however, that institutional safeguards against misuse of discretion are either unnecessary or impossible to define. Two of them, in particular, seem to be relevant. First, an appropriate articulation of procedures covering the whole spectrum, from the highest (constitutional) level of 'rule', to the lowest (operational) level of 'discretion'. Monetary policy covers such a wide range of decisions and actions that there is enough material to fill each step in the range. Second, an institutionally independent central bank is an important defence against the temptations of short-sightedness and demagogy.

98   EUROPE'S MONEY

(iii) *If the quality of the currency deteriorates, the government's ability to gain seigniorage profits is reduced accordingly.*

We use the term seigniorage, not inflation tax, to stress that we refer to the gain accruing to the government from the rent in issuing a non-interest-bearing liability, and not to the additional tax which it can levy by engineering inflation.

If demand for real money balances expressed in low-quality currencies is reduced, this means that the government will be able to finance a smaller part of its operations by issuing money. The tax base on which seigniorage is paid is reduced. If the government tries to increase the 'tax rate' by engineering inflation, it will further reduce the tax base and a point will be reached where the tax revenue will start to decrease. The extent of inflation financed by any given amount of monetary creation will grow correspondingly.

Although, as is made clear above, we are not considering a monetary liability of the central bank (base money) which yields a seigniorage profit directly to the issuer, but rather bank liabilities and trade contracts, the matter is still relevant for two reasons. Firstly, the production of the privately issued liabilities will require, at some state, the use of some base money. Secondly, the whole point of looking at international agents who can indulge in a high degree of currency substitution is just to be able to have an 'early diagnostic' of dollarization phenomena, i.e. to detect the incipient signs of substitution of a 'foreign' for a 'national' low-quality currency. Thus even if the substitution of one currency for another in bank deposits or trade contracts is not directly conducive to seigniorage losses, it is still a warning of future problems.

There are, however, problems of a technical nature in having a high-quality currency widely used for international purposes. 'Internationalization' of a currency tends to generate a new kind of instability in the demand for money. Shifts in currency preferences will superimpose themselves on the shifts in preference between money and other financial assets, making monetary control more complex.

The international economy

The above propositions are relevant for the monetary authorities of an open economy, but do not contain sufficient elements to ensure the smooth functioning of an international economy composed of economically interdependent but politically sovereign countries.

(iv) *The paradigm of oligopolistic competition points to some elements that are relevant when dealing with a multi-currency reserve system. These include potential instabilities, the need for co-operative*

action, and the scope for discretionary decisions taken with the aid
of international organizations.

We have given above empirical and conceptual reasons for regarding
central banks as oligopolistic producers engaged in quality and price
competition for the product they sell (i.e. money). This is not to say
that the money industry is necessarily characterized by instability.
Most oligopolistic theoretical models are stable, and examining industrial oligopolistic markets, one does not find conclusive evidence of
instability. It remains true, however, that the actions of central banks
are interconnected and that potential instability exists.

For example, substitution away from a currency whose quality has
deteriorated will lead to demand for other currencies. If the move is from
a small or medium-sized economy/currency, the effects will presumably be modest, and no significant reaction will be generated. However,
if the move is from a large country, then the effect can be sufficiently
large to cause other countries to react. The possibility of a circular
chain of actions and reactions is therefore established. Although in the
absence of direct evidence and of a more formal model this argument
cannot be pushed too far, it seems fair to relate some of the monetary
events of the 1970s, in particular the actual and potential shifts
between the US dollar, the Deutschmark and the yen, to shifts in the
perceived relative qualities of these three countries. These shifts in
turn triggered off feedbacks and counter-feedbacks which could be
responsible for some of the monetary upheavals of the last decade.

If the effects of the actions of any oligopolist cannot be assessed
without making some assumptions about the reactions of other producers, the industry-wide equilibrium depends even more directly on
the feedbacks. The potential instability of an oligopolistic system
means that this equilibrium may not be achieved through the natural
play of market forces and that, instead, a state of uncertainty, instability and even economic warfare may prevail. If this is damaging in
a national context, it is particularly dangerous in the international
financial field, for two reasons: first, that no established 'government'
functions exist at the international level, and second, that financial
and monetary relationships need a framework of stability and certainty.
This points to the strong necessity for international co-operation in the
area of money and finance. When considering the possible mechanisms
to bring about co-operative actions in the international financial sphere,
it is clear that two solutions exist to deal with interdependence: rules
and discretion.

The Bretton Woods system which enshrined the leadership of the
United States in international treaties was an example of oligopoly
organized by *rules*. Another example, which is however more an ideal

than a reality corresponding to any historical experience, is the rule
given by completely free floating exchange rates. Neither of these
systems seems viable in present day circumstances. US leadership
has given way to a polycentric world in which not only other, already
industrialized countries have a voice, but also newly industrialized
ones. The inability of a freely floating system to survive in practice
leads to doubts about its usefulness.

If the possibility of dealing with interdependence by means of rules
does not exist, then the only alternative is to resort to *discretion*,
i.e. to devise solutions to problems when they arise, and to base policy
choices on circumstances. This is very much what happened in national
policies. It is also the prevailing mode in international relationships,
where discretion takes the form of policy co-ordination among the
governments and authorities of different countries, helped by international organizations and institutions.

The adequacy of international institutions for this purpose can be
assessed from a short-term or a long-term perspective. From a short-
term perspective, the existing arrangements seem unlikely to undergo
substantial changes or improvements, and the main objective is to
extract from them the best they are able to give. In this sense, it may be
said that such arrangements work satisfactorily on the whole.

From a longer-term point of view, however, the existing arrangements do not seem to offer a solution to the problem of governing
a multi-country economy, whether regional or world-wide. This is
because they lack the necessary authority instruments to take or
enforce action when required. It is not a lack of procedural rules that
makes the exercise of policy co-ordination so difficult. Difficulties
arise from the fact that national authorities have to respond to elec-
torates who do not express the same priorities at the same time, and
who do not always advocate objectives that are mutually consistent
internationally. Moreover, the complexities of the policy process and of
its widely differing institutional framework make co-ordination quite
difficult, even when broad policy orientations are compatible.

V. Summary

Two *empirical facts* are highlighted in this chapter.

(i) High-inflation countries tend to be characterized with respect to
    low ones by more pronounced volatility in an extensive range of
    monetary and real variables: the rate of inflation, exchange and
    interest rates (nominal and real), money aggregates, relative infla-
    tion, and dispersion of inflationary expectations. Thus, countries
    which have stabilized inflation seem to have achieved a relative
    stabilization of all the other variables as well. Conversely, countries

which have failed in one respect seem to have failed in the others as well. This allows an overall classification of currencies in terms of their 'quality', or stability.

(ii) The international use of a currency, both for financial and trade purposes, is not independent of its quality: over and above the use implied by the size of the issuing country, high-quality currencies are over-used and low-quality ones are under-used.

The suggested *interpretation* of these facts is that:

— the overall association between the level of inflation and the overall quality of a currency can be explained, provided one combines the long-term neutrality of money with short-term, non-neutral effects and recognizes that the instability of monetary variables is not the cost to be paid for the stabilization of such variables, but is either the result of a faulty macro-economic policy, or of an unfavourable economic structure.

— the over-use of high-quality currencies and the under-use of low-quality ones is consistent with the hypothesis that currencies are demanded for the contribution they make to overall economic efficiency by lowering transactions costs, and that the more predictable their value, the higher this contribution is.

The empirical evidence, and the arguments used to explain it, suggest that the 'industry' in which 'international money' is supplied cannot be characterized either by monopoly or by perfect competition. It seems more appropriate to deal with some intermediate oligopolistic market form, and this obliges us to acknowledge the interdependence between the actions of the oligopolistic firms in this market: the central banks.

Some *policy considerations*, drawn from the empirical evidence and its interpretation are:

(i) the cost of monetary instability appears to be high enough to induce operators who are not 'locked in' a national currency to reduce significantly the use of low-quality currencies and to increase the use of high-quality ones;

(ii) if the government sacrifices too frequently its long-term task of providing a stable currency to achieve short-term objectives, it gradually destroys the very possibility of pursuing an effective counter-cyclical policy;

(iii) if the quality of the currency deteriorates, the government's ability to gain seigniorage profits is reduced accordingly;

(iv) the paradigm of oligopolistic competition points to some elements that are relevant when dealing with a multi-currency reserve system. These include: potential instability, the need for co-operative action, and the scope for discretionary decisions taken with the assistance of international organizations.

Appendix

Competing currencies: quality and price factors in the change of the share of each currency in total real money balances

Here we propose an approach to analysing the effect that changes in the relative quality and relative price of a currency have on its share in total real money balances. In order to simplify the exposition, we have limited the competing currencies to two.

In this approach money is demanded for its monetary services, i.e. for the contribution it makes to production and consumption activities. Monetary services are produced with a linearly homogeneous Cobb-Douglas technology. The arguments of the production function of monetary services are real money balances and the 'quality' of a currency. Quality can be interpreted as predictability of the value (however expressed) of the currency. This interpretation is consistent with the idea that the higher the predictability of the value of a currency, the greater its contribution to economic efficiency (reduction of transaction costs).

Demand for monetary services has the same structure as the ordinary demand for money function. The monetary services provided by the two currencies are perfect substitutes and quality is the only factor which makes the productivity of one currency in producing monetary services different from that of the other currency. We assume equilibrium in the market for monetary services, and all prices are exogenous.

A model[36] which presents these features is:

supply of monetary services $N^s = \mu_1^\alpha B_1^\beta + \mu_2^\alpha B_2^\beta$ (1)

demand for monetary services $N^D = y^\gamma (P_N/P)^\delta$ (2)

definition of the price of money $P_{M_i} = 1 + R_i - r_i$ (3)

perfect substitutability of monetary services $\dfrac{P_{N_1}}{P_1} = \dfrac{P_{N_2}}{P_2} = \dfrac{P_N}{P}$ (4)
provided by the two currencies

equilibrium in the market for monetary services $N^s = N^D$ (5)

The first equation states that the total supply of monetary services is equal to the sum of monetary services provided by currency 1 and those provided by currency 2. The supply of monetary services provided by each currency is, in turn, a linearly homogeneous Cobb-Douglas (i.e. $\alpha + \beta = 1$), which has as arguments real money balances ($\mu_i : i = 1, 2$) and quality-predictability ($B_i : i = 1, 2$). Since we are only interested in changes in relative quality between currency 1 and currency 2, we set B_2 constant and we normalize it to one.

Equation (2) says that demand for monetary services is a positive function ($\gamma > 0$) of a scale variable (say, permanent income) and a negative function ($\delta < 0$) of the relative price of monetary services, i.e. the price of monetary services (P_N) divided by the aggregate price level, P.

Equation (3) defines the cost of holding one unit of money as one plus the rate of interest on an asset which provides no monetary services (R_i), minus the financial rate of interest on money (r_i). The rate of interest on money will be zero on assets such as cash. It will be positive on bank deposits, either because an explicit rate of interest is paid, or because deposits are paid for in kind, e.g. free banking services.

To avoid unnecessary complications, it is assumed that open interest rate parity holds for the returns on illiquid assets i.e.:

$$(R_1 - R_2) = \text{expected change in the exchange rate between}$$
$$\text{currency 1 and 2.}$$

Only under this condition will the opportunity cost of holding money assets in currency 1 with respect to illiquid assets be equal to $(R_1 - r_1)$ and the opportunity cost of holding money assets in currency 2 be equal to $(R_2 - r_2)$.)

Equation (4) establishes that, due to the perfect substitutability of monetary services, the price of monetary services is the same when expressed as a ratio to the aggregate price level. The aggregate price level in currency 1 is normalized to be unity.

Equation (5) defines the existence of equilibrium on the market for monetary services.

Given this model, we want to establish: (1) the effect which a change in the relative quality of currency 1 will have on its market share; (2) the effect which a relative change of its price will have on its share.

Optimization conditions imply that the marginal physical productivity of money multiplied by the price of monetary services be equal to the price of money.

That is to say:

$$N^s(\mu_i)P_{N_i} = P_{M_i} \tag{6}$$

where $N^s(\mu_i) = \dfrac{\partial N^s}{\partial \mu_i}$ is the marginal productivity of currency 1.

We can write, using (4) and (6), and remembering that we have normalized $P_1 = 1$,

$$\frac{PM_1}{N^s(\mu_1)} = P_{N_1} = \frac{P_{N_2}}{P_2} = \frac{P_{M_2}}{P_2 N^s(\mu_2)} = \frac{P_N}{P} \tag{7}$$

but from (1) we have

$$N^s(\mu_1) = \alpha \mu_1^{(\alpha-1)} B_1^{\beta} \tag{8}$$

$$N^s(\mu_2) = \alpha \mu_2^{(\alpha-1)} \tag{9}$$

where we have used the fact that we have normalized $B_2 = 1$.

Substituting (8) and (9) into (7) we have

$$\frac{P_{M_1}}{\alpha \mu_1^{(\alpha-1)} B_1^{\beta}} = \frac{P_{M_2}}{\alpha \mu_2^{(\alpha-1)} P_2} = \frac{P_N}{P} \tag{10}$$

which we can substitute in equation (2).

Reshuffling (10), we can express the amount of real money balances in one currency as a function of the amount of real balances expressed in the other currency to respect maximization conditions {equation (6)}

$$\mu_1^{(\alpha-1)} B_1^{\beta} = P_2 \frac{P_{M_1}}{P_{M_2}} \mu_2^{(\alpha-1)} \tag{11}$$

Substituting (10) into (2), and (1) and (2) into (5) we have

$$\mu_1^{\alpha} B_1^{\beta} + \mu_2^{\alpha} = y^{\gamma} \left(\frac{P_{M_1}}{\alpha \mu_1^{(\alpha-1)} B_1^{\beta}} \right)^{\delta} \tag{12}$$

Defining $m_1 = \ln \mu_1; m_2 = \ln \mu_2; b = \ln B_1; p = \ln (P_2 P_{M_1}/P_{M_2})$ we can rewrite (11) and (12) as:

$$(\alpha - 1)m_1 = p + (\alpha - 1)m_2 - \beta b \tag{11a}$$

and

$$\exp\{\alpha m_1 + b\beta\} + \exp(\alpha m_2) = y^{\gamma} P_{M_1}^{\delta} \alpha^{-\delta} \exp\{-\delta\left[(\alpha - 1)m_1 + b\beta\right]\} \tag{12a}$$

Substituting the expression for m_2 derived from (11a) into (12a), and remembering that $\alpha + \beta = 1$ due to the assumption of constant returns to scale, we have:

$$\exp\{\alpha m_1 + b\beta\} + \exp\left[\alpha(m_1 + \frac{p}{\beta} - b)\right] = y^{\gamma} P_{M_1}^{\delta} \alpha^{-\delta} \exp\{\delta\beta(m_1 - b)\} \tag{13}$$

Taking the derivative of (13) with respect to b we have:

$$\frac{\partial m_1}{\partial b} = \frac{\mu_2^{\alpha} - \beta(1 + \delta)N}{(\alpha - \delta\beta)N} \tag{14}$$

where we can see that the sign of $\partial m_1/\partial b$ is indeterminate, and real

money balances denominated in currency 1 may
increase because of an increase in its quality.
notice that N, monetary services, μ_2, real money,
in currency 2, and β the exponent of 'quality' input
function of monetary services, are all constrained to be pos.

δ, however, which is the exponent of the 'price' term in the
for monetary services, is negative. This result confirms Klein's conci.
sion that the demand for real money balances can increase or decrease
due to an increase in quality. In fact, an increase in quality makes
each unit of currency more efficient in producing monetary services
and therefore the same amount of monetary services can be supplied
with a smaller quantity of money balances and this reduces their
demand. However, an increase in quality reduces the unit price of
monetary services and this increases their demand. The net effect of
these two offsetting tendencies is indeterminate. From (14) it can be
seen that one sufficient, but not necessary, condition for $\partial m_1/\partial b$ to
be positive is $(1 + \delta) < 0$, i.e. $|\delta| > 1$. But note that δ is the interest
rate elasticity of the demand for monetary services. Therefore, a sufficient condition for money balances denominated in currency 1 to
increase, due to an increase in its relative quality, is that the demand
for monetary services be elastic with respect to the 'price of monetary
services'. (If there were only one currency, $(1 + \delta) < 0$ would be
a necessary condition. The introduction of a competing currency
can therefore be seen to relax the conditions required for an increase
in the quality of a currency to lead to an increase in demand for it.)

To sum up, even if currencies are competing with one another to
produce monetary services, an increase in the quality of a given
currency does not necessarily increase the demand for it.

Using (11a) and (12a) by analogy to what was done for μ_1, we
can calculate the effect on the demand for real balances denominated
in currency 2 of an improvement in relative quality of currency 1.

$$\frac{\partial m_2}{\partial b} = \frac{-\mu_1^\alpha B^\beta}{(\alpha - \delta\beta)N} < 0 \tag{15}$$

Equation (15) gives the change in the real balances denominated in
currency 2 due to an increase in the relative quality of currency 1. This
derivative is always negative, implying that currency 2's real balances will
unequivocally decrease if the relative quality of currency 1 improves.

At this stage, we still do not know the effect of a change in relative
quality on the share of the two currencies. To do so we define the share
of currency 1 as:

$$\lambda = \frac{\mu_1}{\mu_1 + \mu_2} \tag{16}$$

and notice that:

$$\frac{\partial \lambda}{\partial b} = \lambda(1 - \lambda)\left(\frac{\partial m_1}{\partial b} - \frac{\partial m_2}{\partial b}\right) \tag{17}$$

Substituting from (15) and (16) above, we have:

$$\frac{\partial \lambda}{\partial b} = \lambda(1 - \lambda) > 0 \tag{18}$$

which shows that the share of currency 1 in total real money balances increases (having imposed strict positiveness of μ_1 and μ_2 we have $0 < \lambda < 1$) when its relative quality increases and, correspondingly, it decreases when its relative quality deteriorates. Thus, although the elasticity of the demand for monetary services might be such that the demand for real money balances denominated in currency 1 decreases when its quality improves, its *share* in total money balances will still increase because the demand of currency 2 will decrease even further.

It is easy to show that $\partial \lambda / \partial P_{M_1} < 0$; that is, that the share of currency 1 decreases if its price, defined as the interest rate on illiquid assets minus the interest rate on money, increases.

In fact, from (11a) and (12a) we have:

$$\frac{\partial m_2}{\partial P_{M_1}} = \frac{\alpha(\beta P_{m_1})^{-1}\mu_1^\alpha B^\beta}{(\alpha - \delta\beta)N} > 0 \tag{19}$$

i.e., the demand for currency 2 increases if the cost of currency 1 increases.

Similarly, we can calculate:

$$\frac{\partial m_1}{\partial P_{M_1}} = \frac{\alpha\beta^{-1}\mu_2^\alpha - \delta N}{P_{M_2}(\delta\beta - \alpha)N} < 0 \tag{20}$$

showing that the demand for currency 1 decreases if its cost increases. Of course, the *share* of currency 1 decreases as a result of an increase in its price, since demand for it decreases and demand for the competing currency increases.

To sum up, there are two factors in our model which influence changes in the share of the two currencies, namely price and quality. An increase in the price of one currency relative to the other reduces its share. A decrease in its quality reduces its share as well 'Dollarization' phenomena, i.e. the substitution of a foreign currency for a domestic currency, can therefore be explained by two factors.

The first factor is that if a currency has a very high rate of inflation which pushes up the rate of interest on illiquid assets (R_i) but does not raise, in the same manner, the rate of interest on money (r_i), then the cost of this money ($R_i - r_i$) increases and agents will tend to substitute it with a cheaper currency, i.e. a currency with a lower opportunity cost. The clearest case in this respect is base money, whose rate of interest is fixed at zero. An increase in the rates of inflation and interest will unequivocally raise the cost of holding money balances in the currency which has been subject to the increase in inflation, and its share will go down.

The second, mutually consistent, explanation is that if a currency suffers a decrease in its quality predictability in the sense that its value, expressed either in foreign currencies or in real goods, becomes more difficult to forecast, then its share in total money balances will go down. This will be so irrespective of the behaviour of the rate of interest paid on the money balances considered. In other words, it will be so even if the cost of holding money does not change because the two rates move uniformly and their difference $(R_i - r_i)$ remains unchanged.

Acknowledgements

When they wrote this chapter, Mr Padoa-Schioppa was Director General and Mr Papadia was Economic Adviser in the Directorate General for Economic and Financial Affairs of the Commission of the EC. Both have now returned to the Banca d'Italia in Rome.

The authors would like to acknowledge Stanley Fischer and Alfred Steinherr for their stimulating advice, comments, and critiques; Chris Smyth for carrying out estimates on their behalf; and the Bank of England, the Bank for International Settlements, the Federal Reserve Board of the United States, and the Federal Reserve Bank of Philadelphia for supplying data.

Notes and sources

[1] Leland B. Yeager (ed.), *In search of a monetary constitution* (Harvard University Press, Cambridge, Mass., 1962).

[2] H. Markowitz, *Portfolio selection*, Cowles Foundation Monograph No. 16 (John Wiley & Sons, Inc., New York, 1959), and J. Tobin, 'Liquidity preference as behaviour towards risk', *The Review of Economic Studies*, Vol. 25 (2), No. 7, pp. 65–86, 1958.

[3] M. Adler and B. Dumas, 'International portfolio choice and corporation finance: a survey', *Mimeo*, December 1981.

[4] Note that variability is defined for the actual and expected rate of inflation, the monetary aggregates, and the interest rate, as the standard deviation of the series. For unexpected inflation, the real and effective exchange rate, and the real rate of interest, variability is calculated on the differences between expected and realized values. Expected inflation and the ex-ante real rates of interest are calculated from survey-based data for the EC countries and the US. The EC data are taken from F. Papadia and V. Basano, 'EC-DG II inflationary expectations survey based inflationary expectations for the EEC countries', *Economic Papers*

No. 1, Commission of the European Communities, Directorate-General for Economic and Financial Affairs, May 1981. US data are taken from the *Livingston Survey*, as provided by the Philadelphia Reserve Bank. For the other countries stationary expectations are assumed, i.e. the expected future rate of inflation is equal to the realized one. The rate of exchange is assumed to be a random-walk and therefore the expected future value is equal to the one achieved at any period.

[5] The degree of integration between national and international financial markets for the same currency is measured as the difference between the rate of interest observed in the Euro-currency market and the one recorded in the domestic financial market.

[6] Note that the exchange rate is defined in such a way that the country ranked first will be the one with the highest (nominal or real) average *devaluation*, while the country ranked last will be the one with the highest average *revaluation*.

[7] The data, taken from the Bank for International Settlements (BIS) *Annual Report*, refer to the domestic currency liability figures in the table 'External assets and liabilities of banks in individual reporting countries and of certain off-shore branches of US banks'. Various issues, Basle.

[8] The data, also from the Bank for International Settlements (BIS) *Annual Report*, are the liabilities in the table, 'Currency breakdown of foreign currency positions of banks in reporting European countries'. The published data were completed by information kindly provided by the BIS.

[9] The data are from the Group of Thirty, *How central banks manage their reserves*, New York, 1982.

[10] The data are from S. A. B. Page, 'The choice of invoicing currency in merchandise trade', *National Institute Economic Review*, 1981, pp. 60–72; and Brian O'Loghlen, 'The use of Community currencies in trade and finance', mimeo, Directorate-General for Economic and Financial Affairs, Commission of the European Communities, Brussels, 1981. They refer to the share of each country's exports/imports denominated in national currency. B. O'Loghlen's work provided the initial stimulus for writing this paper.

[11] As explained in Section IV and in the Appendix, the share of each currency in total real money balances is the variable which is of interest. It is known that PPP holds over the medium/long term but not in the short term and, in particular, that overshooting phenomena occur. This will bring about temporary increases in the share of revaluing countries with respect to the share measured from real values. However, since averages over a period of nine years are used in the empirical analysis, these transitory discrepancies need not worry us.

[12] Of course, this assumes, quite arbitrarily, that there is a one-to-one relationship between 'size' and 'use'. Better results could arguably be obtained by relaxing this condition.

[13] The rank correlation coefficients between excess use and quality was calculated for some other quality measures given in Table 1. The positive association is generally confirmed, with the exception of the international reserves held by industrialized countries. For 'use' defined from liabilities of domestic banks held by non-residents, for example, the following coefficients were estimated:

rank coefficients between excess use and quality measured as variability of:	unexpected inflation	M2	short-term interest rate	effective exchange rate
	.333	.248	.200	.321

[14] Regression analysis was chosen rather than rank correlation analysis because

there appeared no obviously plausible way to apply the latter. However, the test should still be interpreted as one of independence of the two phenomena rather than a fully fledged estimation. A more satisfactory 'trade use' variable would have been the share of 'world trade', rather than that of a given country's trade, denominated in each currency. This would have taken into account the use of each currency by third parties. However, data on this variable were impossible to gather.

[15] S. A. B. Page, 'The choice of invoicing currency in merchandise trade', *National Institute Economic Review*, 1981, pp. 60-72; and Brian O'Loghlen, 'The use of Community currencies in trade and finance', mimeo, Directorate-General for Economic and Financial Affairs, Commission of the European Communities, Brussels, 1981, give an exhaustive treatment of the issue.

[16] The result stands up to different definitions of quality.

[17] We are in good company, however, since the point was originally raised by A. Okun, 'The mirage of steady inflation', *Brookings Papers on Economic Activity*, No. 2, 1971, pp. 485-98.

[18] This hypothesis was expressed and tested positively by L. Leiderman, 'Monetary accommodation and the variability of output, prices, and exchange rates', *Carnegie-Rochester Conference Series on Public Policy 16*, 1982, pp. 47-86, eds. Karl Brunner and Alan Meltzer.

[19] As done by Stanley Fischer, 'Relative price variability and inflation in the United States and Germany', *European Economic Review*, 18, 1982, pp. 171-96.

[20] A Cukierman and P. Wachtel, 'Differential inflationary expectations and the variability of the rate of inflation: theory and evidence', *American Economic Review*, June 1969, pp. 444-74.

[21] See among others: R. Parks, 'Inflation and relative price variability', *Journal of Political Economy*, 1978, Vol. 86, No. 1, pp. 79-95; D. R. Vining, jr. and T. C. Elwertowski, 'The relationship between relative prices and the general price level', *The American Economic Review*, Vol. 66, No. 4, September 1976, pp. 699-708; D. Logue and T. Willet, 'A note on the relation between the rate and variability of inflation', *Economica*, Vol. 43, May 1976, pp. 151-8; A Cukierman, 'Relative price variability, inflation and the allocative efficiency of the price system', *Journal of Monetary Economics* 9, 1982, pp. 131-62; F. Padoa-Schioppa, 'Inflazione e prezzi relativi', *Moneta e Credito*, 1979, Vol. XXXII, No. 128, pp. 457-77.

[22] It is interesting to recall that such a 'strange theory' was backed up by: (1) a 'former Minister of Finance and a celebrated economist'; (2) the President of the Reichsbank; (3) the German economic press; and (4) the Statistical Bureau of the Reich! The quotation is taken from the English version of two articles originally published in 1925 and 1926 in Italian. See C. Bresciani-Turroni, *The Economics of Inflation* (George Allen & Unwin Ltd., London, 1937) p. 155.

[23] Ibid., p. 173.

[24] Stanley Fischer, 'Seigniorage and the case for national money', *Journal of Political Economy*, 1982, Vol. 90, No. 21, pp. 295-313.

[25] An equivalent formulation of this argument is to posit the demand for real balances as a negative function of the nominal rate of interest or the expected inflation. This is the point made by P. Cagan, 'The monetary dynamics of hyper-inflations', in *The Quantity Theory of Money—A Restatement*, Milton Friedman ed. (The University of Chicago Press, 1956). Further analysed by M. Bailey, 'The welfare cost of inflationary finance', *The Journal of Political Economy*, Vol. LXIV, No. 2, April 1956, pp. 93-110, and reconsidered by T. Sargent and N. Wallace, 'Some unpleasant monetarist arithmetic', *Federal Reserve Bank of Minneapolis Quarterly Review*, Autumn 1981, pp. 1-17. The same explanation has been invoked recently by A. Cukierman, K. Lennan, and F. Papadia, 'Inflation

caused redistributions in five European countries: 1974–81', mimeo, Directorate-General for Economic and Financial Affairs, Commission of the EC, Brussels, 1982. They use it to explain the fact that in European countries in which inflation is high, the ratio of money balances to income is lower than in low-inflation countries.

[26] See M. Mussa, 'The welfare cost of inflation and the rôle of money as a unit of account', *Journal of Money, Credit and Banking*, Vol. 9, No. 2, May 1977, pp. 276–86. Also S. Fischer and F. Modigliani, 'Towards an understanding of the real effects and costs of inflation', *Weltwirtschaftliches Archiv*, 1978, Vol. CXIV, pp. 810–33.

[27] As far as bank deposits are concerned, an explanation of the shares of the various currencies in the portfolio of agents, according to the Capital Asset Pricing Model, has been put forward and empirically estimated by M. Adler and B. Dumas, 'International portfolio choice and corporation finance: a survey', mimeo, Dec. 1981. The results, however, are so far removed from reality that, although interesting in themselves, they do not provide an empirically useful tool.

[28] For an analytic presentation of this argument, see S. Fischer, 'Money and the production function', *Economic Inquiry*, Vol. 12, 1974, pp. 517–33. Also E. Fama and A. Farber, 'Money, bonds and foreign exchange', *The American Economic Review*, Vol. 69, No. 4, September 1979, pp. 639–49.

[29] The numerous ways in which inflation reduces the usefulness of any given currency are examined by S. Fischer and F. Modigliani op. cit. and also in S. Fischer, 'Towards an understanding of the costs of inflation: II', *Carnegie-Rochester Conference on Public Policy 15*, 1981, pp. 5–42.

[30] B. Klein, 'The demand for quality-adjusted cash balances: price uncertainty in the US demand for money function', *Journal of Political Economy*, 1977, Vol. 85, No. 4, pp. 691–715.

[31] This adaptation of Klein's model is intuitively plausible in that it confirms the common sense statement that the market share of a goods item, be it a real goods item or a currency, depends positively on its quality. The variation is also consistent with the empirical results of M. Blejer, 'The demand for money and the variability of the rate of inflation: some empirical results', *International Economic Review*, Vol. 20, No. 2, June 1979, pp. 545–9. Blejer, assessing the model based on data relating to small open economies (Argentina, Brazil, Chile), found that the use of the 'national' currency decreased when its quality decreased.

[32] S. Fischer, 'Towards an understanding of the costs of inflation: II', op. cit.

[33] e.g. D. Logue and T. Sweeney, 'Inflation and real growth: some empirical results', *Journal of Money, Credit and Banking*, Nov. 1981, Vol. 13, No. 4, pp. 497–501. Also P. Baffi, 'Perspectives on inflation', preliminary draft, mimeo, 3 October 1980; and C. Bresciani-Turroni, *The Economics of Inflation*, op. cit.

[34] M. Friedman, 'Inflation and Unemployment', *Journal of Political Economy*, Vol. 85, 1977, pp. 451–72.

[35] F. Hayek, 'Denationalization of money', *Hobart Paper, No. 70*, Institute of Economic Affairs, London, 1970.

[36] This model is an elaboration of that by B. Klein. See note 31. The difference is that there are two currencies competing here rather than one as in the closed economy model by Klein. Furthermore, the demand and supply functions of monetary services are given a specific structure, whereas they were more general in Klein's formulation.

3

Structural Changes in the Banking System and the Determination of the Stock of Money

CHARLES GOODHART*

Introduction

The pace of structural change

The structure of the banking system is currently in the midst of profound change. Some aspects of this have already been largely completed, for example banks' switch to liability management. Some are still in progress, like the continuing shift away from fixed-rate lending to variable-rate lending—though this shift has reflected worsening inflation, and could cease, or even reverse, were inflation conquered. Other changes are still in the pipeline—their outline may already be discernible, but they have not yet fully taken effect; these last include prospective changes in the structure of retail deposit business and the form of payment transmission technologies. This chapter considers these changes and explores their implications for monetary control, notably for the achievement of target rates of growth for certain specified monetary aggregates.

There is clearly now in process a set of structural and technological changes, which appear likely to alter the form of banking and financial intermediation. Structural changes of this magnitude within the banking industry seem to come in waves. One such wave occurred during the course of the nineteenth century, when there was a major extension of payment services from currency alone to chequeable deposits with the banking system. Banks developed from a rudimentary state at the beginning of the century to a stage by its end which in form, structure, and basic technology remained broadly constant until the 1960s. Whereas an economist surveying monetary and banking developments through the nineteenth century would have had to concentrate on structural changes, describing and accounting for the historical evolution of financial institutions and discussing the changing conceptual form of money itself, it is possible for economists studying money and banking from the end of the nineteenth century to about

* Bank of England.

1970 to treat structural changes as of relatively minor significance, occurring sufficiently slowly and gently over time not to become a central element in the main analytical record. For example, Friedman and Schwartz in *Monetary Trends in the United States and United Kingdom*,[1] are aware of the importance of structural changes during the century (1870-1970), but argue that, '. . . many elements in the financial structure remain the same throughout the period and have been common to both countries'.

Indeed, at the end of the 1970s, the structure and form of *retail* financial services were still looking much the same as they had done by about the beginning of the twentieth century, at least in English-speaking countries. The branch banking system, the cheque book, the system of cheque clearing, the provision of mortgages through specialized housing institutions (the building societies in the UK), the provision of insurance services by insurance companies, etc., which were already in place at the end of the nineteenth century, remained largely unchanged. It is the thesis of this chapter, however, that we have now entered into a period of more rapid structural change, so that analysis of financial development will once again have to pay serious attention both to structural changes and to consequential conceptual reconsiderations, rather than undertaking analytical studies on the basis of an assumption of a largely unchanged monetary system.

The causes of structural change

These current structural changes are mainly caused by three inter-related factors: high, variable, and unpredictable inflation, leading to high and variable nominal interest rates; the existence (in some countries) of restrictive and burdensome regulations discriminating against certain forms of financial (banking) intermediation; and finally the rapid development of technology, speeding up and cheapening the flow, retrieval, and analysis of information. These factors interact. For example, the high and variable inflation brings high and variable interest rates, which in turn make certain of the restrictions on banking inter-mediation—e.g. in the form of non-interest-bearing reserve requirements and limits on interest payments—more burdensome, while the development of information flows, via the new technology, allows financial flows to be shifted more easily into channels where such regulations have less effect.

The pace of structural change has therefore tended to be greatest in those countries where inflation, and thus also interest rates, have been quite high (though this is not by itself sufficient to generate structural change, since one can point to several high inflation countries where it has not taken place), where discrimination against certain forms of financial intermediation has been burdensome (but where there has been freedom for entrepreneurs to shift to other forms of financial intermediation without general constraint and intervention from the state), and where progress in information technology has been greatest. It is therefore no surprise to find such change has probably been greatest in the United States. In the UK the rate of inflation and its variability have been more extreme than in the US, but the constraints imposed by the authorities on banking intermediation were considerably eased in 1971 (and again in 1980 with the abandonment of the 'corset'), and the pace of structural change has been somewhat slower than in the US. Structural changes of a broadly similar kind are also proceeding at quite a rapid rate in other English-speaking countries—e.g. Australia in the aftermath of the Campbell Report,[2] and in Canada and South Africa.

In continental Europe however, the pace of such structural change to date appears to have been somewhat slower than in the English-speaking countries. There are differing reasons for this. In certain countries, such as Greece, and to a somewhat lesser extent in France and Italy, the scope of regulation has been so pervasive that the possibility of shifting the flow of financial intermediation to avoid the burden of regulation hardly becomes possible. Thus one factor encouraging structural change tends to be absent.[3]

In certain other European countries, for example the Federal Republic of Germany and Switzerland, the average rate and variability of inflation, one of the other elements forcing the pace of structural change, has been less virulent, thus reducing the incentive towards structural change within the financial system.[4] Of course, the institutional forms and legal arrangements under which banking and deposit-taking operate have a generalized effect on the evolution of each country's banking system.

The forms of structural change

The first major changes to the *domestic* banking system began in the late 1960s in the United States, with the switch from *asset management* to *liability management*.[5] This occurred before the onset of rising and variable inflation, and was initially mainly adopted as a means of avoiding the constraints on growth and on the expansion of bank balance sheets caused by the exhaustion of 'surplus' public sector debt on the asset side, and by the restrictions on the rate of interest that could be offered on retail-type deposits on the liability side (Regulation Q). This development, in part following the example of the already rapidly growing Euro-markets, was also encouraged and facilitated by the development of computers and other advances in information technology and proved highly efficient; it soon spread to other countries' domestic money markets. These developments and their consequent implications for monetary control are described relatively briefly (because they are already well known and appreciated) in the following section.

The next set of structural changes considered here mainly represents a response to the rising, high, and variable rates of inflation that developed during the 1970s. The main feature of these changes involves the shift by both borrowers and (bank) lenders away from *fixed* rate lending to *variable* rate lending. As will be described, once such a shift towards variable rate lending has taken place, then the contemporary *level* of interest rates comes to have a less direct influence both on the demand of borrowers for funds and on the supply of funds by (bank) lenders. This is obviously so because the initial rate of interest no longer holds throughout the period of the loan, but can be expected to vary, generally in line with variations in inflation, at shorter, usually pre-arranged roll-over dates, throughout the life of the loan. The contemporary level of interest rates will continue to have a (lesser) effect on credit markets, both indirectly through its generalized effect on demand and activity (perhaps especially through its effects on exchange rates), i.e. through changing macroeconomic conditions, and also through some residual effect on the demand for individual channels of credit. Nevertheless, an increasingly important influence on the demand and the supply of bank credit under these conditions becomes not so much the general level of interest rates, but the spread charged by the bank, i.e. the margin between the going market rate for (wholesale) deposit funds and the market rate for loans, for example as expressed by the margin over LIBOR (London Inter-Bank Offer Rate) in the Euro-markets.

The final set of structural changes considered here involves innovations in the form of retail banking and transmission mechanisms. The application of improved technology is now bringing cash management techniques that were initially only available to wholesale banking customers increasingly into the area of retail deposit banking. This could have the effect of further blurring the already fuzzy distinction between transactions and savings balances, with perhaps the bulk of transactions balances, other than cash, bearing market-related interest rates. A still wider range of differing forms of liquid asset holdings available for retail depositors may be devised, encompassing differing combinations of payments services and interest rates. The effect of technology in cheapening transmission mechanisms may encourage and facilitate a wider range of competition in retail banking activities. Again, technological developments, by cheapening certain forms of transmission mechanisms, should lead to a faster rate of growth in these forms rather than others. For example, it is possible that a much larger proportion of payment transactions will be made through the means of plastic or other cards and be met initially out of credit facilities, rather than from low or zero-interest-yielding transaction balances. So the immediate buffer of funds available to families in order to undertake immediate transactions may well come to reside in a pool of credit facilities, carried on behalf of the individual transactor by the institution(s) looking after the individual's cash management, rather than in deposit balances as in the past.

The final section of this chapter deals with the implications for financial control and monetary targetting of these latter two forms of structural change.

I. Liability management

Historical development

At the end of the Second World War, banks in certain major countries, notably the US and UK, emerged with swollen holdings of public-sector debt, proportionately much larger than they had normally held in their balance sheets, and equivalently much lower holdings of loans to the private sector. This was a result of the pattern of financing during the war. The data for the proportionate holdings of public- and private-sector debt in banks' assets for the UK and US are shown in Table 3.1 below.

These 'excess' holdings of public-sector debt provided the banks with a cushion with which to absorb the growing demands of private-sector borrowers and a source of flexibility, enabling banks to adjust to the changing demands of borrowers, while at the same time continuing to respond passively to inflows of deposits obtained at interest rates constrained either by regulations, such as Regulation Q (which set ceiling interest rates that could be offered by banks on various forms of deposits), or by oligopolistic arrangements (as in the cartel in the UK until 1971, and in Canada until 1967). In short, banks adjusted to cash-flow pressures primarily by asset management, particularly by varying their holdings of public-sector debt, while rates on their deposit liabilities were constrained *not* to react fully to variations in market rates.

In such a constrained system, control over the total size of bank deposit liabilities (though *not* over the growth of bank lending to the private sector—which was in some cases subject to additional direct controls, i.e. ceilings on advances, and direct requests), was relatively easy. Open market sales by the authorities, when they wished to be restrictive, would squeeze the cash base of the banks and encourage them to sell off their holdings of public-sector debt. The direct and indirect effect of such open market operations (the indirect effect being the subsequent induced sales by the banks), would lead to a rise in the yields on longer-dated public-sector assets and to yields on marketable

TABLE 3.1

Proportion of UK and US banks' assets held in public- and private-sector debt

At end-December	UK-London clearing banks		US commercial banks	
	Public[1] %	Private[1] %	Public[2] %	Private %
1939	31.7	44.9	30.2	32.2
1946	60.0	19.0	53.4	23.5
1950	49.1	27.7	42.0	33.8
1955	47.1	28.9	35.3	41.1
1960	26.7	44.5	30.5	46.9
1965	17.6	53.2	26.0	54.5
1970[3]	12.1	61.0	22.8	54.4

[1] Public-sector debt comprises British Government securities (BGS) and Treasury bills and Treasury deposit receipts. Available sources included local-authority debt as private-sector debt. Certain items, notably cash, special deposits, money at call and short notice, premises, and other fixed and working capital, etc., are excluded from this table, so the figures do not add up to 100%.

[2] Public-sector debt comprises US Government securities and state and local government securities.

[3] Average of mid-December 1970 and mid-January 1971.

Sources: D. K. Sheppard, *The Growth and Role of UK Financial Institutions 1880–1962* (Methuen and Co. Ltd., London, 1971); *Bank of England Quarterly Bulletin*; *Federal Reserve Bulletin*.

securities rising generally relative to deposit rates.[6] Moreover, because a rise in market rates, engineered by the authorities in the pursuit of monetary control, would cause such rates to rise relative both to non-interest-bearing and also to interest-bearing deposits, owing to the limited flexibility of the latter, the growth rates of both narrow and broad money tended to be strongly positively correlated, though their respective demand-for-money functions tended to have differing interest elasticities. So movements over quarters and over years of broad and narrow money were relatively similar, and their relationships with movements on nominal incomes, their velocities and demand-for-money functions, tended to exhibit somewhat similar features during these early post-war years, from 1945 until the mid-1960s.

This extra cushion of flexibility, provided by public-sector debt holdings, was largely exhausted by the mid-1960s, as can be seen in Table 3.1. In the United States, the banks then developed the ability to borrow very large sums of money on marketable instruments, e.g. certificates of deposit (CDs), on market-related terms.[7] The resulting growth of such wholesale funds was extremely rapid and quickly spread to other countries, such as Canada and the United

Kingdom (see Figure 3.1). In the UK this occurred most strongly after the direct constraints on bank lending were removed in 1971 as part of the shift to the new system of Competition and Credit Control.

Monetary control

The advent of such liability management in wholesale money markets drastically affected the authorities' ability to control the total size of banks' books. Previously, with banks engaging in asset management while generally accepting external constraints on interest rates on deposits, the authorities were in a position to enforce shifts in *relative* interest rates by varying the *general* level of market rates. Thus when they wished to be restrictive and increased the general level of interest rates, market rates generally would rise relative to bank deposit rates, because the latter were more or less constrained, thus inducing an outflow of funds from bank deposits to other assets, and so forcing banks to sell their surplus reserve assets, in this case generally their 'excess' holdings of public-sector debt. But once the banks shifted to liability management, it became very much more difficult for the authorities to shift relative interest rates unfavourably against *all* bank deposit rates[8] when they raised the general level of market rates. Once the banks turned to liability management, however, a cash outflow (whether because of an increase in the demand for bank loans, or as a result of a fall in retail deposits—with the latter perhaps caused by the authorities raising interest rates in pursuit of a more restrictive policy), could be met by the banks by compensatory increases in interest rates on wholesale deposits in order to obtain the required funds to meet the demand for additional loans, or to replace a deposit drain.

So, while retaining control over the general level of interest rates, the authorities now found it much harder to maintain control over the relativities between market rates and those deposit rates for wholesale funds which the banks were using aggressively in order to fund their books. As long as banks could find profitable lending outlets for funds, they would bid for deposits in wholesale markets in order to provide the finance for such lending. For the individual bank, access to such markets appeared to provide it with a much more elastic and flexible source of funds than had previously been available. Even for the banking system as a whole, particularly in open economies without exchange controls on international capital movements, the development of such markets will presumably have raised the elasticity of shifts of funds in response to *relative* interest differentials. Consequently, as the supply of funds to banks could be adjusted to meet demand, so control over the total size of banks' books came to depend increasingly on the interest elasticity of demand for bank lending, an interest elasticity

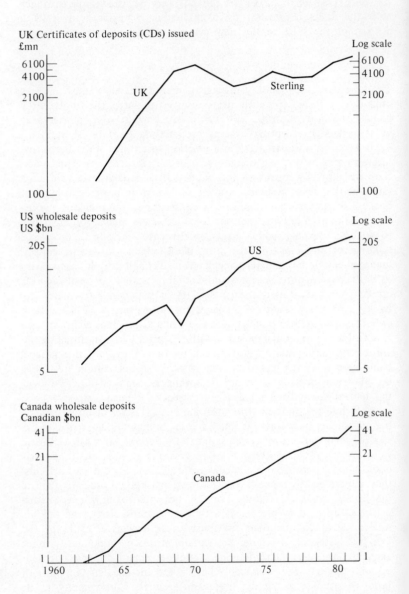

Fig. 3.1: The growth of wholesale liabilities.

which was always somewhat uncertain and low in the short term. Moreover, assessment and analysis of such interest elasticity of demand for bank borrowing was distorted by the authorities' own use of credit controls (and of various forms of moral and other suasion on banks) to restrain bank lending at particular times, and indeed by the possible application of various forms of non-price limitation on credit availability by the banks themselves. So there were probably periods when the market for bank credit did not clear. Accordingly, attempts to estimate demand and supply functions for bank loans, particularly their interest elasticity, were complicated. Moreover, as will be described in the next section, this elasticity was further affected by the switch from fixed-rate loans to variable-rate lending.

Previously, under asset management, the interest elasticity of demand for broad money depended on the authorities' ability to vary the *relativity* between bank deposit rates and market rates, as the authorities operated to control the general level of short-term market rates. Now, with liability management, the effective interest elasticity on broad money came to depend much more on the interest elasticity of the demand for bank loans, i.e. the major element in the asset books of banks. Consequently the elasticity of demand for broad money fell sharply in response to general changes in market interest rates. It was not that the responsiveness of banks, or bank customers, to interest rates declined; indeed their general reaction to relative rate differentials, if anything, became even more sensitive. Rather the authorities' ability to vary the general *level* of interest rates had significantly less impact on the relevant *differentials* once liability management came into play. As a result, the response of the overall balance sheets of banks, i.e. the variation of their total loans and deposits, to changes in interest rates became less elastic and also less predictable, since it would depend largely on how banks themselves would react to the authorities' pressures. (By the same token, the reactions of the system in response to changes in the level of base money, in the form of changes in interest rates as well as quantitative changes, became somewhat more volatile and less predictable.) The LM curve, with money broadly defined, became more vertical, but also more subject to unpredictable supply-side shifts.

This led to a change in the previous relationship between narrow money, normally termed M1, and broader monetary definitions, with the latter including large elements of wholesale deposits bearing market-related interest rates. Whereas the advent of liability management changed the relationship between movements in the general level of interest rates and broad money, the relationship between narrow money (M1) and incomes and interest rates remained largely unchanged, since at this time (i.e. the 1960s and 1970s) the determination of interest rates on the various components of M1 remained largely constrained by regulation or convention.

Under liability management, a rise in the demand for credit would tend to raise the general level of interest rates, but the banks would then raise rates on wholesale deposits even further in order to provide funds to meet that rise in credit demand. Thus, under these circumstances, the total of interest-bearing deposits would rise, and often the total of broad money would increase, while M1 would unambiguously fall. Whereas with asset management, prior to the end of the 1960s, there was a generally positive correlation between narrow and broad money, after the advent of liability management through the course of the 1970s there was often either no correlation between narrow and broad money, or even in some cases signs of a negative correlation. While this generalization holds for the Anglo-Saxon countries, i.e the US, UK, Canada, and also Switzerland, it does not hold in the case of France, Japan, and the Federal Republic, as shown in Table 3.2. It may be that in France and Japan the continuation of credit ceilings (*encadrement du crédit* and window guidance respectively) constrained the development of liability management. I cannot explain the Federal Republic result, except in so far as the risks of extending loans on a fixed-rate term led German banks to ration credit availability as interest rates rose. These shifts in the relationship between the quarterly and annual percentage changes of movements in narrow and broad money between the 1960s generally and the 1970s are shown in Table 3.2.

This structural change made control over the growth of broad money more difficult and caused problems in some of the countries which focused on such wider monetary aggregates. However, this change in banks' behaviour had no effect on the determinants of narrow money, so in those countries in which the authorities were targetting mainly, or exclusively, on narrow money, this had little or no effect on their ability to achieve their chosen monetary targets. But in the countries which adopted broad money targets, notably the UK, there were varying responses to the declining ability of the authorities to control their chosen broad monetary aggregates through the use of their main instrument, i.e. the control over the general level of interest rates.

In some cases, as in Italy,[9] the authorities reverted to direct controls over bank lending. In other cases the authorities tried to restrain, or rescind, the freedom of the banks to bid freely for wholesale deposits. An example of the latter was the 1972 Winnipeg agreement in Canada. Perhaps the most sophisticated attempts to apply direct controls to the rate of growth of total bank lending and total bank deposits are to be found in France with their penalties on marginal bank lending[10]

TABLE 3.2

Correlation between percentage changes in broad and narrow money

	Correlation coefficient	
	1960s[2]	1970s[2]
(a) Correlation between *annual* percentage changes in broad and narrow money[1]		
Canada	0.60	−0.13
Switzerland	0.45	−0.54
UK (using £M3)	0.95	−0.39
(using M3)	0.97	−0.45
US	0.64	0.26
FRG	0.79	0.82
France	0.92	0.86
Japan	0.87	0.97
(b) Correlation between *quarterly* percentage changes in broad and narrow money[1]		
Canada	0.71	0.30
Switzerland	0.91	0.65
UK (using £M3)	0.91	0.55
(using M3)	0.92	0.46
US	0.93	0.85
FRG	0.94	0.82
France	0.90	0.93
Japan	0.52	0.93

[1] For the UK between M1 and £M3 or M3 as shown. For other countries figures are taken from *International Financial Statistics* (IFS) for money and quasi-money: i.e. narrow money = currency outside banks and private-sector demand deposits; broad money = narrow money plus residents' time, savings, and foreign currency deposits.
[2] Because of data problems the periods used are in some cases slightly different from those shown.

(the *encadrement du crédit*) and in the UK with the Supplementary Special Deposits Scheme (the Corset) which penalized the marginal rate of growth of interest-bearing deposits above some allowable trend.

With the growth of bank lending to the private sector often representing a reasonable proxy for the growth of total bank credit, and with the growth of deposits of domestic non-bank residents representing a reasonable proxy for the growth of total bank liabilities and with total bank liabilities equal to total bank assets as an identity, there can at times be room for confusion in countries with broad monetary targets whether their main concern was with credit expansion or monetary expansion. An example of this occurred in the UK during the course of 1981. An overshoot in the £M3 target was tolerated in part on the grounds that this resulted from a switch in the provision of mortgage lending from building societies to banks. However, if the focus of the target was on the monetary liability side, then it should have made no difference what changes in credit markets may have formed the counterpart to the increase in monetary liabilities. Alternatively, it could be argued that bank deposit liabilities were such close substitutes with building society deposits that a switch of funds between such holdings would be largely immaterial. But if so, the appropriate target should not be £M3, but a wider aggregate encompassing both sets of liquid assets. The adoption of a target for PSL2[11] (which is such a wider aggregate) in addition to £M3 in 1982 supports the second interpretation.

In most countries with broad monetary targets, the weight of opinion has been that the main focus should be on the liability monetary side, rather than on the credit market side.[12] In such cases one response to liability management, in conditions of sizeable and unpredictable shifts in the demand for bank lending, has been to devise, to encourage, and to maintain conditions in which increases in bank lending to the private sector, relative to the target rate of growth, could be financed through banks, but in what could be described as 'non-monetary' ways.

For example, in both the Netherlands and the Federal Republic sizeable proportions of bank liabilities are held in forms which are considered to be of sufficiently long maturity, with sufficient constraints on early withdrawal, to be described as non-monetary in form. Thus in the Netherlands, when there was such a large demand for bank credit as to threaten the monetary target, the authorities have on occasion brought into play a form of credit ceiling which directly limits neither the banks' ability to issue additional loans, nor the size of the banks' balance sheets in total. Instead, it limits the extent to which the banks can fund the additional lending by monetary liabilities, therefore requiring them to raise the yield on 'non-monetary' liabilities, and thus attract the additional funds into such 'non-monetary' form.

In France the rules governing restricted lending allow the proceeds of bond issues (and equity issues) by banks to be on-lent without restriction; and banks take full advantage of this when market conditions are favourable. As in the Netherlands, this gives the larger banks with easier access to the bond market a competitive advantage. Demand for such bonds increased in 1981 when the authorities restricted the rate of interest that could be offered on certain domestic deposits. Similarly, in the Federal Republic the system works in such a way that shifts in the demand for bank credit are frequently met through non-monetary financing.

In the UK, however, there has been much less development by the banks, or bank customers, of holdings of longer-term savings deposits with the banking system.[13] No such development occurred in the UK even when there was a clear advantage to the banks in attracting such longer-term deposits under the Corset system because deposits with a maturity over two years would not have been caught by the Corset. It is not clear why such a market for longer-term savings deposits with banks has not grown up in the UK. One factor may possibly be because the building societies had already established a sufficient market in such deposits. Another factor may be the wider range of government savings instruments available for personal investors in the UK compared to most other countries in Europe.

In so far as shifts over the boundary from assets designated as 'monetary' into those designated as 'non-monetary' leaves the economic position and opportunities of deposit holders largely unchanged (and the above qualification should be emphasized), it could then be argued that 'control' established in this way, by encouraging possibly quite small shifts in the maturity holdings of bank deposits, is somewhat cosmetic in its overall economic effect. Admittedly, shifting the public's asset holdings outwards along the maturity spectrum must always be regarded as restrictive. Nevertheless the extent of such real shift[14] may not be measured well by concentrating on any one, or even a few, aggregates; on the other hand trying to assess 'liquidity' as a whole, à la Radcliffe, leads into a conceptual and statistical quagmire. It can however be argued that the continuing stability and satisfactory performance of demand-for-money functions of the different Ms, and the stability and predictability of the velocity of these Ms, such as they may be, represents an econometric test of how far such shifts in asset holdings involve real changes in economic behaviour, or are largely cosmetic.

Playing the yield curve

On occasion it has been suggested that, if the authorities' ability to control the broad monetary aggregates through varying the general level of market rates has become impaired as a result of liability management (or in terms of monetary-base control, if the variability and uncertainty of changes in interest rates in response to changes in the base have become greater), then the authorities could restore some of their ability to control the broad monetary aggregates by altering the shape of the yield curve, rather than by trying to vary just the general level of rates. Unfortunately what is gained on the one hand in terms of making deposits less attractive to deposit holders when long yields are raised relative to short yields, tends by the same token to induce borrowers to shift short, borrowing more from banks and less from capital markets. When faced with an excess demand for funds by borrowers and an insufficiency of deposits, banks will respond by raising deposit rates, thereby offsetting, in so far as they can, the shift in the yield curve set in motion by the authorities.

In contrast some observers in the UK have suggested that the appropriate response for the authorities when they try to be restrictive is to raise short yields relative to long ones, in order to persuade borrowers to shift from banks back into capital markets. But such a tilt in the yield curve would (perversely) attract asset holders short, e.g. by selling (or not buying) long-dated (government) bonds, in order to add to their bank deposits. Again, with an excess of deposit funds and an insufficiency of demand from borrowers, banks would tend to lower their general level of rates, again tending to offset the tilt in the yield curve which the authorities might try to establish. Although there may be occasional market opportunities[15] for operating in such a way as to encourage *both* borrowers and depositors to shift longer by appropriate market tactics, the exercise does not seem to me easy, obvious, nor probably long sustainable.

II. Inflation, variable rate lending, and the importance of the spread

Maturity transformation and interest rate risk

One of the main functions of financial intermediaries is to provide depositors with deposit liabilities of a maturity which the depositors want, while at the same time lending on their funds on maturity terms acceptable to their borrowers. In general, the preferred maturity of depositors and borrowers do not match, so the maturities of liabilities and assets on the books of financial intermediaries differ, i.e. financial intermediaries undertake maturity transformation. In some specialized cases, where the financial intermediaries are acting as long-term savings institutions concentrating on the provision of life insurance or pensions, the liabilities held by such intermediaries may on average be longer than their assets. More generally, and particularly in the case of monetary institutions, the usual preference of depositors is for the holding of short-term claims, or deposits, on the (banking) institutions, while borrowers have a preference for loans on more extended terms. In some cases the extent of maturity transformation is restricted by legislation, as in Italy where the 1936 Banking Law broadly restricts lending by banks to a maximum term of eighteen months. In the UK a large proportion of bank lending is undertaken in overdraft form, which is nominally repayable on call by the banks, but in practice is outstanding for an indefinite period.

Thus banks, and other non-bank financial intermediaries (NBFI), engage in maturity transformation. This involves the intermediaries in various kinds of risk, particularly interest-rate risk if the interest rates on their assets/liabilities are fixed for the duration of the maturity. This risk arises because, with their liabilities generally on a shorter-term basis than their assets, a rise in the general level of interest rates would force them to re-finance lending, undertaken earlier at lower (fixed) rates, on the basis of funds obtained later at higher interest, thus enforcing a running loss. With assets longer than liabilities, and both undertaken on a fixed-rate basis, any unforeseen rise in nominal interest rates would bring about an unexpected loss to the banks, while any unforeseen fall in interest rates would lead to a windfall gain.

More generally, interest risk arises whenever there is a mismatch in the periodicity over which interest rates on assets and liabilities are fixed. This can occur even when there is no *maturity* transformation, i.e. if the maturity of the assets and liabilities is the same, but there is some resetting of interest rates on one side of the balance sheet, which is not similarly matched on the other. This interest-rate risk is obviously greater when nominal interest rates become more variable and unpredictable. The variability of nominal interest rates will tend to rise with an increased variability in the rate of inflation. (Such variability may also be greater, at least in the short run, if the authorities are trying to maintain continuous control over the path of monetary growth, rather than allowing monetary variations to respond in an accommodating manner to short-term fluctuations in money-market conditions.) Over the last decade, and more particularly in the last few years, the variability of nominal interest rates has increased, and this has had serious effects on those institutions sticking to fixed-rate financing. The plight of the savings and loan associations (S&Ls) in the US is a prime example of the dangers of continuing with fixed-rate financing in a conjuncture subject to sizeable and unforeseen fluctuations in the level of nominal interest rates.

It is possible to obtain protection from interest rate risks of this kind by the adoption of some form of variable-rate lending, in which lending rates are not fixed, but change over time in response to changes in market conditions.[16] There are various ways in which interest rates on longer-term loans can be varied over time in response to such changing conditions. The rate can be varied administratively by the lending institutions, as in the case of building societies in the UK: but leaving rates to be varied at the administrative fiat of the lending institution may in normal circumstances be regarded as leaving the borrower potentially subject to exploitation. However, the particular institutional position and historical traditions of building societies (as mutual funds) has enabled the administrative variation of their lending rate to be generally acceptable in the UK.

Alternatively, interest rates could be related to the current rate of inflation, plus a margin to provide a real rate of return. Indeed indexation of this kind, often described as 'monetary correction', has been adopted in several countries with especially high and variable inflation rates, such as Brazil and other countries in South America. Nevertheless, indexation has not been widely adopted, despite the onset of higher and variable inflation rates, in major industrial countries.[17] The more usual relationship between a variable lending rate and market conditions is to have the lending rate tied to the going market rate for large wholesale funds, with the rate varied at pre-arranged adjustment dates. Thus a two-year loan might represent in effect a series of three-month loans at the going wholesale three-month deposit rate, plus negotiated spread. Such floating rate loans originally emerged in the Euro-markets.[18]

This latter step greatly reduces the interest rate risk, notably to the lender, but also, in general, to the borrower if his loan would otherwise have been on a fixed term without break clauses. For the lending intermediary, it reduces the risks of undertaking maturity transformation. With the norm being for their financial claims to have a longer maturity than liabilities, the usual historical tendency has been for the profits of financial intermediaries to be squeezed as interest rates rise. This has been dramatically demonstrated with the S&Ls in the US, and still occurs in countries largely persisting with fixed-rate lending, for example the Federal Republic. Many West German banks took a long time to recover from losses made from long-term fixed-rate lending in 1978, and subsequently financed by increasingly expensive deposits. Swiss rates on such lending also tend to be sticky, with changes largely determined administratively. So the banks can lose out severely in times of rising interest rates, while not necessarily gaining equivalently in the converse situation when administered rates are lowered more rapidly.

In countries, though, which have historically worked on a variable rate basis, or have come increasingly to use this technique,[19] a reverse effect on profitability may now hold. With a proportion of deposits continuing to bear a fixed rate of interest (notably sight or demand deposits, the majority of which still have a zero interest rate in the UK and most other countries), more assets than deposit liabilities may now be on a variable rate basis. In this case then, profits tend to rise as interest rates rise, since the interest rate on a larger proportion of deposit liabilities maintains a fixed rate. This has become known in the UK as the endowment effect.[20] Thus banks (essentially the clearing banks) having a sizeable proportion of zero-interest-rate demand deposits receive larger 'endowment' profit as interest rates rise. This effect however is subject to erosion over time, as funds are switched from non-interest-bearing deposits to higher yielding assets. (The implications of this for monetary control are discussed further in the next section.)

The switch to variable rate lending is as important to the borrower as it is to the banks. The borrower will benefit most when the (unpredictable) developments causing changes in the variable rate are closely correlated with changes in the borrowers' cash flow. If there is a likelihood that fluctuations in the borrowers' cash flow and in variable rates might be negatively correlated, then the adoption of variable rate financing could well *increase* borrowers' risks. It was the rise in Euro-dollar interest rates at a time when export earnings came under severe pressure that highlighted this latter possibility internationally. Recent experience of cash flow pressures on companies at a time of high nominal interest rates reiterates the same lesson domestically.

Nevertheless, the conjunction of variable inflation and variable interest rates has led a sizeable proportion of borrowers to prefer to switch on to a variable rate basis. In practice, the 1970s were a decade when it would, with the benefit of hindsight, have been highly profitable for most companies to have borrowed on a fixed rate basis. Yet it was just in this period when, in the UK at least, virtually none did, and the long-term debenture market in the UK became moribund. In some part this was, perhaps, because company treasurers as a group 'got it wrong', believing that the current level of medium- and long-term interest rates was unnaturally high, just at a time when it was, in reality, due to rise even higher. Yet, even those who may have realized that there was a good chance that interest rates would rise further felt themselves unable to borrow at such high rates, because of the risk that rates might come down, and that they would be landed with unacceptably high fixed-rate borrowing, particularly with the outlook for profits, even in nominal terms, becoming more uncertain. Moreover, the risk appeared greater, in so far as their colleagues elsewhere were not themselves borrowing. To stick one's neck out in a risky venture by oneself is much more dangerous than to stick one's head out as a member of a large group. So, the rising rate of inflation, and with that the rising medium- and long-term interest rates, led to the virtual demise of the debenture market for companies in the UK.

There is, however, now some question whether companies (except perhaps really large companies) would go back to raising long-term fixed-rate debt on the capital market, even if inflation and nominal interest rates should come back down. With the demise of the debenture market, companies have turned increasingly to the banks for their medium-term finance.[21] There is a possibility that the banks have now developed a superior product to the capital market. The costs of capital transactions on the debenture market are high (especially in view of the fixed costs involved in new issues for medium and smaller companies). When there is a need to deal with many small purchasers there is a concomitant requirement to provide them with sufficient information and sufficient protection. Thus there is a need in the capital market for an expensive prospectus, and the whole process of financing a large new debenture issue with underwriting and sub-underwriting is expensive. Dealing with banks in the provision of medium-term funds, even with a banking syndicate when there is a lead bank, may be considerably cheaper and easier than facing the transactions costs of the debenture market. So even if inflation and nominal interest rates should now fall appreciably, there is still some likelihood that the banks will continue to take a larger share of such medium-term lending than was the case in the 1960s. With lower inflation and lower nominal interest rates, the form of such medium-term lending by banks could revert to being at fixed rather than at variable rates, perhaps thereby also inducing UK banks to seek medium-term fixed-rate deposits rather more keenly than in the past. The extent of continued involvement by the banks in this area will, however, in part depend on how spreads (and fiscal conditions) develop. During periods of low interest rates, endowment profits are low and spreads tend to be higher, forcing borrowers into the capital market. The reverse was true during the 1970s.

The effects of the switch to variable-rate lending

The change from fixed-rate lending to variable-rate lending will have reduced the interest sensitivity of borrowers to variations in the level of nominal interest rates.[22] Unless the expected duration of the borrowing is rather short, the shift to variable-rate lending means that the timing of the borrowing no longer matters greatly. With fixed-rate lending, it is obviously of crucial importance to seek to arrange the borrowing when the interest rate is relatively low, or believed to be, because that low rate will pertain throughout the life of the borrowing. Equally there will be a considerable advantage in avoiding borrowing at times when the rate, persisting throughout the life of the loan, is thought to be temporarily high. With variable-rate lending, it no longer will matter to the borrower whether the rate is thought to be temporarily high or temporarily low. If a loan is expected to be of a duration as long as an expected cycle of interest rates, then the borrower will even out the swings and the roundabouts in that cycle. So the current, momentary *level* of market interest rates no longer matters as greatly to a medium-term borrower.[23]

Instead, what now matters much more to the borrower is the spread that he is charged above the general market level of rates. Indeed the spread between the variable rate charged on loans and the rate paid on short-term deposits represents, in an important sense, the cost of intermediation. The cheaper the cost of intermediation, the larger the volume will be. In the US of course, large customers can directly enter the commercial paper market, as borrowers or lenders, if the cost of bank intermediation becomes too large. Large companies, especially multi-nationals, can generally turn to the Euro-markets if domestic intermediation costs rise too far.

The cost of bank intermediation for large customers has come down so far over the course of recent years that many, indeed most, large customers who can enter wholesale markets probably now have both debit and asset positions outstanding at the same time with the banking system. It is no longer the case that all banking customers with outstanding debts to the banks will seek to run these down as far as they can, so long as they have spare assets available. This is, perhaps, most obvious in the case of sovereign borrowers, who will continue to wish to maintain gross positive reserve positions, often in the form of holdings in the Euro-dollar markets, and yet also wish to borrow for general development when the terms are attractive.

The same is increasingly true now for corporate clients, who may be running gross asset and debit positions considerably in excess of their net position (whichever sign that may have) with the banking system. During the course of the last few years in which the company sector in the UK has been under severe cash-flow pressure, it has still built up its gross liquidity ratio. The lower the spread, the more attractive it will be for such customers to maintain liquidity on the basis of borrowed funds and to meet their additional financial requirements by borrowing, rather than by running down their existing deposit holdings. Indeed at the limit, if the spread is zero, given that liquidity has some utility, the demand for both bank lending and deposits would theoretically be infinite. Owing to the existence of rigidities and distortions in certain interest rates, there have occasionally been times in the UK in the years since 1971 when the interest rate on bank borrowing has actually fallen temporarily below an interest rate on deposits of a similar maturity, so that there was even a turn to be made by borrowing in order to re-deposit. This has been termed 'round-tripping'.

Thus one of the increasingly important determinants of the volume of both bank borrowing and bank deposits, given the widespread adoption of variable-rate lending, is the spread required by banks. The importance of the spread as a determinant of the rate of increase of intermediation has been clearly recognized in the case of the Euro-markets.[24] The importance of the spread as a determinant of the

volume of bank borrowing and deposits is, however, rather less clear
as yet in most domestic money markets, but some research has been
done in the Bank of England on the determinants both of the rate of
growth of broad money (£M3) and also on the demand for loans, which
suggests that variations in the spread may have a significant effect. The
effect of the spread on the total of loans and deposits is, however,
difficult to quantify, in part because it depends on reactions to relatively small variations in the differential between two highly-correlated
variables, and also because adequate data on actual rates at which transactions, borrowing and depositing, are undertaken are frequently not
available, nor sufficiently accurate, for the purpose of econometric
testing.

A reduction in spreads will tend to raise the rate of growth of the
banks, which are, in effect, thereby pricing their products more com-
petitively. But by the same token a reduction in spreads reduces profit
margins, and therefore erodes capital ratios—the ratio of the capital
stock to the volume of business being undertaken. An increase in competition, a desire for growth for its own sake, and confidence in the
soundness of the business being undertaken (a belief that risk of bad
debts are low) will all tend to squeeze the size of spreads. A natural
danger for the banking industry is that a successful run of years of
financial operations will encourage an erosion of capital/asset ratios
to a stage at which a deterioration in economic conditions generally,
leading to an increase in bad debts, could cause difficulties for the
banking system. One could, therefore, envisage a cycle with misplaced
confidence eroding capital adequacy, and then being found to have
been excessively optimistic, so that the capital position is impaired
yet further by bad debts. The resulting shock to confidence would
induce a subsequent recovery in spreads and profit margins, which
would have the effect of bringing about a (sudden) slow-down in the
rate of expansion of financial intermediation, or even some decline.[25]

Capital and reserve ratios and the size of banks

In the above analysis the overall size of banks' books is seen as depending on the volume of capital resources that the banks are able to attract
and on the ratio of total assets/liabilities to such capital that they seek
to maintain. The size of the banking business, as with other financial
intermediaries, is viewed as being determined essentially in the same
way as the size of any other business, depending on the volume of basic
resources (essentially capital) that it can employ and the opportunities
available to the industry for the employment of such resources. These
opportunities exhibit themselves for financial intermediaries in the
form of the interest rates available and the lending and deposit business
that they can undertake in financial markets. Shifts in the extent of

competition, and therefore in spreads, i.e. the cost of intermediation, may encourage bank customers to increase both their holdings of claims on the banks and their liabilities to the banks, and may, therefore, alter the velocity of the broader monetary aggregates at any rate. So, increasing competition could raise the ratio of broad money to nominal incomes, subject to such constraints as the maintenance of capital adequacy places on such a trend.

To some extent, changes in velocity may be a function of changing conditions within the banking business, rather than necessarily having any wider economic significance, though concern may remain that the apparent shift in the liquidity of the private sector's asset portfolio could affect future economic developments and hamper the authorities' ability to control such developments. Shifts in velocity for broad money that are accompanied by changes in banks' capital adequacy ratios may also provide some indication of changing financial risks, of the ebb and flow of competitive pressures, and perhaps of financial strength (or fragility). While it is difficult to establish any strong case for a particular ratio of capital to risk assets being an optimum, an equilibrium, or a desideratum, nevertheless it is possible to chart whether the financial exposure of the banking system is becoming greater or less.

It may be argued that the market will act to deter excessive financial risk-taking by the banking system by reducing the equity value of those banks which the market feels have been taking an excessively risky position. It is difficult, however, to feel confident that the market will be able to, or will generally, act in this way. Assessment of the trade-off between higher earnings and greater risk is not easy for the general public to make. The market lacks detailed information about the nature of the particular business of individual banks,[26] and the banks for reasons of competitive secrecy are unlikely to be prepared to give such information publicly and openly. In addition, there are many who believe that the market's time-horizon is relatively short, that it suffers from myopia, and that it is too prone to extrapolate short-term developments, frequently forgetting longer-term traditional norms of safety in the pursuit of a 'quick buck'.

On such grounds, there is, of course, an argument for prudential controls in order to restrain the degree of fragility and risk adopted by the banking system and to ensure the sufficiency of capital adequacy and the maintenance of sufficiently large spreads in the business. With the move of wholesale banking business into the international arena, with easy substitution into financial channels abroad (in place of domestic banking), there is, moreover, good reason in theory for some international harmonization of prudential controls over capital adequacy, though it would be difficult in practice. Otherwise those countries which allow their banks to maintain the lowest ratios of capital will also enable them to offer the lowest spreads, to become 'unfairly' competitive, and to grow in size relative to the banks in those countries undertaking a more prudent position. If, however, banks in the countries allowing a riskier position were then to get into trouble, the resulting effects on the banking business, and on the world economy generally, could spill over, e.g. into those countries where the banks had maintained a more prudent position.

If the size of banks' books is therefore determined by their access to capital resources and their capital/deposit ratios, what role is left for the monetary base as a determinant of the overall size of bank deposits? Of course, in many countries banks are only required to hold reserves against a section, or proportion, of their deposits, notably their demand deposits or transaction balances. So perhaps it could already be said that banks' access to reserves does not determine the *overall* size of their books. But even in the case of countries where reserves are required against total deposit liabilities, how does this requirement affect the overall size of their business?

First, any countries undertaking monetary base control would observe a rise, possibly a sharp rise, in interest rates as the 'reservable' deposits rose, above their target rate of growth. (Though such a rise in interest rates—not perhaps of the same speed or magnitude—would also generally occur even with a more discretionary reaction to monetary growth greater than the target.) This would affect and depress the general level of activity in the economy in the normal way. This reduction in economic activity, combined with some residual direct effect of interest rates on the demand for bank borrowing, would have the effect of reducing the growth and size of banks' business.

Perhaps more importantly, required reserves, if they do not bear a market interest rate, represent a form of tax on banking business. The higher interest rates go, the higher is the burden of this tax on banking. So relatively high required reserves, bearing low or zero interest rates, will directly act to reinforce the restrictive effect of rising interest rates. This 'tax' on banking intermediation will vary both with the size of the required reserves and with the general level of market interest rates. Indeed it has been argued by some, for example Davis and Lewis in Australia,[27] that following the abolition of administratively fixed interest rates, the authorities need the support of a variable tax on banking intermediation (in conditions of liability management, variable rate lending, and market-related interest rates), in order to maintain sufficient control over monetary growth. While one can see the advantages of having such a tax, the impact of which would vary with the level of interest rates, it would also have the disadvantages common to all such taxes of giving rise to reallocations of resources and avoidance. In particular, there would be a tendency, when such tax appeared particularly onerous, for intermediation to be shifted into other channels. Accordingly, if the burden of such tax tended to be high for more than short periods, there would be an increasing tendency for financial intermediation to be shifted abroad, or through other non-banking routes, which in turn would affect the velocity of the controlled banking sector and the proportion of financial intermediation done by it. Over time this would weaken and lessen the effect of the control itself.

III. Technology and the retail depositor

Electronic banking?

Currently we appear to be on the verge of several new applications of electronic and computer technology to banking practices, especially retail banking processes. In recent years there has been a veritable flood of articles, not only in the specialized banking journals, but also in the press more widely, recording the technical possibilities and, increasingly, the commercial application of these new developments. A whole new glossary of technical terms and acronyms is having to be learned by those interested in the banking industry, e.g. EFT (Electronic Funds Transfer). Perhaps the most visible innovation has been the recent surge in the use of ATMs (Automated Teller Machines), notably— but not only—in the US, where they are evolving from their earlier humble guise as simple cash dispensers into a more advanced form of machine that can carry out a wider range of operations, broadly replacing the function of the human bank clerk, or teller. Such operations include the receipt of cash and cheques, the provision of statements, the provision of travellers' cheques, and the automatic processing of standard loan applications.

A more advanced concept, though its use is only just beginning, is that of home banking, whereby the individual depositor or family of depositors can access their own bank's computer through a machine attached to their television set. This enables them to communicate with the computer, to receive information, and to send instructions.[28]

Other developments are extending the use of the plastic card, which had its origin as a source of credit. It is now also being used as a debit card in ATM and point-of-sale (POS) machines, communicating directly with bank computers. Another technique—that codes additional information onto the card itself so that it contains data on the remaining available funds in machine-readable form—is being used in telephone kiosks by British Telecom and, more ambitiously, as a general payment card in some regional experiments in France.

Another set of developments involves accelerating, cheapening, and simplifying the transfer of information, notably payments instructions, between banks. There are several examples of this kind of development. In the US settlement systems are provided by the Federal Reserve (Fed Wire) and by the private sector (Bank Wire for domestic payment and CHIPS—Clearing House Inter-Bank Payments System—for payments between New York banks). In Japan the Zenyin system provides an inter-bank transfer service and there is a similar system in France. The UK banks will shortly be launching CHAPS (Clearing House Automated Payment System), a highly sophisticated inter-bank payment service. Internationally, SWIFT (Society for Worldwide Interbank Financial Telecommunication), jointly owned by banks in many countries, provides financial message services, but without settlement facilities.

These innovations carry an aura of technological glamour and have an excitement in their own right. What is perhaps less easy to assess is exactly how these developments are likely to change the behavioural patterns of bank customers and users of financial intermediary services, and what consequential implications these changes may therefore have for those involved with monetary control. For the purpose of this latter type of analysis it may be desirable to try to classify and characterize the effects of these changes in an economic and analytical framework. For this purpose I shall use the simplest of economic classifications, that is the division into the effects on supply and on demand, in order to consider how these changes may affect the supply of financial intermediary services, and subsequently the demand by bank customers for such services.

Structural changes in the supply of financial services

In the same manner as technological changes improve productivity in other industries, they should raise productivity in the provision of intermediary services, thereby reducing costs and the requirement for both labour and capital in a system 'drowning in a sea of paper'. In so far as input factor costs go down, the cost of intermediation, i.e. the spread, can be reduced without imperilling profit margins, thereby encouraging some further extension of the volume of intermediation. However, this development is likely to be gradual and perhaps will not do much more than act as a counterweight to the otherwise rising labour costs of processing the rising flood of paper transactions. Considerably more important for the developing shape of the financial system will be the likelihood that the technological changes may drastically alter the relative cost structure of providing transmission services (and other elements of retail banking) for differing potential suppliers of such services.

Previously the provision of retail financial services required the

physical presence of custom-built branches, combining bricks and
mortar, office equipment (e.g. processing machines of varying degrees
of sophistication), and human operators. The provision of such
a branch network was extremely expensive. This gave an advantage
to those institutions with an established branch network, such as the
banks and also the Post Office. It would require a vast outlay of capital
in order to establish from scratch a branch system sufficiently widespread to provide effective competition. So, once established, the main
systems offering retail financial services tended towards oligopoly,
protected from competition by economies of scale and the high costs
of entry. There is, however, an exception to this, but an exception
which was brought into being artificially by government intervention
and legislation. This is to be found in the US where the 1927
McFadden Act prevented inter-state branching, and where limitations
on branching, both Federal and within certain states, has resulted in
a fragmented banking system.

Now these retail financial transmission services *may* be capable of
being provided more cheaply, without such a massive initial outlay
of capital and with far less labour input. ATMs can be set up in place
of branches. The transmission network, in the form of electronic equipment, can also be linked in with other, already existing non-financial
activities, e.g. a chain of department stores or even a large chain of
garages. At the extreme, home banking, as exemplified by the
Verbraucher Bank in the Federal Republic, would allow all users of
the network, wherever situated in the country, to be linked electroni-
cally to a single financial and computer centre. In a sense each home
then becomes its own personalized branch of the single bank.

The implication of this is that setting up a large-scale network to
transfer payment instructions over that net could now become cheaper.
Even so, the installation of a new network would remain exceedingly
expensive, and it would be extremely risky for a newcomer to seek to
challenge those already established in the provision of retail payments
services. In the US, these developments may at the outset have the
effect of binding the artificially segmented banking system into larger
effective groupings. This could occur because ATMs, not counting
legally as separate branches, can be set up across state borders.[29]
There is therefore some pressure on banks in adjoining states to co-
ordinate in setting up ATMs which can be accessed by users of those
banks in many states. This could have the effect of bringing about some
common operations of banks joining in the single ATM franchise. It
may also allow other (non-banking) institutions to enter the industry
and to compete more effectively and directly with the established
providers of retail banking services. Merrill Lynch and Sears Roebuck
are examples in the US. In the UK, building societies, such as the

Abbey National and the Leicester Building Society, have taken some
initial steps in the provision of payment services, although at the
moment they are using the banks' transmissions systems, and other
building societies are considering possible future developments in that
direction. In some cases the services provided by building societies may
be offered in conjunction with a bank. The possibility of cheaper entry
into the provision of retail services in the UK may encourage certain
banks, e.g. US banks, which have not previously sought to enter into
this part of the banking industry, to do so.[30]

In so far as new competitors enter into the provision of retail
banking (whether from other parts of the banking system that had
previously not provided such services, or from outside the banking
system as presently designated; whether previously financial intermediaries, as in the case of building societies and Merrill Lynch, or
not, as in the case of Sears Roebuck), this development will, of course,
bring into further question the present statistical boundaries between
the differing financial institutions, and more fundamentally the
adequacy of the present definitions of banks and deposit-takers. All this
may allow a rather wider range of currently differing institutions to
become general providers of retail financial services. But in addition
to such providers of general retail financial services, there is likely to
remain a continuing sizeable penumbra of more specialized, and
generally wholesale, financial institutions concentrating on wholesale
banking, for example, or on operations in futures markets, or on
money-market brokerage, or perhaps specializing in the provision of
mortgage finance. There would also be continuing room for providers
of financial services for special groups, etc.

The above outline of possible future developments is based on the
expectation that technology will in due course cheapen information
flows over a single widespread network. It is difficult, however, to see
now just how far or how fast such developments may alter the shape
and form of the supply of retail financial intermediary services. There
are obstacles in the way. One of these is that the technological changes
cheapen information flows over a *single* network, but the use to the
customer of any one individual network also depends crucially on
the ability to transfer information and instructions between the one
single electronic network and other related networks. For example,
the use of an existing retail financial system, such as Lloyds Bank in
the UK, would be far less effective and serviceable for the retail depositor if he could not receive payments from customers of other banks, or
make payments to customers of other banks, or only do so at an
exorbitant cost. In the UK the main retail clearing banks have joined
together, through the cheque-clearing system, to provide one single,
overall, transmission network. At its initiation, some thought that the

development of the Giro through the Post Office system might provide a separate financial network, but in practice the Giro has not been able to attract a sufficiently large number of customers to form a wholly separate network and it has now joined the main clearing system. In many other European countries, however, the Giro network and the banking clearing system are completely separate. In the UK, because of our historical experience, we still tend to think of one single clearing network as the norm. This need not be so; there could be a multiplicity of separate networks, with or without effective and efficient links between them.

So the question arises whether, if a new competitor wanted to set up a new individual network, it could join the existing clearing system, or whether it would have to seek to develop an entirely separate clearing system. The position in differing countries on this issue depends on their particular historical and institutional situation. For example in the US, the banking system is so fragmented that the new large competitors in the provision of financial intermediary services, such as Merrill Lynch, can frequently find a relatively small bank within the clearing system that is prepared to act as their point of access into the existing clearing network. The situation in several other countries with a more concentrated retail banking system, where the clearing system is dominated by large oligopolistic retail banks (e.g. the UK, Canada, and Australia) is *potentially* different. In these cases the existing retail banks *might* be in a position to raise the cost of entry into the clearing system for a new competitor, subject to legal and other factors preventing restrictive trade practices.

In so far as the main retail banks sought to restrict competitors' entry onto the existing clearing network, then they should in theory be able to restrain competition and/or require the duplication of main clearing systems, with resulting important implications for efficiency, allocation of resources, etc. It is on this latter question that important issues for the regulatory authorities in many countries are quite likely to arise. However, the pressure of competition between existing retail banks may well be such that newcomers will be able to find an existing bank which is willing to sponsor them.

The effect on the demand for financial services

Besides customers benefiting generally from improving productivity and a cheapening of the provision of financial services, these technological innovations should provide specific advantages to customers for retail financial services in the form of easier access to cash, credit, and information on the depositor's cash-flow position. There will be easier access to cash through the medium of ATMs, especially those that are available through-the-wall and therefore open at all times, even when the institutions themselves are shut. In so far as it becomes easier and less costly in time and effort to replenish cash holdings, so that the costs of running out of cash are less because there are more available sources to provide additional cash funds, then the expectation is presumably that average personal holdings of cash will be less and the frequency with which cash is replenished will be somewhat greater, even though easier access to cash may slow the trend towards making payments in other non-cash media.

Moreover, the existence of cash dispensers, and even more so of ATMs offering wider services in places of work such as large factories and office blocks, is likely to be a factor in shifting the habits of the work-force away from wage payments in cash into wage payments in paper, or, perhaps, increasingly in forms of electronic direct transfer. Besides making the banking habit more widespread, this tendency is likely to bring about some further reduction in the usage of cash.

The larger proportion of purchases which in future may be paid for through the medium of the plastic card should also tend to reduce cash usage. In the UK, at any rate, during the course of the last four years or so, the usage of cash has fallen quite sharply below that which would have been predicted on the basis of earlier, well-fitting, econometric equations. Our present view is that this shortfall in currency holdings has arisen because of the accelerating trend towards wage payment in other than cash form and, perhaps, to some growing usage of plastic cards for making transactions.

Although the means of making payments may increasingly depend on the plastic card, it is currently starting from a low base.[31] Initially such plastic cards primarily provided the user with a form of short-term credit on an interest-free basis until the first payment date, and thereafter in the form of a consumer loan at relatively high interest rates. But in future the increasing development of card-operated payments (e.g. POS) may more frequently instigate adjustments in the depositors' current accounts with banks. In those countries which have a tradition of extending overdrafts, such card-initiated payments may be honoured so long as the overdraft does not run above a certain, probably pre-specified, borrowing limit. The usage of plastic cards, whether they are formally credit or debit cards, may have the effect of further increasing access to automatic credit for most depositors and card users. In so far as such a credit line is effectively automatic, and is known to be so by the customer, his access to immediately available funds clearly includes the extent of that credit line.

So, the 'true' money stock, as Keynes noted long ago, should in theory include such unused credit lines. The adjustment, therefore, to unforeseen cash flows may be buffered in the short run as much by shifts in customers' debt position (their overdraft) with banks as in variations in their credit position (their deposit accounts). Already in the case of large customers, it is arguable that it is changes in their *net* position with banks that better represent the changes in their overall liquidity position. The further development of plastic cards could imply that short-term variations in individuals' cash-flow positions will as easily be met by variations in their borrowing from banks as in variations in their deposit balances. It could be the net position of the customer with the bank that would absorb these shocks, rather than just changes in the deposit balance. Thus it may become increasingly misleading to focus on variations on the deposit side of the banking system alone as an indication of the financial position of bank customers. Moreover, in so far as the 'true' money stock is effectively increased by any addition to such credit facilities, the lower may be the average balance that depositors will still need to feel that they should hold in their deposit accounts. So easier access to credit facilities, via plastic cards or otherwise, may tend to reduce the ratio of demand (sight) deposits to incomes and expenditures.

Easier, quicker, and cheaper access to information for the individual on his cash flow will also presumably allow depositors to economize on lower-yielding transactions balances by facilitating and expediting shifts between higher-yielding savings balances and transactions balances. However, the main, and more important, change in this respect is that a combination of competition, technological change, and in some cases deregulation (as in the US), is likely to induce financial intermediaries to offer more competitive interest rates that vary more closely in line with market rates on balances that remain usable for transactions.

A whole new range of techniques having this effect has become available in the US. These include negotiable orders of withdrawal (NOW) and automated transfer from savings (ATS) accounts, money market mutual funds (MMMFs), cash management accounts (as run by Merrill Lynch), and bank offerings of short-term re-purchase agreements (RPs) —whereby banks invest any surplus balances in transactions accounts in interest-bearing, very short-term overnight funds, and then make these balances available for transactions on the next day—and sweep accounts, which have the same general effect. RPs and sweep accounts have been offered for some time to larger, corporate customers, but the further development of technology and competition could increasingly induce banks to offer these services to smaller and smaller customers, though their popularity to these customers will depend on the continuation of high nominal interest rates.

These various developments have differing distorting effects on the data. NOW and ATS accounts are included in M1. The rate at which depositors transfer savings into these accounts will distort the historical comparability of the M1 series; this has indeed been acknowledged by the Federal Reserve in its interpretation of the data for the purposes of monetary policy. The funds 'deposited' in MMMFs are generally included in M2. However, the funds which have been shifted into cash-management accounts are not included in the narrower or wider monetary aggregates, while the funds which are shifted into RPs are included in M2 only if they are overnight RPs issued by banks.

Such developments are also beginning to appear in the UK. Two of the main clearing banks, Midland and Lloyds, are test-marketing special arrangements whereby depositors can obtain interest on balances which they can transfer into cash (e.g. through a cash dispenser), but which cannot be used for the whole range of transmission services, e.g. in the form of writing cheques on these. A much smaller bank, a subsidiary of the Co-op Bank, is providing interest on transactions balances at nearly market rate. These balances can, however, still be used for the whole range of transactions services. As already noted, the building societies are also dipping a toe into this area of providing payment transmission services. The likelihood must be that this trend will continue further, since a combination of competitive forces and available technology, as well as the example from the US and possibly other countries, will further encourage it. On the other hand a fall in nominal interest rates—as inflation falls—would reduce the pressure for change.

This trend towards the payment of a market-related interest rate on transactions balances is, however, restrained and moderated in the UK by the present nature of the tax regime. The provision of transmission services, e.g. in clearing cheque payments, is extremely costly.[32] Most depositors do not bear these costs themselves, and are generally unaware of the extent, or even perhaps the existence, of such costs. This occurs because under UK arrangements the transactions costs are offset against *notional* interest payments on non-interest-bearing demand deposits. This provides an advantage to many depositors, since, if both the interest payments and the transactions costs were specifically and separately charged, under present fiscal arrangements there would be tax to pay on the interest on demand deposits, but the transactions costs would not be allowable against tax. The Inland Revenue will not allow the individual transactions costs generated by the individual depositor to be offset against his specific interest receipts on his personal deposit. Accordingly in the schemes that have been devised so far to offer interest payments on bank current accounts, the interest is paid only after debiting for an *average* charge, averaged over all customers, or alternatively, as with the Midland, the interest is only offered on such forms of deposit which are restricted in the nature of the payments which they can be used for, and therefore in the transactions costs generated.

The extent and speed of the spreading of the payment of market-related interest rates on transactions balances will depend both on the continuation of high and variable inflation and interest rates,[33] and on the particular institutional and fiscal arrangements in each country. Nevertheless the interaction of competitive pressures and the developing technological capacity are likely to make this a continuing trend. What are the implications?

First, during the period in which these innovations are being introduced, some instability in the functional relationships between the monetary aggregates affected and general economic developments is to be expected. Holdings of 'traditional' transactions balances, both cash and ordinary zero-yielding sight balances, will probably grow more slowly—relative to nominal incomes—while holdings of these newer forms of interest-bearing balances, capable of being used for making payments, will grow quickly initially, drawing funds both out of 'traditional' transactions balances and from 'traditional' savings deposits. The rapidity of this growth, and the extent to which such balances may be drawn from 'traditional' transactions or from savings deposits, will not be easily predictable. The apparent growth rates of the narrow aggregates may come to depend crucially on the precise statistical definition adopted in each case, with markedly differing growth rates for the differing definitions, e.g. non-interest-bearing (nib) M1 and M1 in the UK; MIA and MIB in the US.

Second, with transactions balances coming to bear a more market-related interest rate, such balances will also become less responsive to variations in the general level of interest rates because an increase in the *general* level will tend to have less of an effect on interest rate *differentials*, i.e. those between the interest rates on transactions balances and on other forms of assets. This does *not* mean that the depositor in the future will become any less sensitive to the pattern of *relative* interest rates. Indeed, with easier access to information, in the form of home banking for example, the depositor of the future is likely to become *more* sensitive to minor variations in relative interest rates between differing assets and liabilities.

As a result, there is almost bound to be some increasing volatility of flows of funds between channels and between assets. The authorities who can only adjust the general overall level of interest rates and cash pressures cannot easily control these flows since they will depend on shifts in interest differentials, and the shifts will depend crucially on the reactions and responses of the various financial intermediaries to the varying pressures on them. What this represents is simply an extension of liability management from wholesale banking increasingly into retail banking. Just as the extension of liability management to wholesale banking impaired the authorities' ability to control the overall size of banks' books, this further development will also impair the authorities' ability to control the narrow monetary aggregates.[34]

All of this will also have major implications for financial intermediaries, particularly for banks. As these developments occur (which may, or may not, take place gradually), the banks will lose their ability to rely on large, solid blocks of low-cost retail deposits, whose variation is subject to the law of large numbers and is largely predictable. So long as this block of low-cost retail deposits exists, it offers endowment profits as interest rates rise (as earlier noted), offsetting the greater risks and bad debts that also increase in periods of high and rising interest rates. Thus the existence of such low-yielding current accounts have provided a counterweight to the fluctuations in the variability of banking risk and profitability over the course of the interest-rate cycle. With the (gradual) erosion of such low-cost retail deposits, banking business will therefore become riskier, as already noted in the US, reinforcing the need to pay more attention to prudential control and capital adequacy.

On the other hand, the endowment effect encouraged banks to expand loans as interest rates rose. In so far as the objective of policy was to control the broader monetary aggregates, this made control more difficult, since banks tended to become more expansionary/ aggressive just when the authorities wished for greater restraint, and vice versa. But it might also be argued that such bank behaviour had some counter-cyclical advantages, in so far as rising interest rates squeezed company profits and made them more dependent on external funds.

While it is the thesis of this section that a combination of technological development, high and variable inflation and interest rates, and competition between financial intermediaries makes the introduction of new forms of interest-bearing transactions balances inevitable, there remains a question of the time-scale involved. There are reasons for believing that the time-scale could be protracted. So long as the bank customer in the UK is receiving 'free banking'—with charges for transmission services offset against notional interest payments—he is likely to be somewhat apathetic about learning/adopting new payments' methods (e.g. POS) whose benefits in cost reduction may accrue mostly to banking profitability. There remain, in the UK at least, legal difficulties to be resolved relating to the use of electronic funds transfer (EFT). Thus, there is established case law and statute in relation to cheques and Bills of Exchange, but there is no equivalent law in regard to the use of a Personal Identification Number (PIN) in conjunction with a plastic card, nor indeed with respect to electronic transfers more generally.

Moreover the adoption of new payments mechanisms and systems will generally require a large initial investment (though not one comparable to the cost of setting up a full set of branches) and will require some large flow of transactions to be profitable. The expense and uncertainties involved may act as some deterrent. On the other hand the successful introduction of such new methods in one country will encourage its spread in other countries; these new methods are now being introduced, if still mainly experimentally, in various countries, primarily in the US. Even in the US, however, the process is retarded by technical and social frictions and by the costs of offering all customers a market rate on their balances. The man (woman) in the street may have a NOW account (paying 5¼%), but overnight 'SWEEP'ing to money-market investments will probably continue to operate initially only with a high minimum balance, while the minimum value for cheques drawn on money market mutual funds (MMMFs) may well remain over $200 or more.

To the extent that the spread of these innovations is slow and steady, it may be possible to make some allowance for the likely shifts in the relationships between the monetary aggregates and economic developments. This is the hope of those who wish to continue to base monetary policy upon the adoption of quantitative targets.[35]

Whether or not that will be the case, time will tell. In the meantime, however, the possibility that a swing in monetary growth may reflect a shift in the pace of monetary innovation rather than a 'real' development will have some influence on the authorities' reactions to such developments. The present changes imply that monetary aggregates should be interpreted and analysed with scrupulous care—on a judgmental, institutional and empirical basis—rather than just mechanically extrapolated from previously fitted equations.

IV. What can the central bank control?

So long as the central bank continues to have a monopoly on the supply of legal-tender currency in the economy, and so long as there remains a demand for such legal-tender currency, the central bank will be able to control and determine the general level of money-market interest rates. If people wish to hold the legal-tender currency of the central bank, either in order to make certain payments in currency form, or as a result of some continuing residual suspicion of the safety of banks and other NBFI (non-banking financial intermediaries), then banks will in their turn need to ensure the convertibility of their deposits (and also their non-legal-tender notes outstanding), into legal-tender currency. They will also therefore need to hold currency in their tills and to hold balances with the central bank. The central bank can therefore continue to operate to effect this cash base in order to influence the general level of short-term interest rates. This has always been the main central bank instrument. This instrument, and this form of control, is not impaired in the slightest by any of the technological or other banking developments described earlier: the only requirement for such control is a continuing demand to hold the (zero-yielding) notes issued by the central bank.

What is more likely to be impaired is the central bank's ability to use either variations in the general level of interest rates, or changes in the level of the monetary base, in order to bring about pre-planned changes in the rates of growth of the various monetary aggregates. In the past, when the central bank altered the general level of interest rates, by the same token it shifted the relative pattern of interest rates in such a way as to make holding deposits with the banking system more or less attractive. Although this coherence between the general level of interest rates and the relativity between rates on non-monetary assets and on bank deposits is now increasingly being broken, the central bank can still have a strong impact on the growth of the monetary aggregates. But in future this impact is as likely to be *indirect*, with the changes in interest rates primarily affecting levels of incomes, expenditures, and exchange rates, and with these general macroeconomic effects feeding back into the demand for bank lending and the money stock. [This contrasts with a direct form of effect, in which changes in interest rates (and/or the monetary base) have an immediate impact on the monetary aggregates (via shifts in interest differentials), which in turn subsequently feed through various transmission routes to effect the level of incomes and expenditures.] Moreover, shifts in the various monetary aggregates will increasingly become a function of changing competitive pressures, and therefore changing relative yields, in a world where technological changes *may* cause these to vary quite sharply. Increasingly the definition of the banking system, the proper definition of money, and the sense of concentrating mainly on the deposit liabilities of the banking system (rather than customers' net positions) will come into question.

Notes and sources

[1] M. Friedman and A. J. Schwartz, *Monetary Trends in the United States and the United Kingdom*, A National Bureau of Economic Research Monograph (University of Chicago Press, Chicago, 1982). See also D. K. Sheppard, *The Growth and Role of UK Financial Institutions 1880-1962* (Methuen and Co. Ltd., London, 1971).

[2] *The Committee of Inquiry into the Australian Financial System, Final Report* (Australian Government Publishing Service, Canberra, 1981).

[3] An alternative to those financial channels subject to internal domestic constraints has always been to shift financial flows abroad to the international Euro-markets. The continuation of comprehensive constraint over domestic financial intermediation, therefore, requires reinforcement with extensive external

exchange controls. Should such exchange controls be abandoned, for example in pursuit of the ideal of free movement of capital over national boundaries, then it would follow that much of the domestic framework of financial control within these countries would rapidly unravel.

[4] Even so, there have been important structural changes in banking in the Federal Republic. There has been increasing competition to attract small-scale deposits, both transactions and savings deposits. And with relatively low inflation not sufficing to prevent sharply varying nominal interest rates, often for external reasons, and high real interest rates, the banks have reacted by shortening the average maturity of their loan books. What is less clear is how far they are also switching their lending onto a variable rate basis, or are restricted from doing so by the authorities.

[5] This switch towards liability management via wholesale markets first occurred in fact in the *international* Euro-dollar market. Thus the first of the wholesale markets to emerge, at the end of the 1950s, was the Euro-currency market, initially mainly centred in London. The first statistics on the operation of the Euro-currency market date back to 1962, when the Bank of England began to collect data on the external liabilities and claims of banks in the UK. This was followed in the 1960s by the development of a market for wholesale funds within the US. Since the main interest of this paper is with the implications of structural changes for domestic monetary control within a single country, our main focus of interest will be on domestic wholesale markets and not on the Euro-currency market.

[6] Even then, there were some limitations to the authorities' willingness to control the rate of growth of the monetary aggregates by this means, because of their fears of the consequences of having to make sufficiently large changes in yields on public-sector debt. Aggressive steps to raise rates of interest, particularly if this was to be in the form of direct action to reduce bond prices, was, for a time at least after World War II, considered dangerous in both the UK and US, and bond market conditions were felt to require sensitive handling. In part this sensitivity was the result of the very high ratios of public-sector debt to nominal incomes in the post-war period. Not only did this entail relatively large interest payments as a proportion of public expenditure, but also very large proportionate maturities in relation to the need for new public-sector debt. Any development which might weaken confidence in the market for this swollen volume of public-sector debt was felt to be inherently dangerous.

[7] Large negotiable CDs, in their present form, have been used as a source of funds since 1961, and those issued by large commercial banks reached a volume of around $20 billion by 1966. Because of the growing sophistication of corporate treasurers, the banks were faced in the mid-1950s with a reduction in the rate of growth of corporate deposits, as funds were diversified into short-term interest-bearing investments such as Treasury bills. Negotiable CDs, with their extensive secondary market, enabled the banks to offer an interest rate on a highly liquid asset. The rate of interest offered on the CDs was not, however, always market-related, because until 1973 Regulation Q interest-rate ceilings applied to negotiable CDs. Two sharp reductions in market volume, in 1966 and 1969, were caused by market interest rates exceeding the ceilings. In 1973, Regulation Q ceilings were lifted for CDs of over $100,000.

[8] In so far as certain deposit rates, e.g. on demand deposits or retail deposits, remained constrained, it continued to be the case that the authorities' control over the general level of interest rates also ensured their control over the relative pattern between such market rates and the *constrained* deposit rates.

[9] The Italian target has been 'total domestic credit expansion' rather than broad money. There is, however, a considerable overlap between these two aggregates.

¹⁰ Similar schemes of lending ceilings and penalties have also been applied in Italy and Ireland.

¹¹ PSL stands for private sector liquidity; PSL2 is the wider, second definition of such liquidity, including building society deposits which are omitted from PSL1.

¹² In those countries with narrow monetary targets, such as Switzerland and Canada, massive variations in bank lending and in the total size of banks' books are frequently accommodated and coexist with maintained control of, and even very slow growth in, the narrow monetary elements.

¹³ The definition of the target aggregate, £M3, however, encompasses all deposit holdings by UK residents, including the relatively small amounts of savings-type deposits of longer maturities.

¹⁴ For example, in Italy the banks are constrained by credit ceilings and other regulations on interest rates, so the authorities have been able to induce a shift of funds out of bank deposits into Treasury bills. How far the resulting slower growth in the monetary aggregates really represents a tightening of policy, and how far this widening of the Treasury bill market really has given monetary policy additional efficacy remains debatable.

¹⁵ For example, if the assets available to savers are mainly in fixed interest form, whereas borrowers predominantly borrow from financial intermediaries on a variable rate basis, then expectations of falling interest rates may lead depositors to want to shift into longer dated assets without provoking a countervailing shift shorter by borrowers.

¹⁶ The protection will be greater the closer the periodicity of the adjustment of lending rates to the adjustment of borrowing rates.

¹⁷ In some cases the reasons why indexation has not been adopted are clear, e.g. official hostility to it, or fiscal arrangements which make it disadvantageous. But there are instances where there appear to be no barriers to its introduction, as in the US. The reasons for the failure of indexation arrangements to emerge there are not fully understood.

¹⁸ The reasons are straightforward: (i) volatile deposit sources and an almost exclusive dependence on the wholesale and inter-bank market when funding loans; and (ii) a large number of market participants, of different nationalities, make it impossible to agree lending conventions. A market rate is an impersonal measure; whereas even agreeing on an appropriate inflation rate on which to base short-term interest rates could raise problems.

¹⁹ Both these conditions would apply to the UK. Historically mortgage lending in the UK by the building societies has been on a variable rate basis. More recently the banks have been moving towards the provision of large volumes of medium-term lending, which again are now increasingly, possibly almost entirely, on a variable rate basis.

²⁰ This endowment effect is, however, considerably reduced if banking profits and accounts are calculated on an inflation-adjusted basis rather than on an historical cost basis. Bank liabilities include capital as well as deposit liabilities so, with total assets equal to total liabilities, banks hold monetary claims on other sectors which exceed their monetary liabilities, i.e. they hold *net monetary assets*. As the rate of inflation rises, these net monetary assets depreciate, and the fall in real profits is especially marked if real interest rates happen to be low as inflation rises. With inflationary expectations apparently lagging behind the reality during the course of the 1970s, this was frequently the case, so despite the high nominal profits induced by the endowment effect, the real profitability of the banking system, particularly on a post-tax basis, was much less. Of course, the same inflation effect on banking profitability also impinges on those financial

intermediaries which have continued to maintain fixed-rate lending; in their case true profitability is doubly affected by the interest rate rise at a time of inflation upsurge.

[21] And this was facilitated in the UK by the removal of direct controls on bank lending.

[22] This assertion can be challenged on theoretical grounds. The most abstract argument is that, even if only fixed-rate lending is available, a borrower could in theory operate in futures markets to transform the fixed-rate contract effectively onto a variable-rate basis. In practice, at least in the past, the absence of a full set of futures markets and transactions costs in the existing markets restricted such opportunities. Additionally, so long as lenders' and borrowers' expectations were symmetrical, it could be argued that both fixed-rate yields and the average of expected variable rates over the relevant period should adjust equally in response to (policy-induced) changes in short rates and in the associated shape of the yield curve, so that the mean expected yield on both would always remain in equilibrium. Such symmetrical response is uncertain. Banks may tie fixed-rate medium-term lending to current prime or base rates, while borrowers may have more regressive expectations about future rates. Probably more important, even if the *mean* expected yield would be the same in either case, the risk of having borrowed on fixed terms at a temporarily unpropitious time will weigh more heavily than in the case of variable-rate borrowing. Experience in other capital markets, e.g. with new issues in equity and debenture markets, suggests that the elasticity of borrowing to such risk considerations and/or to asymmetric expectations of borrowers and lenders may well be considerable, i.e. that new issues are more sensitive to the current level of equity and debenture prices than might have been expected on the basis of rational, symmetric expectations.

[23] Furthermore, the development of a broad market in financial futures should allow risk-averse borrowers and lenders to shift such interest-rate risks to speculators. In so far as the (perceived) variability of interest rates increases as the level of nominal interest rates (and inflation) rises, this capacity to shift risk via the futures market might facilitate the continuation of more bank intermediation in the face of high and rising nominal interest rates and inflation, and thus further reduce the interest elasticity of the provision of bank loans.

The abolition of legal or administrative ceilings on interest rates on lending —e.g. owing to usury laws—will also allow bank lending to continue more strongly as nominal interest rates rise.

The main influence on the demand for borrowing is, presumably, the post-tax real cost. In most countries the tax system is only partially, if at all, inflation adjusted. So long as the borrower has profits, or income, available against which nominal interest can be offset, an equal rise in inflation and nominal interest rates actually *reduces* post-tax real rates of interest. While the level of nominal interest rates has some independent effect, e.g. via front-end loading of real interest payments and income gearing, the unadjusted form of the tax system in most countries must have further reduced the responsiveness of the demand for bank borrowing to variations in the level of nominal interest rates, when these have accompanied variations in the (perceived) rate of inflation.

[24] The evidence shows that the volume of newly announced syndicated medium-term Euro-credits expanded very rapidly at the same time as spreads were falling (e.g. see R. B. Johnston, 'Banks' international lending decisions and the determination of spreads on syndicated medium-term Euro-credits', *Bank of England Discussion Paper*, No. 12, London, September 1980). But, arguably, the supply of intermediation services by banks should be a positive function of the spread, *ceteris paribus*. Having allowed for credit risks, etc., the

residual trend of spreads was still downwards in the 1970s, which can be explained by increasing international banking competition. This trend may continue as marginal banks continue to enter the market, but the supply function *should* slope upwards after some 'equilibrium' has been reached. On the side of borrowers, the econometric evidence shows that the demand for syndicated medium-term Euro-credit is quite spread-sensitive, much more so than with respect to the level of short-term interest rates (LIBOR).

One complication is that, in addition to the spread, the charge for financial intermediation is taken in the form of various fees and initial charges. Indeed, in some cases, because the spread is seen as a public indication of relative credit standing, some borrowers in the Euro-markets have a preference for a package with higher fees and a lower published spread.

[25] In the Euro-market, spreads rose very sharply following the banking crises in the summer of 1974, and reached historically high levels in 1975 and 1976. At the same time, despite the massive increase in global payments imbalances, there was a fall in the rate of expansion of syndicated medium-term Euro-currency loans.

[26] For example, 'hidden reserves', varying provisions (general and specific) for bad debts, deferred taxation provisions, problems of inflation adjustment, etc., can make outside assessment of the conditions of individual banks from their published accounts a difficult exercise.

[27] K. T. Davis and M. K. Lewis, notably in their paper on 'Can Monetary Policy Work in a Deregulated Capital Market', in the Campbell Inquiry Symposium, *The Australian Economic Review*, 1st Quarter 1982, pp. 9-12.

[28] The home screen obviously cannot dispense cash. Cash could be sent by post instead, but in so far as this is slow and/or unreliable, the home screen needs to be complemented by ATMs.

[29] ATMs cannot, however, take deposits across state lines.

[30] Whereas the introduction of ATMs seems likely to reduce the cost of entry into the retail financial market, it can be argued that other technological innovations, e.g. home banking and POS, may increase the competitive dominance of existing large banks because of the high initial costs and the large banks' competitive ability to induce large retail outlets to join their payments' networks.

[31] In the UK Monopolies Commission Report of September 1980 on 'Credit Card Franchise Services', Cmnd 8034, HMSO, London, 1980, it was stated that in 1976 credit cards accounted for only 0.3% of all payments (by adults) over 50p, 1.5% for payments of £5 and over, and 2.1% for payments of £25 and over (para. 2.22, p. 21). They also provided a table (2.1, p. 11) showing the amounts of such credit outstanding at end-years, 1976-9. During this period credit cards grew proportionately more strongly than other forms of consumer lending, rising from 5.5% of all such lending at end-1976 to 9.7% at end-1979. Subsequent data are not available because of disclosure problems, but it may be that increased nominal interest rates since 1979 have retarded the faster rate of growth of this relatively expensive form of borrowing.

In the US the proportion of transactions effected by money and credit varied only slightly during the 1970s. The share of purchases using currency and demand deposits remained about 70% over the decade.

[32] In 1977 the Price Commission found, in their Report on 'Banks: Charges for Money Transmission Services', HMSO, London, April 1978, that 'the costs of these [money transmission] services were amply covered by imputed income from deposits [when LIBOR (London Inter-Bank Offered Rate) was high]. At the time of writing, with LIBOR around 6¾ per cent the result for the banks cannot be better than neutral ...'. See Chapter 11, para. 11.4, p. 49.

Subsequently in 1981, David Lomax arguing in 'The Case against the Banking Levy', mimeo, Banking Information Service, London, 1981, p. 5, claimed that the cost of providing such services had increased yet further 'because the workload has increased while the balances have declined in real terms, the up-to-date figure [for the equivalent cost of providing money transmission services] is about 9 per cent . . .'. Currently, even a figure of 10% has been mentioned publicly.

[33] The payment of interest at such market-related rates has been generally available for some time in Italy, but has not yet been introduced in most other European countries. In several other countries, e.g. Belgium, Switzerland, and the Netherlands, a very low and sticky interest rate is available on current accounts, but it is not a market-related rate. West German banks, like British banks, pay nothing.

[34] Moreover, the multifarious forms in which transactions/savings balances can be packaged and offered by varying institutions—some of them outside the monetary sector, some of them even perhaps physically abroad—could make reserve requirements and monetary-base control virtually impossible to operate.

[35] On this, see S. H. Axilrod, 'Monetary Policy, Money Supply, and the Federal Reserve's Operating Procedures', *Federal Reserve Bulletin*, January 1982, pp. 17 f.

PART III

FISCAL CONSTRAINTS ON
MONETARY CO-ORDINATION

4

A Comprehensive Balance Sheet and Permanent Income Accounting Framework for the Public Sector: Theory and Applications

WILLEM H. BUITER*

I. Introduction

This chapter studies budgetary, financial, and monetary policy evaluation and design using a comprehensive wealth and income accounting framework. The focus is on the public sector accounts, but inevitably some attention is paid to the private and overseas sectors. A stylized comprehensive balance sheet for the public sector and its 'flow' counterpart—the change in real public-sector net worth—is constructed and then compared with the conventionally measured balance sheet and flow-of-funds accounts. A comprehensive list of the symbols used in this chapter is appended.

The conventionally measured public sector balance sheet typically contains only marketable financial assets and liabilities. On the asset side it omits such items as the value of the stock of social overhead capital, the value of government-owned land and mineral rights, the present value of future planned tax revenues, and of future seigniorage from money creation. On the liability side it omits the present value of social insurance and other entitlement programmes.

The conventionally measured public sector financial surplus, even when evaluated at constant prices, presents a potentially very misleading picture of the change in the real net worth of the public sector. One reason is that capital gains and losses on outstanding stocks of government assets and liabilities are not included in the flow of funds. These include capital gains or losses due to relative price changes (e.g. changes in the real value of mineral rights), changes in the real value of nominally denominated public sector debt due to inflation, and changes in the real value of foreign-currency-denominated assets and liabilities caused by exchange rate changes.

---

* London School of Economics and National Bureau of Economic Research.

A second reason is that changes in tax and entitlement programmes, in the future revenue base, and in discount rates, etc., may significantly alter the planned or expected future streams of taxes and benefits and their present value. Capital gains' and losses on such implicit, non-marketable assets and liabilities are part of the Hicks–Simon concept of permanent income but are excluded from the flow of funds accounts.

The differences between the conventionally measured and the comprehensive accounts can be very large. In inflationary periods large conventionally measured public sector deficits may be more than matched by the inflation-induced reduction in the real value of the government's nominal liabilities. Changes in the conventionally measured current-account deficit of the balance of payments may be offset or enhanced by changes in the value of external assets and liabilities associated with exchange rate changes. Changes in social security legislation may alter the future flows of benefits and contributions. With efficient, forward-looking financial markets, such policy changes will not merely alter *future* rates of return—when the financial implications of current legislation become visible and directly measurable, say through changes in the amount of public sector borrowing. They will also have an effect on *current* financial asset prices and rates of return because larger anticipated future deficits may raise current interest rates.

After presenting the comprehensive and conventionally measured accounts for the public sector, the private sector, and the overseas sector, I propose some very general rules for policy design. These derive from a not unreasonable policy norm or objective and from rather minimal and uncontroversial assumptions about private-sector behaviour. To translate these general (and perhaps rather vague) rules into concrete policies is a task that is well beyond the scope of this chapter. A wealth of country-specific knowledge will be required in each case.

The essence of the argument is that in a first-best world, private agents, governments, and international organizations would decide on their spending, saving, lending, production, and portfolio allocation programmes constrained only by comprehensive wealth or permanent income. Single-period or other short-run 'budget constraints' would not represent further effective or binding constraints on economic behaviour.

The perfect internal and external capital markets required to implement the first-best solution do not exist. Private agents are constrained by the illiquidity and non-marketability of certain assets (e.g. pension rights, human capital, and expected future tax cuts). A dearth of suitable collateral often renders unfeasible the borrowing required to spend in line with permanent income. These cash-flow constraints, illiquidity, credit-rationing, lack of collateral, the non-marketability of

certain assets and liabilities, and a host of other capital-market imperfections force the actions of private agents and national governments
to depart from the behaviour that would be optimal if only comprehensive net worth or permanent-income constraints had to be taken into
account.

Flow-of-funds accounting on a cash or transaction basis and the
analysis of balance sheets consisting only of marketable claims is useful precisely because it will help to identify the conditions under which
the behaviour of economic agents is likely to be constrained by factors
other than comprehensive net worth.

Within a national economy, conventional accounting helps to decide
when and how the national authorities, through appropriate fiscal,
financial, and monetary measures, can help private agents to avoid or
overcome obstacles to spending and saving in line with permanent
income (in the case of households) and impediments to production in
pursuit of long-run profit or social net benefit (in the case of firms).
Within the international economy it serves to identify the conditions
under which international organizations should extend or restrict
credit to nation states to enable them to develop in line with their
long-run potential. Financial evaluation exercises, such as the IMF's
financial programming, should therefore start from two sets of accounts.
The first contains the conventional cash-based flow-of-funds accounts,
the SNA income–expenditure accounts, and the conventional balance
sheets of marketable assets and liabilities. The second set of accounts
contains the comprehensive balance sheets or wealth accounts outlined in the chapter and their 'flow' counterparts describing the changes
in real sectoral net worth over time and thus permanent income—
the ultimate accrual-based accounts.

Both national governments and international agencies should design
fiscal, financial, and monetary policies so as to induce an evolution of
the conventionally measured balance sheet and flow-of-funds accounts
that permits private agents, and national economies, to approximate
the behaviour that would be adopted if comprehensive wealth or
permanent income were the only binding constraints on economic
behaviour.

Conventional financial planning is, therefore, an essential input
into optimal (or even merely sensible) policy design. Without a set of
comprehensive wealth and permanent-income accounts, however,
financial analysis does not possess the minimal data base required for
proper policy evaluation and design. Conversely, without the conventional accounts, analyses based just on the comprehensive wealth and
permanent-income accounts will fail to take into account many of the
actual binding constraints on economic behaviour.

'Stabilization policy', as viewed in this chapter, is potentially useful and effective even if goods and factor markets clear continuously. The existence of capital-market imperfections (that prevent private agents from spending in line with permanent private disposable income and nations from spending in line with national permanent income) is necessary to allow scope for stabilization policy: policy actions or rules designed to permit the smoothing of consumption over time by removing or neutralizing constraints on spending other than permanent income. Successful stabilization policy keeps disposable income in line with permanent income and ensures an adequate share of disposable financial wealth in comprehensive wealth.

Another necessary condition for potentially desirable stabilization policy is that governments have access to capital markets on more favourable terms than private agents, or more generally that governments have financial options that are not available to private agents. The same applies in an international setting for certain international agencies *vis-à-vis* national governments. The existence of Keynesian effective-demand failures due to disequilibria in goods and factor markets would, of course, strengthen the case for stabilization policy.

This view of stabilization policy implies that it is the government's financing policies—changes in its tax-transfer-borrowing and money-creation mix—that should be used rather than variations in its spending programme on goods and services. The latter should aim to achieve the best feasible public–private consumption mix out of national permanent income.

II. A stylized set of public sector accounts

Table 4.1 contains a stylized and simplified 'comprehensive' balance sheet for the public sector. Many definitional problems are ignored: e.g. throughout this chapter the terms 'government' and 'public sector' are used interchangeably.[1] It is assumed that a very heterogeneous set of assets and liabilities can somehow be expressed in common-value terms. This in spite of the fact that some of the assets are not marketable (K^{soc}) or, even if potentially marketable, may lack a current observable market price (K^G). Some assets and liabilities are neither marketable nor tangible, and merely represent implicit, non-contractual (and reversible) political commitments (T and N).

Referring to T, N, and A^M as present discounted values of future streams of payments or receipts involves a rather cavalier use of certainty equivalence: the conditional mathematical expectations of the uncertain future revenues or outlays are discounted using 'risk adjusted' discount rates. If, for example, future tax revenues are highly uncertain, T would be correspondingly small. The relevant horizon is, in principle, infinite.

TABLE 4.1
The comprehensive consolidated public-sector balance sheet at current (market or implicit) prices

Assets		Liabilities	
$p_{K^{soc}}K^{soc}$	Social overhead capital (non-marketable)	B^H	Net interest-bearing debt denominated in domestic currency, held by residents
$p_G K^G$	Equity in public enterprises (partly potentially marketable)	B^F	Net interest-bearing debt denominated in domestic currency, held by non-residents
$p_R R^G$	Land and mineral assets (marketable)		
eE^*	Net foreign-exchange reserves	eB^{*H}	Net interest-bearing debt denominated in foreign exchange, held by residents
T	Present value of future tax programme, including social security contributions, tariff revenue, etc. (implicit asset)	eB^{*F}	Net interest-bearing debt denominated in foreign exchange, held by non-residents
pA^M	Imputed net value of the government's cash monopoly	$p\tilde{B}^H$	Net interest-bearing index-linked debt held by residents
		$p\tilde{B}^F$	Net interest-bearing index-linked debt held by non-residents
		H	Stock of high-powered money
		N	Present value of social insurance and other entitlement programmes (implicit liability)
		W^G	Public sector net worth

For many purposes it is better not to try to reduce marketable and non-marketable, implicit and explicit claims to a common-balance-sheet measure of value. Instead each of the items in the balance sheet will be modelled as having potentially distinct behavioural effects. The proper way of handling this will depend on the specifics of the model and application under consideration.

For a first pass at the problem of comprehensive wealth and income accounting in the public sector, the heroic balance sheet of Table 4.1 does, however, have its uses.

Most of the items in the balance sheet are self-explanatory. Public sector overhead capital is assumed to yield an implicit rental $r^{\text{soc}}p_{K\text{soc}}K^{\text{soc}}$ which corresponds to the item pG^{soc} (public-sector consumption of social overhead capital services) on the debit side of the public sector current account. $p_G K^G$ is the balance-sheet counterpart of the operating surplus of the public-enterprise sector in the public-sector current account. This may well be a negative item for some of the secular public-enterprise loss makers, in which case it should be moved to the liability side of the balance sheet. The present value of current and capital grants is not entered separately; it can be viewed as subsumed under N or T. Net foreign exchange reserves E^* are entered separately as an asset rather than netting them out against

$$B^{*\text{F}} \text{ or } B^{*\text{F}} + \frac{B^{\text{F}}}{e} + \tilde{B}^{\text{F}}\frac{p}{e}.$$

For simplicity, only nominal capital-certain bonds and real capital-certain bonds are considered.[2]

The treatment of money in this presentation of the comprehensive wealth accounting framework deserves some elaboration. The reason for adopting the approach is that it represents the simplest way of introducing a non-trivial role for money. Specifically, it prevents the economy from becoming identical to a barter economy when, in Section VI, we consolidate the accounts of the public and private sectors in our investigation of debt neutrality: money as a social asset, producing liquidity and convenience services, does not disappear when private- and public-sector assets and liabilities are netted out. However the usefulness of the comprehensive wealth accounting framework does not depend on the acceptability of this approach to modelling money.

Money has value to the private sector because it yields a flow of imputed, non-pecuniary liquidity and convenience services. Let ρ^{M} be the non-pecuniary rate of return on money. The value to the private sector of their money holdings is given by V^{M} in equation (1):[3]

$$V^{\text{M}}(t) = \frac{1}{p(t)} \int_t^\infty H(t)\hat{\rho}^{\text{M}}(u,\,t) \exp\left(-\int_t^u \hat{i}(s,\,t)\mathrm{d}s\right) \mathrm{d}u. \qquad (1)$$

Assuming that the pecuniary and non-pecuniary yields on money and bonds are equalized at the margin, we also have:

$$\rho^{\text{M}} = i = r + \frac{\hat{p}}{p}. \qquad (2)$$

Equations (1) and (2) imply that:

$$V^{\text{M}} = \frac{H}{p}.$$

Let Π^M be present discounted value of the expected future flow of profits to the government from operating the printing presses. Assuming that cash can be produced costlessly, this is given by:[4]

$$\Pi^M(t) = \frac{1}{p(t)} \int_t^\infty \hat{H}(u, t) \exp\left(-\int_t^u \hat{i}(s, t) ds\right) du. \qquad (4)$$

Integrating (4) by parts we get:[5]

$$\Pi^M(T) = -\frac{H(t)}{p(t)} + A^M(t) \qquad (4')$$

where

$$A^M(t) = \frac{1}{p(t)} \int_t^\infty \hat{i}(u, t)\hat{H}(u, t) \exp\left(-\int_t^u \hat{i}(s, t) ds\right) du. \qquad (5)$$

Thus $A^M(t)$, the net value of the government's cash monopoly, can be interpreted as the present discounted value of the interest income the central bank expects to earn at each future date on a portfolio of government bonds equal in value to the stock of high-powered money at that date.

The conventionally measured public-sector balance sheet typically omits from Table 4.1 all non-marketable and non-financial assets and liabilities, that is, K^{soc}, K^G, R^G, T, N, and A^M.

Table 4.2 gives the current and capital accounts of the public sector whose balance sheet is given in Table 4.1.[6] They are stylized SNA accounts and have a number of significant shortcomings when used uncritically as a guide to the changes over time in the balance sheet — especially as regards the evolution of *real* public-sector comprehensive net worth and its components.

For simplicity I have assumed that government consumption G^c and the imputed rental services from social overhead capital have the same price, p.[7] A uniform depreciation rate δ for different types of capital is also imposed. Foreign-exchange reserves are assumed to pay the same interest rate as other foreign-currency-denominated financial claims. All of these assumptions are for illustrative purposes only.

The 'public sector budget constraint', rediscovered by macroeconomic theorists in the early 1970s, is obtained by consolidating the current and capital accounts of Table 4.2. Imputed income and consumption are netted out. Deflating by the general price level yields the conventionally measured public sector financial surplus (at constant prices) given in equation (6):

$$\frac{\tau}{n} - \frac{n}{p}G^c - \frac{p_{K^{soc}}}{p}\delta K^{soc} - \frac{p_G}{p}\delta K^G - i\left(\frac{B^H + B^F}{p}\right)$$

TABLE 4.2
Public-sector income and expenditure and capital finance accounts at current (market or implicit) prices

Current account

Debit		Credit	
$p(G^c + G^{soc})$	Government consumption, including imputed rental from social overhead capital	tax receipts, including social security contributions	τ
$\delta(p_{K^{soc}}K^{soc} + p_G K^G)$	capital consumption	profits from public enterprises and ownership of natural resources	$r^G p_G K^G + r^R p_R R^G$
n	transfer and benefit payments	interest received	ei^*E^*
$i(B^H + B^F) + ej^*(B^{*H} + B^{*F}) + rp(\dot{B}^H + \dot{B}^F)$	interest paid	imputed return from social overhead capital	$r^{soc} p_{K^{soc}}K^{soc}$
S^G	surplus on current account		

Capital account

Debit		Credit	
$p_{K^{soc}}(\dot{K}^{soc} + \delta K^{soc}) + p_G(\dot{K}^G + \delta K^G)$	gross investment in structures and equipment	surplus on current account	S^G
$-[\dot{B}^H + \dot{B}^F + e(\dot{B}^{*H} + \dot{B}^{*F} - \dot{E}^*) + p(\dot{B}^H + \dot{B}^F) + \dot{H}]$	net financial investment	capital consumption	$\delta(p_{K^{soc}}K^{soc} + p_G K^G)$
$p_R \dot{R}^G$	net purchases of existing assets		

$$-\frac{e}{p}i^*(B^{*H}+B^{*F}-E^*)-r(\tilde{B}^H+\tilde{B}^F)+r^G\frac{p_G}{p}K^G$$

$$+r^R\frac{p_R}{p}R^G \equiv \frac{p_{K\text{soc}}}{p}\dot{K}^{\text{soc}}+\frac{p_G}{p}\dot{K}^G+\frac{p_R}{p}\dot{R}^G-\frac{1}{p}(\dot{B}^H+\dot{B}^F)$$

$$-\frac{e}{p}(\dot{B}^{*H}+\dot{B}^{*F}-\dot{E}^*)-(\dot{\tilde{B}}^H+\dot{\tilde{B}}^F)-\frac{\dot{H}}{p}. \tag{6}$$

Even this 'real' surplus, however, is likely to be a poor indicator of the change in the real net worth of the public sector, as defined from the balance sheet in Table 4.1. This change in the real net worth of the government is given in equation (7):[8]

$$\frac{d}{dt}\left(\frac{W^G}{p}\right) \equiv \frac{p_{K\text{soc}}}{p}\dot{K}^{\text{soc}}+\frac{p_G}{p}\dot{K}^G+\frac{p_R}{p}\dot{R}^G$$

$$-\frac{1}{p}(\dot{B}^H+\dot{B}^F)-\frac{e}{p}(\dot{B}^{*H}+\dot{B}^{*F}-\dot{E}^*)$$

$$-(\dot{\tilde{B}}^H+\dot{\tilde{B}}^F)-\frac{\dot{H}}{p}+\frac{1}{p}(\dot{T}-\dot{N})+\dot{A}^M$$

$$+\left(\frac{\dot{p}_{K\text{soc}}}{p_{K\text{soc}}}-\frac{\dot{p}}{p}\right)\frac{p_{K\text{soc}}}{p}K^{\text{soc}}+\left(\frac{\dot{p}_G}{p_G}-\frac{\dot{p}}{p}\right)\frac{p_G}{p}K^G$$

$$+\left(\frac{\dot{p}_R}{p_R}-\frac{\dot{p}}{p}\right)\frac{p_R}{p}R^G+\frac{\dot{p}}{p}\left(\frac{B^H+B^F+H}{p}\right)$$

$$-\left(\frac{\dot{e}}{e}-\frac{\dot{p}}{p}\right)\frac{e}{p}(B^{*H}+B^{*F}-E^*)$$

$$-\frac{\dot{p}}{p}(T-N). \tag{7}$$

Comparing the right-hand side of equations (6) and (7), we observe that the difference between 'real' or constant price surplus and the change in real net worth is due to capital gains and losses, Ω, and to changes in the value of the implicit assets and liabilities, Δ, where

$$\Omega=\left(\frac{\dot{p}_{K\text{soc}}}{p_{K\text{soc}}}-\frac{\dot{p}}{p}\right)\frac{p_{K\text{soc}}}{p}K^{\text{soc}}+\left(\frac{\dot{p}_G}{p_G}-\frac{\dot{p}}{p}\right)\frac{p_G}{p}K^G+\left(\frac{\dot{p}_R}{p_R}-\frac{\dot{p}}{p}\right)\frac{p_R}{p}R^G$$

$$+ \frac{\dot{p}}{p}\left(\frac{B^{\mathrm{H}} + B^{\mathrm{F}} + H}{p}\right) - \left(\frac{\dot{e}}{e} - \frac{\dot{p}}{p}\right)\frac{e}{p}(B^{*\mathrm{H}} + B^{*\mathrm{F}} - E^*) - \frac{\dot{p}}{p}(T - N)$$

(8a)

and

$$\Delta = \frac{1}{p}(\dot{T} - \dot{N}) + \dot{A}^{\mathrm{M}}.$$

(8b)

As regards Ω, the statement that the change in wealth or net worth equals savings plus capital gains will not come as a surprise to anyone. The importance of accounting fully for capital gains and losses on existing government assets and liabilities in order to obtain a correct understanding of the short-run and long-run implications of past, present, and prospective budgetary, monetary, and financial policies has not, however, been universally appreciated.

Considerable interest attaches to behaviour by an economic agent, sector, or group of sectors that leaves real comprehensive net worth unchanged. Such agents or sectors consume their permanent income and their behaviour is (*ex ante*) permanently sustainable. For policy design, policies aimed at keeping total national (public plus private) consumption in line with national permanent income, i.e. policies focusing on the comprehensive balance-sheet accounts of a consolidated public and private sector, are of special relevance. These are considered in Section VI.

While there certainly exist valid reasons for optimal consumption to depart from permanent income, such divergences must necessarily be temporary, with overshooting and undershooting of the permanent income benchmark cancelling in present value terms. Focusing on spending behaviour consistent with constant real comprehensive net worth should, therefore, come naturally in policy evaluation and design. Note that equations (7), (8a), and (8b) represent *ex post* or realized measures only. For planning, including consumption planning, the *ex ante* measures are relevant. They are obtained by replacing actual changes in prices by anticipated changes in prices and equations (7) and (8a), and by substituting anticipated changes in the value of implicit assets and liabilities for actual changes in equations (7) and (8b). In what follows, *anticipated* capital gains and losses replace the *ex post* measures whenever planned private- or public-sector behaviour is discussed.

III. Amortization of public debt through inflation and currency depreciation

Consider first changes in the public sector balance sheet due to 'pure' or general inflation. This is defined as a situation in which all money prices (including the prices of real capital assets) change at the same rate, i.e.

$$\frac{\dot{p}_{K^{\mathrm{soc}}}}{p_{K^{\mathrm{soc}}}} = \frac{\dot{p}_{\mathrm{G}}}{p_{\mathrm{G}}} = \frac{\dot{p}_{\mathrm{R}}}{p_{\mathrm{R}}} = \frac{\dot{p}}{p}$$

(For reasons of space we ignore capital gains or losses on the implicit assets and liabilities T and N due to inflation.)

Inflation-induced changes in real public-sector net worth Ω' are given by:

$$\Omega' = \frac{\dot{p}}{p}\left(\frac{B^{\mathrm{H}} + B^{\mathrm{F}} + H}{p}\right) + \left(\frac{\dot{p}}{p} - \frac{\dot{e}}{e}\right)(B^{*\mathrm{H}} + B^{*\mathrm{F}} - E^*)\frac{e}{p} \quad (9a)$$

The closed economy

In a closed economy the last term on the right-hand side can be ignored and the reduction in the real value of the outstanding stock of nominally denominated government liabilities is given by Ω'.[9]

$$\Omega'' = \frac{\dot{p}}{p}\left(\frac{B^{\mathrm{H}} + H}{p}\right) \quad (9b)$$

Proper wealth accounting requires that the amortization of public debt through inflation should be put 'below the line' in measuring the financing of the government's net 'real' borrowing.[10] Above the line, a higher rate of inflation will (if interest rates are free) swell the measured deficit as nominal interest rates rise with the rate of inflation. If the Fischer hypothesis holds and real interest rates are invariant with respect to the rate of inflation, the increased nominal interest payments associated with a higher rate of inflation will be matched exactly by the reduction in the real value of the government's stock of nominally denominated, interest-bearing debt, Ω''', defined by

$$\Omega''' = \frac{\dot{p}}{p}\frac{B^{\mathrm{H}}}{p} \quad (9c)$$

Subtracting Ω''' from the conventionally measured deficit gives the deficit 'at real interest rates'—what the conventionally measured deficit would have been had all interest-bearing debt been index-linked. In models that do not exhibit 'Ricardian' debt neutrality, changes in the real value of the stock of government interest-bearing debt are the major proximate determinant of 'financial crowding out'—the displacement of private capital formation by government borrowing, holding constant the size and composition of the government's real spending programme. The exact nature (degree, scope, and time pattern) of financial crowding out will, of course, be 'model-specific'.

A number of simple examples will be analysed in a sequel to this chapter.[11]

The central (and obvious) point is that *ceteris paribus* private agents (whose portfolio demands are for real stocks of assets if agents are free from money illusion) will absorb additional issues of nominal government bonds equal to the erosion in the real value of their existing holdings due to (anticipated) inflation, without requiring any increase in the real rate of interest. Such government borrowing, therefore, does not raise the degree to which the public sector competes with the private sector for real investible resources.

The *ceteris paribus* clause of the previous paragraph includes a given stock of real money balances. Additional monetary financing equal to the inflation tax on existing money balances $(\dot{p}/p)(H/p)$ leaves real money balances unchanged. A conventionally measured deficit equal to Ω'', financed by borrowing an amount $(\dot{p}/p)(B^{\mathrm{H}}/p)$ and by money creation equal to $(\dot{p}/p)(H/p)$, is therefore consistent with constant real interest rates and a constant degree of aggregate financial crowding-out pressure.[12] Note that substracting Ω'' from the conventionally measured deficit yields a somewhat wider concept of the deficit at 'real interest rates', since the real rate of return (ignoring non-pecuniary liquidity and convenience services) on high-powered money bearing a zero nominal interest rate is minus the rate of inflation.[13]

The argument for public-sector inflation accounting in the closed economy can be summarized succinctly using a simplified version of equations (1) and (2). We ignore G^{soc}, K^{soc}, and R^{G}, assume that $p_{\mathrm{G}} = p$ and define $G^{\mathrm{I}} = \dot{K}^{\mathrm{G}}$ (net investment by public-sector enterprises) and $\tilde{\tau} = (\tau - n)/p$ (real taxes net of transfers and other benefits). If we assume in addition that $r = i - \dot{p}/p$, then the conventionally measured government budget constraint is given by:

$$\frac{\dot{M} + \dot{B}^{\mathrm{H}}}{p} + \dot{\tilde{B}}^{\mathrm{H}} \equiv G^{\mathrm{c}} + G^{\mathrm{I}} + \delta K^{\mathrm{G}} - \tilde{\tau} + \left(r + \frac{\dot{p}}{p}\right)\frac{B^{\mathrm{H}}}{p} + r\tilde{B}^{\mathrm{H}} - r^{\mathrm{G}}K^{\mathrm{G}}.$$

(10)

The change in the real value of the stock of interest-bearing debt is given by:

$$\frac{\mathrm{d}}{\mathrm{d}t}\left(\frac{B^{\mathrm{H}}}{p} + \tilde{B}^{\mathrm{H}}\right) \equiv G^{\mathrm{c}} + G^{\mathrm{I}} + \delta K^{\mathrm{G}} - \tilde{\tau} + r\left(\frac{B^{\mathrm{H}}}{p} + \tilde{B}^{\mathrm{H}}\right) - r^{\mathrm{G}}K^{\mathrm{G}} - \frac{\dot{H}}{p}.$$

(11)

The deficit measure relevant for aggregate financial crowding-out pressure on private capital formation given in equation (11) will, of course, depend on the amount of monetary financing the authorities are permitting. Useful benchmarks are (a) monetary financing sufficient to keep the real money stock constant:

$$\frac{\dot{H}}{p} = \frac{\dot{p}H}{p\,p};$$

and (b) monetary financing consistent with a zero trend rate of inflation:

$$\frac{\dot{H}}{p} = \gamma \frac{H}{p}.$$

where γ is the natural rate of growth.[14]

Equation (11) answers the questions as to whether the fiscal stance (defined by G^c, G^I, and $\tilde{\tau}$) and the monetary target (defined by $\dot{H}/p$) imply aggregate financial crowding-out pressure, i.e.

$$\frac{\mathrm{d}}{\mathrm{d}t}\left(\frac{B^H}{p} + \tilde{B}^H\right) > 0,$$

or crowding-in pressure, i.e.

$$\frac{\mathrm{d}}{\mathrm{d}t}\left(\frac{B^H}{p} + \tilde{B}^H\right) < 0.$$

This issue can be addressed in the short run (for a single period), in the medium term (by applying (11) sequentially for as many periods as one is interested in), or in the steady state. Note that inflation-induced capital gains or losses on non-indexed bonds cancel the inflation premium in the nominal interest payments: in (11) all debt service is evaluated at real rates of interest.[15]

For aggregate crowding-out pressure on total national (private plus public sector) capital formation, a useful simple measure is (noting that $G^I = \dot{K}^G$):

$$\frac{\mathrm{d}}{\mathrm{d}t}\left(\frac{B^H}{p} + \tilde{B}^H - K^G\right)$$

$$= G^c - \tilde{\tau} + r\left(\frac{B^H}{p} + \tilde{B}^H - K^G\right) + [r - (r^G - \delta)]\,K^G - \frac{\dot{H}}{p}. \quad (12)$$

The conventional deficit measure is further modified in (12) by subtracting-out net investment by public-sector enterprises. Interest payments on net non-monetary liabilities $(B^H + B^H - K^G)$ are evaluated at the real interest rate r. If the net rate of return on public enterprise capital $(r^G - \delta)$ exceeds the opportunity cost of borrowing (r) the 'corrected' deficit is further reduced. If the opposite prevails, the 'corrected' deficit is larger by an amount $(r - (r^G - \delta))K^G$.

The decline in the real value of total public-sector tangible net worth is given by:

$$\frac{d}{dt}\left(\frac{H + B^H}{p} + \dot{B}^H - K^G\right)$$

$$= G^c - \tilde{\tau} + r\left(\frac{B^H}{p} + \dot{B}^H - K^G\right) + [r - (r^G - \delta)]K^G - \frac{\dot{p}}{p}\frac{H}{p}. \quad (13)$$

This could be called the inflation-corrected government current-account deficit. Debt-service payments and receipts on all assets and liabilities (including money) are evaluated at real rates of return.[16]

Some idea of the magnitude of the overstatement of the government's true borrowing by the conventionally measured deficit under inflationary circumstances is provided by Table 4.3a for the United Kingdom and Table 4.3b for the United States.

In 1981 the public-sector borrowing requirement in the United Kingdom was £10.6 billion and the public-sector financial deficit £7.5 billion.[17] The inflation correction in that year amounts to about £11 billion, using a variety of estimates. The inflation-corrected deficit was actually a surplus. If one notes that during 1981 the UK economy was also experiencing the worst recession since the 1930s, there can be no doubt that the inflation-corrected and cyclically-adjusted (trend or permanent) deficit was actually a very sizeable surplus. It is a matter of some practical importance whether that constitutes wise counter-cyclical fiscal policy.

The United States during the period 1979–81 also had an inflation-corrected balanced federal budget. Any reasonably cyclical correction for 1981 produces a large inflation-corrected, cyclically-adjusted surplus. High US real interest rates in 1981 can only be explained by the fiscal stance if one postulates large anticipated future inflation-corrected, cyclically-adjusted deficits.

For the nine other European Community countries an (imperfect) estimate of the inflation correction is presented in Table 4.3c. Only for the Netherlands is the inflation correction applied to external plus internal debt. For all other countries only domestically-held debt is considered. This is especially serious for Denmark, where less than 7.5% of the public debt was held domestically in 1981. For Ireland, 64% of the public-sector debt was held domestically in 1981, for Greece 81%, for Belgium, the Federal Republic of Germany, and the UK about 88%, and for France 97%. No figure for Italy is given.

While it is probably safe to assume that most of the domestically-held debt is denominated in domestic currency, the same cannot be expected to hold for the externally-held debt. The entries for Denmark are therefore virtually useless as a measure of capital gains and losses on the public debt induced by variation of inflation and exchange rates. The data for Ireland and to a lesser extent Greece are also inadequate.

TABLE 4.3a

Correcting the UK public-sector deficit for inflation

Year	Public sector debt (MV)	PSBR		PSFD		Inflation correction (1)	Inflation correction (2)	Inflation correction (3)
	GDP %	£ billion	GDP %	£ billion	GDP %	£ billion	£ billion	£ billion
1967	81	1.9	4.6	1.5	3.8	0.5	0.6	1.0
1968	77	1.3	3.0	0.9	2.0	1.4	2.0	1.2
1969	70	−0.4	−1.0	−0.5	−1.1	1.2	2.0	1.3
1970	67	0.0	0.0	−0.7	−1.3	2.1	2.7	1.4
1971	59	1.4	2.4	0.3	0.53	3.0	3.2	1.5
1972	58	2.1	3.2	1.5	2.4	3.3	3.2	1.7
1973	49	4.2	5.8	2.8	3.8	3.0	4.0	2.3
1974	43	6.4	7.7	4.7	5.7	7.0	9.3	3.3
1975	41	10.5	9.9	7.7	7.3	10.3	11.9	3.9
1976	43	9.1	7.3	8.3	6.6	7.5	7.4	5.0
1977	47	6.0	4.2	5.9	4.1	10.1	9.3	5.8
1978	44	8.4	5.1	8.1	4.9	6.2	6.4	6.5
1979	42	12.6	6.6	8.1	4.2	12.3	13.8	8.2
1980	36	12.2	5.4	9.7	4.3	9.6	12.1	10.5
1981	38	10.6	4.1	7.5	2.9	10.8	11.7	11.8

Notes: MV: market value; PSBR: public-sector borrowing requirement; PSFD: public-sector financial deficit; Inflation correction (1): annual rate of inflation × market value of public-sector debt (mid-year); Inflation correction (2): annual rate of inflation × nominal value of public-sector debt; Inflation correction (3): based on assumption of a 2% long-run real interest rate.
     Source: Marcus Miller, 1982.

TABLE 4.3b
US federal deficits and debt since 1967
(in billions of $ US)

Year	Total federal budget and off-budget deficit fiscal year (1)	Par value of public securities held by private investors end of fiscal year (2)	Par value of public debt securities held by private investors end of fiscal year; 1967 prices (3)	Inflation correction (4)	Public debt GNP ratio (5)
1967	8.7	204.4	204.4	5.9	0.26
1968	25.2	217.0	208.3	9.1	0.25
1969	−3.2	214.0	194.9	11.6	0.23
1970	2.8	217.2	186.8	12.8	0.22
1971	23.0	228.9	188.7	9.8	0.21
1972	23.4	243.6	194.4	8.0	0.21
1973	14.9	258.9	194.5	16.1	0.20
1974	6.1	255.6	173.1	28.1	0.18
1975	53.2	303.2	188.1	27.6	0.20
1976	73.7	376.4	220.8	21.8	0.22
1977	53.6	438.6	241.7	28.5	0.23
1978	59.2	488.3	249.9	37.6	0.23
1979	40.2	523.4	240.8	59.1	0.22
1980	73.8	589.2	238.7	79.5	0.22
1981	78.9	665.4	244.3	69.2	0.23

Notes: Column (3) = Column (2) deflated by c.p.i.; Column (4) = Column (2) × proportional rate of change of c.p.i.
Source: Economic Report of the President, 1982.

TABLE 4.3c

Loss in real value of public debt held by residents, 1973-83 (% of GDP)

	1973	1974	1975	1976	1977	1978	1979	1980	1981
Belgium (1) (3)	4.2	9.6	6.9	4.8	4.1	2.7	3.7	5.4	(6.1)
Denmark	:	−2.9	−0.6	−2.0	−1.8	−0.9	−1.1	−0.7	0.1
Federal Republic of Germany (1)	−0.5	−0.3	−0.1	0.1	0.2	0.2	0.5	0.6	(0.9)
Greece (2)	4.4	2.0	2.3	1.9	2.2	2.8	5.5	5.6	7.3
France (1)	0.6	1.1	0.8	0.9	0.8	0.9	1.2	1.3	(1.3)
Ireland (2)	6.1	9.9	10.0	11.8	6.4	5.2	11.1	12.0	14.7
Italy	5.6	10.5	5.9	12.0	7.0	6.8	11.0	12.0	(11.2)
Luxembourg (2) (3)	1.1	1.6	1.8	1.4	0.8	0.7	1.1	(1.3)	(1.6)
Netherlands (1) (4)	3.5	4.2	3.6	3.3	2.1	1.6	2.2	3.1	(3.4)
EC	2.3	3.9	3.6	3.8	2.7	2.3	3.9	4.1	3.9

Notes: (1): losses calculated on the basis of the net debt of general government; (2): losses calculated on the basis of the gross debt of central government; (3): calculation carried out on the basis of domestic-currency debt; (4): calculation carried out on the basis of the total (domestic and external) debt.

The estimate of the loss in real value of public debt is obtained by multiplying the amount of the debt by the rate of change in the consumer price index during the year.

Source: Commission of the EC, *Annual Economic Review*, 1982–3. Estimates are consistent with the Commission's economic forecasts.

For the remaining countries no wildly misleading impression is conveyed by Table 4.3c. The magnitude of the inflation corrections in 1980 and 1981 for such countries as Ireland, Italy, Greece, and Belgium is quite remarkable. It is also interesting to note that for 1981 the inflation correction (3.4% of GDP) and the cyclical correction given in Table 4.4 below (3.9% of GDP) together match the public-sector borrowing requirement of 7.4% of GDP in the Netherlands. This suggests that there was no collapse of fiscal control in that country in 1981.[18]

The open economy

In an open economy, governments can borrow and lend domestically or abroad. Their financial assets and liabilities can be denominated in foreign or domestic currency or be index-linked. Consider equation (9a). The real value of public-sector debt denominated in domestic currency is reduced by domestic inflation whether this debt is owned by the private sector or the rest of the world. While *ceteris paribus* inflation also reduces the real value of foreign-currency-denominated financial claims, exchange-rate depreciation increases it. If purchasing power parity (p.p.p.) holds, i.e.

$$\frac{\dot{p}}{p} - \frac{\dot{e}}{e} = \frac{\dot{p}^*}{p^*}$$

and through choice of units, $ep^* = p$, equation (9a) becomes

$$\Omega' = \frac{\dot{p}}{p}\left(\frac{B^{\mathrm{H}} + B^{\mathrm{F}} + H}{p}\right) + \frac{\dot{p}^*}{p^*}\left(\frac{B^{*\mathrm{H}} + B^{*\mathrm{F}} - E^*}{p^*}\right). \quad (9a')$$

With p.p.p., reductions in the real value of foreign-currency-denominated public-sector debt can be calculated by multiplying the foreign rate of inflation into the real value of net foreign-currency-denominated liabilities.

Consider the following stylized representation of the position of a number of small, open, developing countries that lack a significant domestic capital market. Government debt is largely placed abroad and tends to be denominated in foreign currency (typically US dollars). In such countries $B^{\mathrm{H}} = B^{\mathrm{F}} = \dot{B}^{\mathrm{H}} = \dot{B}^{\mathrm{F}} = B^{*\mathrm{H}} = 0$. The conventionally measured public-sector deficit is:[19]

$$\frac{\dot{H}}{p} + \frac{e}{p}(\dot{B}^{*\mathrm{F}} - \dot{E}^*)$$

$$= G^{\mathrm{c}} + G^{\mathrm{I}} + \delta K^{\mathrm{G}} - \tilde{\tau} + \frac{e}{p}i^*(B^{*\mathrm{F}} - E^*) - r^{\mathrm{G}}K^{\mathrm{G}}. \quad (14)$$

If, in addition, only the government borrows overseas, $(\mathrm{d}/\mathrm{d}t)(B^{*\mathrm{F}} - E^*)$ equals the current-account deficit (in terms of foreign currency) of the balance of payments:

$$\frac{e}{p}(\dot{B}^{*\mathrm{F}} - \dot{E}^*) = -X + \frac{e}{p}i^*(B^{*\mathrm{F}} - E^*). \qquad (15)$$

Here X denotes real net exports of goods and services (excluding debt service), plus net transfers and grants from abroad.

Compare the current-account balances of two countries, identical in real terms but facing different rates of world inflation. If r^* is the world real rate of interest, $i^* = r^* + \dot{p}^*/p^*$, i.e.

$$\frac{e}{p}(\dot{B}^{*\mathrm{F}} - \dot{E}^*) = -X + \frac{e}{p}\left(r^* + \frac{\dot{p}^*}{p^*}\right)(B^{*\mathrm{F}} - E^*). \qquad (15')$$

If the world real rate of interest is independent of the inflation rate and if p.p.p. prevails, the current account deficit of the country facing the higher rate of world inflation $(\dot{p}^*/p^*)^1$ will exceed that of the country facing the lower rate of world inflation $(\dot{p}^*/p^*)^2$ by an amount

$$\left[\left(\frac{\dot{p}^*}{p^*}\right)^1 - \left(\frac{\dot{p}^*}{p^*}\right)^2\right]e\left(\frac{B^{*\mathrm{F}} - E^*}{p}\right),$$

which is equal to the difference in external debt-service payments. This difference in current-account balances should, however, have no real consequences since the higher debt-service item above the line is matched below the line by the larger reduction in the real value of its external liabilities: higher world inflation means faster amortization of external indebtedness. Thus

$$\frac{\mathrm{d}}{\mathrm{d}t}\left[\frac{e}{p}(B^{*\mathrm{F}} - E^*)\right],$$

the change in net real external liabilities, is the same in the two economies. The country facing the larger current-account deficit owing to higher world inflation should be able to borrow to finance its higher external interest payments.[20]

What we have seen in recent years, of course, is an increase in world real interest rates (r^*). This does require adjustment rather than, or in addition to, merely financing, with the relative weights on adjustment versus financing depending on the extent to which the increase in world real interest rates is perceived as permanent rather than transitory. Also, to the extent that countries have borrowed long-term rather than short-term (or at variable interest rates), unanticipated changes in interest rates will result in (once and for all) real capital gains or losses on external debt. Finally, significant departures from p.p.p. have been the rule, especially since the breakdown of Bretton Woods. Thus, even with a given world real interest rate r^*,

a country's real external indebtedness will increase whenever there is
an increase in

$$\frac{\dot{p}^*}{p^*} - \left(\frac{\dot{p}}{p} - \frac{\dot{e}}{e}\right),$$

the excess of the world rate of inflation over the domestic rate of
inflation minus the percentage depreciation of the exchange rate.

Many other kinds of open economies can be analysed starting from
the general framework of equations (6), (7), and (9a), but the general
principles should be clear from the simple example just analysed.

IV. Budgetary policy and monetary growth:
the eventual monetization of deficits

If bond financing of deficits causes concern about crowding-out of
private capital formation and, in the open economy, about possible
adverse consequences for external indebtedness, monetization of
deficits is a source of concern because of its inflationary implications.
We saw that it was necessary to correct the conventionally measured
budget deficit for the effects of inflation and exchange-rate appreciation on the real value of outstanding stocks of public-sector financial
assets and liabilities in order to assess (changes in) the extent to which
the public sector competes for investible resources with the private and
overseas sectors.

Similar adjustments are required to understand the monetary
implications of the deficit, as will be shown in this section.

The closed economy

From the simplified government budget constraint in equation (10),
we obtain the following expression for the proportional rate of growth
of the nominal money stock.[21]

$$\frac{\dot{H}}{H} = V\left[\frac{G^c + G^I + \delta K^G - \tilde{\tau}}{Y} + \left(r + \frac{\dot{p}}{p}\right)\frac{B^H}{pY} + r\frac{\tilde{B}^H}{Y} - r^G\frac{K^G}{Y} - \frac{\dot{B}^H}{pY} - \frac{\dot{\tilde{B}}^H}{Y}\right]$$

(16)

where $V \equiv pY/H$ is the income velocity of circulation of money. To
evaluate the implications of the fiscal stance for monetary growth, we
must specify paths both for public spending and taxation and for non-
money financing. A particularly useful benchmark financing policy is
one which keeps constant the real values of all government assets and
liabilities (other than money) per unit of output. This would be a
policy of constant crowding-out pressure per unit of output. These
constant liability- (or asset-) output ratios need not be the historically

inherited ones. The exercise can be applied to evaluating the longer-run implications for monetary growth after the debt-output ratios have achieved some desired long-run (or even steady-state) values. Given this rule,

$$\frac{G^{\mathrm{I}}}{K^{\mathrm{G}}} = \frac{\dot{\tilde{B}}^{\mathrm{H}}}{\tilde{B}^{\mathrm{H}}} = \gamma$$

and

$$\frac{\dot{\tilde{B}}^{\mathrm{H}}}{\tilde{B}^{\mathrm{H}}} = \gamma + \frac{\dot{p}}{p}.$$

Equation (16) then becomes:

$$\frac{\dot{H}}{H} \equiv V\left[\frac{G^{\mathrm{c}} - \tilde{\tau}}{Y} + (r - \gamma)\left(\frac{B^{\mathrm{H}}}{pY} + \frac{\tilde{B}^{\mathrm{H}}}{Y} - \frac{K^{\mathrm{G}}}{Y}\right) + [r - (r^{\mathrm{G}} - \delta)]\frac{K^{\mathrm{G}}}{Y}\right]. \quad (17)$$

Defining the longer-run fiscal stance by given constant values of $B^{\mathrm{H}}/(pY)$, $\tilde{B}^{\mathrm{H}}/Y$, and K^{G}/Y and by given, but not necessarily constant, paths of G^{c}/Y and $\tilde{\tau}/Y$, we can see from (17) that longer-run monetary growth is governed by a deficit concept that differs from the conventionally measured deficit in a number of ways.

First, the reduction in the real value of the stock of nominal government bonds due to inflation is subtracted from the conventional measure. Second, in a growing economy the real stocks of government assets and liabilities can grow at the natural rate γ while leaving the asset-output or debt-output ratios constant. The net debt-service term in (17) therefore involves the real, growth-adjusted interest rate $r - \gamma$. Under inflationary conditions this can be significantly less than $i = r + \dot{p}/p$, the nominal interest rate. Note that in order to infer the long-term implications for monetary growth (and thus for inflation) of the fiscal stance, an inflation correction is applied only to the interest-bearing component of the government's nominal liabilities. The conventionally measured deficit should not be reduced by the erosion of the real value of the nominal stock of high-powered money balances, $(\dot{p}/p)(H/p)$. The reason is that constancy of the real value of all (monetary and non-monetary) government debt per unit of output is consistent with any deficit and any rate of inflation.

Large conventionally measured (even if cyclically adjusted) deficits that correspond to small inflation-corrected deficits (or even surpluses)[22] reflect *current* high inflation. They do not indicate the inevitability of high crowding-out pressure or high rates of monetary growth in the future. Even without correcting for real growth, an inflation-corrected (trend) surplus means that (a) with zero money financing, there would be (aggregate) crowding-in, and (b) with a bond-financing policy of zero (aggregate) crowding-in, there would be negative monetary-base growth.

Equation (17) by itself does not permit one to draw any conclusions about the effects of, say, changes in fiscal stance on monetary growth. Positive economic models are required to incorporate the effect of any parameter changes on endogenous variables such as velocity, V, real rates of interest, r and r^G, and even the natural rate of growth γ. Such analysis is simplest in very classical monetarist models, such as Sargent and Wallace's,[23] in which velocity, the real interest rate, and the natural rate of growth are constants, but (17) can be incorporated in models of any hue. (See also Buiter.)[24]

The open economy

From the simplified open-economy budget constraint we obtain the expression for the percentage growth rate of the nominal money stock given in equation (18):

$$
\frac{\dot{H}}{H} = V\left[\frac{G^c + \delta K^G - \tilde{\tau}}{Y} + \left(r + \frac{\dot{p}}{p} \right)\left(\frac{B^H + B^F}{pY} \right) + r\left(\frac{\tilde{B}^H + \tilde{B}^F}{Y} \right) \right.
$$
$$
+ \frac{i^*e}{pY}(B^{*H} + B^{*F} - E^*) - r^G\frac{K^G}{Y} + \frac{\dot{K}^G}{Y} - \frac{1}{p}\left(\frac{\dot{B}^H + \dot{B}^F}{Y} \right)
$$
$$
\left. - \left(\frac{\dot{\tilde{B}}^H + \dot{\tilde{B}}^F}{Y} \right) - \frac{e}{p}\left(\frac{\dot{B}^{*H} + \dot{B}^{*F} - \dot{E}^*}{Y} \right) \right]. \tag{18}
$$

To evaluate the longer-run monetary implications of the fiscal stance, we again assume that all stock-flow ratios on the right-hand side of (18) are kept constant. Equation (18) then reduces to:

$$
\frac{\dot{H}}{H} = V\left\{ \frac{G^c - \tilde{\tau}}{Y} + (r - \gamma)\left(\frac{B^H + B^F}{pY} + \frac{\tilde{B}^H + \tilde{B}^F}{Y} - \frac{K^G}{Y} \right) \right.
$$
$$
\left. + \left[i^* - \left(\frac{\dot{p}}{p} - \frac{\dot{e}}{e} \right) - \gamma \right]\left(\frac{B^{*H} + B^{*F} - E^*}{pY} \right)e + [r - (r^G - \delta)]\frac{K^G}{Y} \right\}. \tag{19}
$$

With p.p.p. this simplifies to:

$$
\frac{\dot{H}}{H} = V\left[\frac{G^c - \tilde{\tau}}{Y} + (r - \gamma)\left(\frac{B^H + B^F}{pY} + \frac{\tilde{B}^H + \tilde{B}^F}{Y} - \frac{K^G}{Y} \right) \right.
$$
$$
\left. + (r^* - \gamma)\left(\frac{B^{*H} + B^{*F} - E^*}{p^*Y} \right) + [r - (r^G - \delta)]\frac{K^G}{Y} \right]. \tag{19'}
$$

The evaluation of the long-term monetization implied by the fiscal stance requires the consideration of a deficit measure which has nominal debt-service payments 'corrected' for the effects of domestic inflation, exchange-rate appreciation, and real growth.

In any particular period the economy may well be far removed from the long-run trend captured in equations (17) and (19) or (19'). Actual monetary growth in the short run will be given by equations (16) or (18). If current inflation is a function only of current monetary growth (as would be the case, for example, if velocity were constant, the price level were perfectly flexible, and output grew at its exogenously given trend rate γ), then $\dot{p}/p = \dot{H}/H - \gamma$. Authorities concerned with inflation in the short run may not be much comforted by the knowledge that the long-run rate of inflation implied by their fiscal stance is low, if current monetary growth and inflation are high. If, as seems more likely, current inflation is a function of current and past monetary growth and *a fortiori* if current inflation depends also on anticipated future monetary growth (as it does in models with forward-looking rational expectations) then the long-run monetary growth expressions in (17), (19), and (19') become the relevant ones even for short- and medium-term policy.

V. The role of implicit assets and liabilities

On the asset side of the public-sector balance sheet we include T, the present value of future planned or anticipated tax revenues, and A^M, the imputed value of the government's cash monopoly. On the liability side was N, the present value of future transfers and benefits under various entitlement programmes. In this section I shall consider how the value of these implicit assets and liabilities changes over time. I shall focus on N. The treatment of T, A^M, and of private sector human wealth (discussed in Section VI) is analytically identical.

N is defined in equation (20):[25]

$$N(t) \equiv \int_t^\infty \exp\left(-\int_t^u \hat{i}(s,t)ds\right)\hat{n}(u,t)\,du. \tag{20}$$

The change in the present discounted value of expected future benefits is given by:

$$\frac{d}{dt}N(t) = i(t)N(t) - n(t)$$

$$+ \int_t^\infty \exp\left(-\int_t^u \hat{i}(s,t)ds\right)\left(\frac{\partial}{\partial t}\hat{n}(u,t) - \hat{n}(u,t)\int_t^u \frac{\partial}{\partial t}\hat{i}(s,t)ds\right)du.$$

$$\tag{21}$$

The first two terms on the right-hand side of (21) show how the present value of future benefits changes if all expectations concerning the future flow of benefits and future interest rates remain the same. The last term shows the effect of changes (at time t) in expectations concerning future benefits $(\partial/\partial t)\hat{n}(u, t)$ and future interest rates $(\partial/\partial t)\hat{i}(s, t)$. As expected, upward revisions in future benefit entitlement raise N, while higher future expected interest rates lower it.

The only item on the right-hand side of (21) that appears in the cash-based public-sector deficit or flow-of-funds accounts is $n(t)$, current benefit payments. $i(t)N(t)$ does not appear because future entitlements are not a marketable interest-bearing liability of the authorities. Changes in planned or expected future benefit entitlements will only appear in the accounts if and when they actually become payable in the future. Yet such 'revaluations' of N are of considerable policy interest.

Even if financial markets are not 'forward-looking', i.e. even if government borrowing affects market rates of return only when it actually occurs, increases in N unmatched by increases in T (or by cuts in other spending programmes) imply increased future borrowing or money issues and thus store up trouble for the future. Financial markets do, furthermore, appear to be linked intertemporally (as formalized, for example, by models of efficient asset market equilibrium incorporating forward-looking rational expectations). A larger anticipated future borrowing requirement will, therefore, affect asset prices and rates of return today. An unanticipated increase in future expected (inflation-corrected) deficits will crowd-out private spending today. The intangible items in the public-sector balance sheet must be taken into account.

VI. The public sector accounts and private behaviour

The private and overseas sectors' accounts

Comprehensive balance sheets analogous to the public-sector balance sheet of Table 4.1 are drawn up for the private sector and the overseas sector in Tables 4.4 and 4.5, respectively. For reasons of space, the private-sector balance sheet consolidates the household sector, the corporate sector, and the private financial sector. For practical applications, further sectoral disaggregation will often be required. The balance sheets require little further explanation. Consumer durables and private residential housing can be viewed as included in K^p, and their imputed service flows as subsumed under private income and consumption in the budget constraint.

For simplicity it is assumed that all claims on, or debts to, the rest of the world take the form of interest-bearing financial claims. Direct

TABLE 4.4
*Private-sector balance sheet
(at current prices)*

Assets		Liabilities	
B^H	net interest-bearing government debt denominated in domestic currency held by residents	T	present value of future taxes
$eB*^H$	net interest-bearing government debt denominated in foreign currency held by residents	W^p	private-sector net worth
$p\tilde{B}^H$	net interest-bearing index-linked government debt held by residents		
H	stock of high-powered money		
N	present value of social insurance and other entitlement programmes		
F^H	net interest-bearing claims on the foreign sector denominated in domestic currency		
$eF*^H$	net interest-bearing claims on the foreign sector denominated in foreign currency		
$p_{Kp}K^p$	value of claims on real reproducible capital, including inventories		
$p_R(\bar{R}-R^G)$	land and mineral assets		
L	present value of future expected labour income		

TABLE 4.5

Overseas-sector balance sheet
(at current prices)

Assets		Liabilities	
B^{F}	overseas holdings of nominal domestic-currency-denominated government bonds	eE^*	net foreign exchange reserves of the government
$eB^{*\,\mathrm{F}}$	overseas holdings of foreign-currency-denominated government bonds	F^{H}	net interest-bearing debt to the domestic private sector denominated in domestic currency
$p\tilde{B}^{\mathrm{F}}$	overseas holdings of index-linked government debt	$eF^{*\,\mathrm{H}}$	net interest-bearing debt to the domestic private sector denominated in foreign currency
		w^{F}	overseas-sector net worth

foreign ownership of domestic real capital or of domestic resources is not considered, but could be added without difficulty. Human wealth, L, the present discounted value of future expected labour income, is a (non-marketable) asset in the household balance sheet. The total national stock of land and mineral rights is assumed to be given by $\bar{R}$.[26]

The conventionally measured private-sector financial surplus (at constant prices) and the change in real private net worth are given in equations (22) and (23), respectively:

$$\frac{\ell}{p} + r^{\mathrm{p}}\frac{p_{K\mathrm{p}}}{p}K^{\mathrm{p}} + r^{\mathrm{R}}\frac{p_{\mathrm{R}}}{p}R^{\mathrm{p}} + \left(r + \frac{\dot{p}}{p}\right)\left(\frac{B^{\mathrm{H}}}{p} + \frac{F^{\mathrm{H}}}{p}\right) + \frac{ei^*}{p}(B^{*\mathrm{H}} + F^{*\mathrm{H}})$$

$$+ r\tilde{B}^{\mathrm{H}} + \frac{n}{p} - \frac{\tau}{p} - C - \delta K^{\mathrm{p}}$$

$$\equiv \left(\frac{\dot{B}^{\mathrm{H}} + \dot{F}^{\mathrm{H}}}{p}\right) + \dot{\tilde{B}}^{\mathrm{H}} + \frac{e}{p}(\dot{B}^{*\mathrm{H}} + \dot{F}^{*\mathrm{H}}) + \frac{\dot{H}}{p} + \frac{p_{K\mathrm{p}}}{p}\dot{K}^{\mathrm{p}} - \frac{p_{\mathrm{R}}}{p}\dot{R}^{\mathrm{G}}$$

$$(22)$$

and

$$\frac{\mathrm{d}}{\mathrm{d}t}\left(\frac{W^{\mathrm{p}}}{p}\right) \equiv \left(\frac{\dot{B}^{\mathrm{H}} + \dot{F}^{\mathrm{H}}}{p}\right) + \dot{\tilde{B}}^{\mathrm{H}} + \frac{e}{p}(\dot{B}^{*\mathrm{H}} + \dot{F}^{*\mathrm{H}}) + \frac{\dot{H}}{p} + \frac{p_{K\mathrm{p}}}{p}\dot{K}^{\mathrm{p}}$$

$$- \frac{p_{\mathrm{R}}}{p}\dot{R}^{\mathrm{G}} + \frac{1}{p}(\dot{L} + \dot{N} - \dot{T}) + \left(\frac{\dot{p}_{K\mathrm{p}}}{p_{K\mathrm{p}}} - \frac{\dot{p}}{p}\right)K^{\mathrm{p}}$$

$$+\left(\frac{\dot{p}_R}{p_R}-\frac{\dot{p}}{p}\right)(\bar{R}-R^G)-\frac{\dot{p}}{p}\left(\frac{B^H+F^H+H}{p}\right)$$

$$+\left(\frac{\dot{e}}{e}-\frac{\dot{p}}{p}\right)\frac{e}{p}(B^{*H}+F^{*H})-\frac{\dot{p}}{p}(L+N-T). \qquad (23)$$

The conventionally measured overseas-sector financial surplus (at constant prices) and the change in the real net worth of the overseas sector are given in equations (24) and (25), respectively:

$$-X+\frac{e}{p}i^*(B^{*F}-F^{*H}-E^*)+\left(r+\frac{\dot{p}}{p}\right)\left(\frac{B^F-F^H}{p}\right)+r\bar{B}^F$$

$$\equiv\frac{e}{p}(\dot{B}^{*F}\,\dot{F}^{*H}-\dot{E}^*)+\left(\frac{\dot{B}^F-\dot{F}^H}{p}\right)+\dot{B}^F \qquad (24)$$

and

$$\frac{d}{dt}\left(\frac{W^F}{p}\right)\equiv\frac{e}{p}(\dot{B}^{*F}-\dot{F}^{*H}-\dot{E}^*)+\left(\frac{\dot{B}^F-\dot{F}^H}{p}\right)+\dot{B}^F-\frac{\dot{p}}{p}\left(\frac{B^F-F^H}{p}\right)$$

$$+\left(\frac{\dot{e}}{p}-\frac{\dot{p}}{p}\right)\frac{e}{p}(B^{*F}-F^{*H}-E^*). \qquad (25)$$

These flow of funds and change in real net worth equations require little explanation. In the case of the private sector, the difference between the financial surplus (at constant prices) and the change in real net worth reflects capital gains and losses on existing marketable assets and liabilities (including capital gains and losses due to inflation and exchange-rate changes) and changes in the value of the intangible and non-marketable items L, N, and T. On the left-hand side of equation (22) we have omitted the implicit liquidity and convenience yield on money balances, $\rho^M H/p = iH/p$, as an item of private consumption and of private income, because only cash transactions are included.

The positive irrelevance and normative relevance of debt neutrality

The simplest theory of the interaction of the private and public sectors is based on the so-called (pre-) Ricardian debt-neutrality hypothesis.[27] This holds that, given the level and composition of the public sector's real spending programme on goods and services, private-sector behaviour will be invariant with respect to changes in the taxation-borrowing mix that finances this spending. Most of the formal models dealing with this issue concern closed barter economies, and the formal invariance propositions tend to be stated in terms of borrowing versus taxing without explicit consideration of monetary financing. The informal lore on the subject does, however, assert the irrelevance for real outcomes of the way in which governments finance their spending for all three financing modes.

The argument underlying this Modigliani–Miller theorem for the public sector *vis-à-vis* the private sector runs as follows. Spending must be financed (in a closed economy) by taxation, borrowing, or printing money. Borrowing is merely deferred taxation. A switch between taxation and borrowing should, therefore, not affect the permanent income and consumption behaviour of rational, well-informed private agents. Monetary financing implies the imposition of an inflation tax which (under suitably restrictive conditions) has the same effect on permanent income as explicit taxes.[28]

With debt neutrality, private-sector spending behaviour for a given programme of public spending on goods and services is constrained only by the consolidated national balance sheet shown in Table 4.6.

TABLE 4.6
Consolidated public- and private-sector balance sheet

Assets	Liabilities
$p_{K\text{soc}}K^{\text{soc}}$ $p_G K^G$ $p_{K\text{p}}K^{\text{p}}$ $p_R \bar{R}$	$W^{\text{p}} + W^G$
$e(E^* + F^{*\text{H}} - B^{*\text{F}})$ $+ F^{\text{H}} - B^{\text{F}} - p\tilde{B}^{\text{F}}$	
L	
pA^{M}	

The distribution of the ownership of the nation's resources between the public and private sectors is irrelevant. The national flow-of-funds account (including non-marketable imputed income and consumption streams) is given in equation (26):

$$\frac{1}{p}[\ell + r^{\text{soc}}p_{K\text{soc}}K^{\text{soc}} + r^G p_G K^G + r^{\text{p}}p_{K\text{p}}K^{\text{p}} + r^R p_R \bar{R}$$

$$+ i^* e(E^* + F^{*\text{H}} - B^{*\text{F}}) + i(F^{\text{H}} - B^{\text{F}}) - rp\tilde{B}^{\text{F}} + iH]$$

$$- \left(G^{\text{c}} + G^{\text{soc}} + C + \frac{\delta}{p}(p_{K\text{soc}}K^{\text{soc}} + p_G K^G + p_{K\text{p}}K^{\text{p}}) + \rho^{\text{M}}\frac{H}{p} \right)$$

$$\equiv \frac{1}{p}[p_{K\text{soc}}\dot{K}^{\text{soc}} + p_G \dot{K}^G + p_{K\text{p}}\dot{K}^{\text{p}} + e(\dot{E}^* + \dot{F}^{*\text{H}} - \dot{B}^{*\text{F}})$$

$$+ \dot{F}^{H} - \dot{B}^{F} - p\dot{B}^{F}]$$

$$\equiv \frac{S}{p}.$$

(26)

The first bracketed term on the left-hand side of equation (26) contains current income, including the imputed return from the government's cash monopoly iH/p. This item is matched in the second bracketed term, containing current consumption, by $\rho^{M}H/p$, the imputed value of the non-pecuniary services of money consumed by the private sector. Those unhappy with our treatment of money can omit both items. The change in real national comprehensive net worth is given by:

$$\frac{\mathrm{d}}{\mathrm{d}t}\left(\frac{W}{p}\right) \equiv \frac{\mathrm{d}}{\mathrm{d}t}\left(\frac{W^{\mathrm{p}} + W^{\mathrm{G}}}{p}\right) \equiv \frac{S}{p} + \left(\frac{\dot{p}_{K\,\mathrm{soc}}}{p_{K\,\mathrm{soc}}} - \frac{\dot{p}}{p}\right)\frac{p_{K\,\mathrm{soc}}K^{\mathrm{soc}}}{p}$$

$$+ \left(\frac{\dot{p}_{\mathrm{G}}}{p_{\mathrm{G}}} - \frac{\dot{p}}{p}\right)\frac{p_{\mathrm{G}}}{p}K^{\mathrm{G}} + \left(\frac{\dot{p}_{K\mathrm{p}}}{p_{K\mathrm{p}}} - \frac{\dot{p}}{p}\right)\frac{p_{K\mathrm{p}}}{p}K^{\mathrm{p}} + \left(\frac{\dot{p}_{\mathrm{R}}}{p_{\mathrm{R}}} - \frac{\dot{p}}{p}\right)\frac{p_{\mathrm{R}}}{p}\bar{R}$$

$$+ \left(\frac{\dot{e}}{e} - \frac{\dot{p}}{p}\right)\frac{e}{p}(E^{*} + F^{*\mathrm{H}} - B^{*\,\mathrm{F}}) - \frac{\dot{p}}{p}(F^{\mathrm{H}} - B^{\mathrm{F}}) + \frac{(\dot{L}/p)}{p} + \dot{A}^{\mathrm{M}}.$$

(27)

The change in real net worth equals saving, S/p, plus capital gains on marketable assets, plus changes in the imputed or implicit value of non-marketable items of wealth. A programme of total national consumption in line with permanent national income means choosing the value of the second bracketed term in (26) such that the expected value of $(\mathrm{d}/\mathrm{d}t)(W/p) = 0$. Such a consumption programme is *ex ante* indefinitely sustainable and serves as a useful benchmark for consumption planning in this debt-neutral economy.

Debt neutrality is bad positive economics. It requires private agents to live for ever or to have operative intergenerational bequest and child-to-parent gift motives in every generation. Perfect capital markets are another necessary condition: future labour income is a source of current spending power on a par with current disposable income and current holdings of government debt.[29]

The economic behaviour that would be generated under debt neutrality is, however, a useful guide to what policy should try to achieve in a world in which a variety of capital-market imperfections prevent the 'unaided' private sector from acting according to permanent income principles.

For example, it is well known that, in the absence of operative private intergenerational transfer motives, changes in the borrowing-taxation mix can redistribute the burden of financing a given government spending programme between generations, even without the existence of capital-market imperfections. If government is motivated by a concern for the utility (i.e. the lifetime consumption patterns) of future generations as well as of the current generation, it can use the budgetary and financial mechanism to induce the current generation to act as if it were constrained by permanent private-sector income rather than merely by the present value of its own lifetime resources.

The endowments listed on the asset side of Table 4.6, the nation's technology (broadly defined) and the international trading and lending or borrowing conditions it faces, represent the unavoidable constraints on the nation's intertemporal transformation of resources. The purpose of financing policy, i.e. the choice of the tax, transfer, borrowing, and money-creation mix for a given real public spending programme on goods and services, should be to avoid additional constraints—cash flow shortfalls, inadequate liquidity, insufficient collateral, non-marketability of assets, credit rationing, etc.—becoming binding or, failing that, to minimize their incidence and consequences.[30]

Through their budgetary and financing policies, governments (within a national economy) and international organizations (within the international economic system) can act as a superior financial intermediary, changing the composition of private-sector or nation–state portfolios, respectively. Well-designed policy interventions of this kind can minimize the extent to which disposable income, current cash flow, and the portfolio of liquid, marketable financial assets become binding constraints on consumption, investment, production, and portfolio allocation, enforcing undesirable departures from behaviour according to permanent income principles. Governments, through their unique ability to impose taxes, through their monopoly of legal tender, and through the superior quality of their debts, have a 'comparative advantage' over the private sector in borrowing to smooth-out income streams.[31] The same, though perhaps to a lesser extent, holds for certain international organizations *vis-à-vis* nation states.

The examples that follow illustrate this role of the government as the natural borrower and its unique ability to restructure the conventionally measured sectoral balance sheets, flow-of-funds, and income–expenditure accounts to permit the economy as a whole to approximate more closely behaviour constrained only by comprehensive wealth or permanent income.

Fiscal aspects of a natural resource discovery

Consider the effects on public-sector and private-sector balance sheets of an oil discovery. We can represent this by an unexpected increase in p_R, the value of property rights in land and mineral assets by, say, $dp_R > 0$. To the extent that these property rights are privately owned and marketable, disposable private net worth increases by $(\bar{R} - R^G)dp_R$. Following permanent income principles, private agents would consume the perpetuity equivalent of this capital gain in each period. If spending were constrained by a dearth of marketable financial wealth to begin with, a temporarily larger increase in private consumption spending would result. The value of public-sector assets increases by $R^G dp_R$. The government could choose to increase its own consumption spending in line with the permanent income equivalent of this capital gain. If it chooses not to do so, it faces the problem of enabling the private sector to raise its spending by the perpetuity equivalent of $R^G dp_R$.

One way to approach this would be to distribute to the private sector (in the form of tax cuts or increased transfer payments) the stream of actual additional oil revenues $r^R(t)R^G(t)dp_R(t)$ as and when they accrue. The present value of such future anticipated tax cuts (or transfer payment increases) is, however, a non-marketable, highly illiquid asset which is singularly poor collateral for private borrowing. If there is a gestation period before the new oil comes on stream and *a fortiori* if development costs have to be incurred before the oil starts to flow, the additional cash flow to the government (and thus to the private sector) may well be negative for a number of years.

Private agents whose current spending is constrained by current disposable income or other forms of illiquidity will therefore be unable to raise their spending in line with their permanent income. A superior fiscal option is for the government to cut taxes (raise transfers) as soon as the new oil wealth is discovered, by an amount equal to the perpetuity equivalent or annuity value of the discovery.[32] This will require additional government borrowing until the moment that actual revenues exceed their permanent value, at which time the authorities will be able to retire the temporary debt issues whose function is merely to relax the spending limits on cash-flow constrained households. With this transformation of future tax cuts into present tax cuts, the nation can consume in line with its new, higher permanent income: the government has transformed future tax cuts into disposable income.

An alternative proposal to handle the same problem has been made by Sam Brittan of the *Financial Times*.[33] His proposal amounts to a capital gift to the private sector by the public sector: the equity in the newly discovered oil riches is transferred to the private sector. If this newly privatized wealth takes the form of marketable financial claims, private spending in line with permanent income is again likely to be encouraged relative to a policy of cutting taxes in line with current oil revenues: the government has transformed future tax cuts into disposable financial wealth.

In this chapter I have used the same symbol T for the present value of the (uncertain) expected streams of future tax payments and receipts, i.e. both for the present value to households of expected future tax payments and for the present value to the government of expected future tax receipts. Similarly, N represented both the household asset and the government liability corresponding to the stream of future benefits.

The presence of an impact on private spending of offsetting changes in, say, T, N, and B^H that would *prima facie* appear to leave household net worth unchanged was then attributed, in a rather *ad hoc* manner, to differences in the liquidity, marketability, and usefulness as collateral of T, N, and B^H. An alternative, but still *ad hoc*, way of avoiding the debt-neutrality conundrum is to assume that households discount future taxes and benefits at a higher rate than the market rate of return on bonds (and at a higher rate than the government discounts its tax revenues and benefit payments). This approach was not adopted here to avoid further growth in the list of symbols and notation. A truly satisfactory treatment of these issues requires the tools of the new microeconomics of credit rationing, collateral, and other capital-market imperfections whose beginnings can be found, for example, in the work of Jaffee and Russell, Benjamin, Webb, and Stiglitz and Weiss.[34]

'Cyclical' corrections to the public-sector deficit

Consider an economy in which the level of economic activity, as measured, for example, by output and employment, cycles around a trend. We do not at this stage assume that these cycles represent Keynesian departures from full employment and normal capacity utilization. They could be regular swings in the natural rate of unemployment.

If we simplify the economy represented by equation (10) even further by ignoring public-sector capital and index-linked bonds, the government budget constraint becomes

$$\frac{\dot{H} + \dot{B}^H}{p} \equiv G^c - \tilde{T} + \left(r + \frac{\dot{p}}{p}\right)\frac{B^H}{p}. \tag{28}$$

$\bar{Y}$, the trend level of output grows at a proportional rate γ. Actual output, Y, cycles steadily around this trend. If the demand for debt is a demand for real debt *per capita*, and if population (in efficiency units) and $\bar{Y}$ grow at the same rate, then government financing will tend to exercise upward pressure on the real interest rate when $(d/dt)(B^H/p\bar{Y}) > 0$ at the given real interest rate and the given real per capita stock of money balances. From (28) we see that

$$\frac{d}{dt}\left(\frac{B^H}{p\bar{Y}}\right) = \frac{G^c - \tilde{\tau}}{\bar{Y}} + (r - \gamma)\frac{B^H}{p\bar{Y}} - \frac{\dot{H}}{p\bar{Y}}. \tag{29}$$

It is a stylized empirical fact that while exhaustive public spending (G^c) tends to grow in line with trend output, taxes net of transfers ($\bar{\tau}$) tend to vary positively with the current level of economic activity. These two relationships can be summarized by

$$G^c = g^c \bar{Y} \qquad 1 > g^c > 0, \tag{30a}$$

$$\bar{\tau} = \theta Y \qquad 1 > \theta > 0. \tag{30b}$$

Substituting (30a, b) into (29) yields

$$\frac{d}{dt}\left(\frac{B^H}{p\bar{Y}}\right) = g^c - \frac{\theta Y}{\bar{Y}} + (r - \delta)\frac{B^H}{p\bar{Y}} - \frac{\dot{H}}{p\bar{Y}}. \tag{31}$$

Similarly, the proportional rate of growth of the money stock, assuming that the authorities keep constant the stock of real bonds per capita or per unit of trend output, is given by

$$\frac{\dot{H}}{H} = V\left(g^c\frac{\bar{Y}}{Y} - \theta + (r - \delta)\frac{B^H}{pY}\right). \tag{32}$$

Thus the current change in $B^H/(p\bar{Y})$ overstates (understates) its trend or long-run average rate of change and the current rate of growth of the nominal money stock overstates (understates) its trend or long-run average rate of growth whenever output is below (above) its trend value.

Even if it is only the current values of $(d/dt)(B^H/p\bar{Y})$ and $\dot{H}/H$ that matter for current crowding-out and current inflation respectively, the trend or long-run behaviour of $d/dt(B^H/p\bar{Y})$ and $\dot{H}/H$—obtained by evaluating (31) and (32) with output at its trend value $\bar{Y}$—will still be of interest to all but the most short-sighted governments.

Furthermore, if current crowding-out is a function of anticipated future changes in $B^H/p\bar{Y}$ and current inflation depends on anticipated future monetary growth (and possibly on past monetary growth as well) current values of $(d/dt)(B^H/p\bar{Y})$ and $\dot{H}/H$ will be a poor proxy for future developments if there are transitory swings in the deficit. From this perspective cyclical corrections are a simple, if *ad hoc*, way of approximating the long-run implications of the fiscal stance for crowding out and monetary growth, i.e., a short-hand way of calculating the permanent deficit.

Evaluating Y and $\bar{Y}$ in (31) and (32) will yield a reasonable approximation to the long-run averages only if the positive and negative deviations of Y from $\bar{Y}$ cancel each other out in the long run, as would be the case, for example, if output followed a regular sinusoidal motion about a trend. If positive and negative deviations of Y from $\bar{Y}$ do not balance on average, the simple cyclical correction will give a biased estimate of the long-run crowding-out pressure and monetary growth implications of the deficit. They will have to be replaced by an explicit averaging of (31) and (32) over long periods of time.

There are good reasons for letting taxes net of transfers vary with the current level of economic activity rather than making them functions of long-run or permanent income. Assume, as seems reasonable, that during the downswing a significant number of private agents are constrained in their spending by current disposable income.[35] By reducing taxes and increasing borrowing during the downswing, public spending during the downswing will be financed to a larger extent by private agents who are not constrained by current disposable income (the purchasers of the bonds). Total consumption will, therefore, decline by less than if taxes (which we assume to fall equally on disposable-income-constrained and permanent-income-constrained private agents) had been kept constant. In the upswing, the additional debt incurred during the downswing can be repaid out of higher than normal taxes.[36] The net result is that consumption is smoothed out over the cycle. This would be desirable on grounds of intertemporal allocative efficiency even if product and factor markets cleared continuously. If there is a wage or price stickiness, Keynesian problems of effective demand failure can occur in addition. Exogenous shocks to demand can set in motion contractionary or expansionary multiplier processes if (some) private agents are constrained in their spending by current disposable income. The usefulness of automatic stabilizers and of countercyclical budget deficits derives from current-disposable-income-constrained private spending and other capital-market imperfections. It is reinforced by output and labour market disequilibrium.

'Cyclical' corrections to the conventionally measured government financial deficits can be significant. Table 4.7 shows some simple but not implausible calculations of the cyclical corrections for eight EC countries. A certain amount of arbitrariness is attached both to the selection of the 'high activity' benchmark years (1973 and 1979) and to the estimate of the rate of growth of high-activity output (the average actual growth rate between the two peak years of 1973 and 1979). There can be little doubt, however, about the importance of the cyclical component in the increase in the government financial deficits between 1979 and the present.

Current disposable income constraints on private consumption need not be absolute. Regular, anticipated cycles in real income do not, of course, imply corresponding cycles in consumption even for individuals who can only borrow on very unfavourable terms in order to consume in excess of their current disposable income. They have the option of accumulating a stock of liquid savings which can be run down and built up again procyclically. Even with uncertain, stochastic swings in the level of economic activity, a buffer stock of liquid financial

TABLE 4.7

The effect of economic activity on general government net borrowing in eight Common Market countries*
(% of GDP)

	Belgium	Denmark	Federal Republic of Germany	France	Ireland	Italy	Netherlands	UK
1970	-0.4	-0.3	-1.8	0.3	0	-0.8	-1.4	0.6
1971	0.1	0.7	-0.9	0.3	0.3	0.3	-0.9	1.1
1972	0.3	0.2	-0.2	0.1	-0.2	0.8	-0.2	1.7
1973	0	0	0	0	0	0	0	0
1974	-1.0	1.7	1.0	-0.1	0	-0.4	-0.3	0.8
1975	0.8	3.4	3.1	1.2	0.9	1.3	1.2	1.8
1976	-0.4	0.9	1.4	0.4	1.6	0.3	0.1	0.9
1977	0.1	0.9	1.1	0.3	0.6	0.6	0.1	0.9
1978	0	0.3	0.7	0.1	-0.7	0.6	0	0
1979	0	0	0	0	0	0	0	0
1980	0	1.2	0.1	0.8	0.9	0.6	1.4	1.4
1981	2.2	2.7	1.3	2.4	2.3	1.7	3.9	3.5

* Actual general government net borrowing minus 'high activity' general government net borrowing as % of GDP. Both 1973 and 1979 were assumed to be 'high activity' years. The trend rate of growth is assumed to equal the average growth rate between these two peak years.

Source: Calculations made by Directorate-General for Economic and Financial Affairs, Commission of the European Communities.

assets may permit a measure of income smoothing. Such private saving strategies are, however, likely to be inferior substitutes for access to borrowing on the terms available to the government.

A further option available to the government is to choose (partial) money financing of cyclical deficit increases rather than borrowing. This option will be more attractive the smaller the number and wealth of private agents that are not constrained by current disposable income and liquidity. The more inelastic the demand for government bonds, the larger the increase in interest rates required to unload additional bond issues on the private sector. (Access to international capital markets may make the total demand for domestic government bonds considerably more interest-elastic than private domestic demand alone.) Such counter-cyclical money issues and withdrawals need not imply any increase in the trend rate of growth of the money stock.

Note that this view of stabilization policy suggests that taxes and transfers, rather than 'exhaustive' public spending on goods and services, should be used to dampen fluctuations in economic activity. Public consumption spending, like all consumption spending, should be smoothed over time in line with permanent income. Public-sector capital formation should have its time profile determined largely by the optimal public-sector consumption programme. Public works and other public spending on goods and services can be effective in regulating the overall level of demand and of economic activity, but are likely to distort the optimal private sector–public sector consumption mix, unlike well-designed changes in the taxation, borrowing, and money-financing mix.

Public-sector asset sales and cosmetic changes in the PSBR

Sales of existing public-sector financial assets do not appear in the SNA public-sector financial surplus, but do appear in the public-sector borrowing requirement (PSBR) and similar transaction records. A 'stock-shift' sale of government-owned natural resources rights $-\mathrm{d}R^{\mathrm{G}}$ or of claims to public enterprise capital $-\mathrm{d}K^{\mathrm{G}}$ to the private sector would not by itself alter public-sector or private-sector net worth. Assuming the government wishes neither to reduce the level of the money stock nor to acquire private-sector capital, the counterpart of a reduction in R^{G} or in K^{G} would be a reduction in B^{H}, $B^{*\mathrm{H}}$, or $\tilde{B}^{\mathrm{H}}$ with $p_{\mathrm{R}}\mathrm{d}R^{\mathrm{G}} + p_{\mathrm{G}}\mathrm{d}K^{\mathrm{G}} = \mathrm{d}B^{\mathrm{H}} + e\mathrm{d}B^{*\mathrm{H}} + p\mathrm{d}\tilde{B}^{\mathrm{H}}$.

There may, of course, be efficiency reasons for wishing to nationalize or denationalize. Total national net worth will be altered by such ownership transfers if the efficiency with which the resources are managed differs between sectors. The financial consequences, however, are virtually nil: bonds in private portfolios are replaced by other financial claims. If the government sells its assets gradually to finance a flow of spending, i.e.

$$p_G \frac{d}{dt} R^G + p_G \frac{d}{dt} K^G < 0,$$

the difference between this policy and one of conventional financing by borrowing is also largely cosmetic.[37] When it borrows, the government incurs an obligation to service the additional debt. When it sells assets, it loses the future income from the assets it sells. It makes little sense, therefore, to attribute economic significance to the distinction between sales of public debt (below the line) and sales of government financial assets (above the line), as is done with PSBR in the United Kingdom.

VII. Conclusion

The general conclusions have been stated in the introduction. In this section I shall confine myself to some more specific and, I hope, practical remarks.

Comprehensive-wealth and permanent-income accounting requires explicit judgments concerning expectations about the future. This arises from the need to evaluate non-marketable and often intangible and merely implicit assets and liabilities, such as future tax and benefit streams. I consider this to be a salutary aspect of comprehensive-wealth accounting. It brings out the distinction between mechanistic book-keeping and recording of transactions, on the one hand, and accounting for economic-policy evaluation and design on the other.

Inflation accounting in the public sector is long overdue. Money illusion in the public sector should cease to be an obstacle to sensible budgetary policy. By themselves, the public-sector financial deficit and the public-sector borrowing requirement (at current or constant prices or as a proportion of GNP) are not very informative statistics. They must be corrected for the change in the real value of the outstanding stocks of interest-bearing public debt to evaluate either the implications of the deficit for financial crowding-out or the 'eventual monetization' implied by the government's fiscal stance. Analogous corrections should be made to the conventionally measured external current-account deficit or surplus to allow for changes in the real value of external assets and liabilities due to changes in the price level and the nominal exchange rate.

To omit government-owned capital and public-sector property rights in land and natural resources from the public-sector balance sheet can give a very misleading picture of the net worth of the public sector and of its present and future fiscal and financial options. This holds true especially for countries where the government owns significant mineral rights (e.g. Norway, the United Kingdom, the United States, and many of the oil-producing nations) and countries in which the nationalized sector accounts for a large share of economic activity (e.g. the United Kingdom and many developing countries). The effect on public-sector net worth of including publicly-owned capital is not self-evident: virtually open-ended commitments to subsidize loss-making public enterprises depress net worth.

The implicit assets and liabilities of the public sector represented by the streams of future tax revenues and of future benefits and transfer payments may well dwarf the marketable financial assets and liabilities in the government balance sheet.

Transitory (e.g. cyclical) deficits and surpluses are a mechanism enabling current-disposable-income-constrained private agents to smooth out consumption and keep it more closely in line with permanent income. By permitting consumption to be maintained in the face of a transitory decline in income, they also mitigate unemployment and excess capacity if price and wage rigidities prevent an instantaneous market-clearing response to demand shocks. It is sound fiscal management for governments to borrow in the downswing 'on behalf of' private agents with less favoured access to capital markets and to retire these countercyclical debt increases during the upswing, regardless of what the rate of inflation happens to be. Alternatively, cyclical increases in the deficit could be financed (partly or wholly) by money creation, to be reversed during the upswing. The optimal financing mix of cyclical (i.e. transitory and reversible) deficits need not be the same as that of permanent deficits.

A consideration of this important issue would require the analysis of specific, detailed models. It is, therefore, well beyond the scope of this chapter, which has tried to focus on general propositions that rely on as few detailed, model-specific properties as possible.

List of symbols

$p_{K\text{soc}}$ price of social overhead capital

p_G price of public enterprise capital

$p_{K\text{p}}$ price of private capital

p_R price of land and natural resource property rights

p domestic general price level

p^* foreign general price level

e nominal exchange rate (domestic currency price of foreign exchange)

i	nominal interest rate on bonds denominated in domestic currency
r	domestic real interest rate
r^G	rate of return on public enterprise capital
ρ^M	non-pecuniary rate of return on money balances
r^R	rate of return from ownership of land and natural resources
r^p	rate of return on private capital
r^{soc}	rate of return on social overhead capital
i^*	nominal interest rate on bonds denominated in foreign currency
r^*	foreign real interest rate
K^{soc}	stock of social overhead capital
K^G	stock of public enterprise capital
R^G	government-owned land and natural resource rights
R^p	privately-owned land and natural resource rights
$\bar{R}$	total natural resource rights
B^H	domestically-held nominal government bonds
B^F	foreign-held nominal government bonds
B^{*H}	domestically-held foreign currency denominated government bonds
B^{*F}	foreign-held foreign currency denominated government bonds
$\tilde{B}^H$	domestically-held index-linked government bonds
$\tilde{B}^F$	foreign-held index-linked government bonds
H	stock of high-powered money
E^*	stock of foreign exchange reserves
N	present value of entitlement programmes
T	present value of tax programmes
L	present value of future expected labour income
W^G	public sector net worth
W^p	private sector net worth
W^F	overseas sector net worth
W	$W^G + W^p = W$
F^H	home-currency-denominated private claims on the overseas sector
F^{*H}	foreign-currency-denominated private claims on the overseas sector

K^{p} private capital stock

A^{M} net value of the government's cash monopoly

G^{soc} government consumption of services of social overhead capital

G^{c} government consumption spending (excluding capital consumption and consumption of imputed services of social-overhead capital)

G^{I} $\dfrac{\mathrm{d}}{\mathrm{d}t}K^{\mathrm{G}}$: net investment in public enterprise capital

τ current taxes

n current transfer and benefit payments

$\tilde{\tau}$ $(\tau - n)/p$

C private consumption

X trade balance surplus, including net international transfer receipts

Y real output

$\bar{Y}$ capacity or trend output

ℓ current labour income

S total national saving

γ natural rate of growth

δ proportional rate of depreciation

V income velocity of circulation of money

$\dot{x} = \dfrac{\mathrm{d}x}{\mathrm{d}t}$

$\hat{x}(s, t)$ value of x expected at t to prevail at s.

Acknowledgements

This chapter was written while I was a visiting scholar in the Fiscal Affairs Department of the International Monetary Fund during August–September 1982. I am indebted to Marcus Miller for unscrambling my thinking on this subject on numerous occasions.

This research is part of the NBER's Programs in International Studies and Financial Markets and Monetary Economics. Financial support from the Leverhulme Trust is gratefully acknowledged. All views expressed are strictly my own.

Notes and Sources

[1] See M. J. Boskin, 'Federal Government Deficits: Some Myths and Realities', *American Economic Review*, Papers and Proceedings, Vol. 72, May 1982, pp. 296–303.

[2] See Marcus Miller, 'Inflation—Adjusting the Public Sector Financial Deficit: Measurement and Implications for Policy', in T. Kay (ed.), *The 1982 Budget*, Blackwell, Oxford, 1982.

[3] Or equivalently by:

$$V^{M}(t) = \int_{t}^{\infty} \frac{H(t)}{\hat{p}(u,\,t)} \hat{\rho}^{M}(u,\,t) \exp\left(-\int_{t}^{u} \hat{r}(s,\,t) \mathrm{d}s \right) \mathrm{d}u.$$

For any variable x, $\hat{x}(s,\,t)$ is the value of x expected at time t to prevail at time s.

[4] Or, equivalently,

$$\Pi^{M}(t) = \int_{t}^{\infty} \frac{\hat{H}(u,\,t)}{\hat{p}(u,\,t)} \exp\left(-\int_{t}^{u} \hat{r}(s,\,t) \mathrm{d}s \right) \mathrm{d}u.$$

[5] It is assumed that for any variable x, $\hat{x}(t_1,\,t_2) = x(t_1)$ for $t_1 \leqslant t_2$: the past and present are assumed known.

[6] See A. F. Ott and J. H. Yoo, 'The Measurement of Government Saving', in G. von Furstenberg (ed.), *The Government and Capital Formation*, Ballinger, Cambridge (Mass.), 1980.

[7] Consumption of the imputed services from social overhead capital can be viewed as a transfer (in kind) from the public sector to the private sector, rather than as an item of public-sector consumption. Alternatively, the services from the stock of public-sector overhead capital could be an input into private production.

[8] No behavioural significance should be attached to the specification of T and N in nominal terms.

[9] Note that $B^{F} = 0$ here.

[10] Clear statements of this proposition can be found in J. Siegel, 'Inflation-induced distortions in government and private saving statistics', *The Review of Economics and Statistics*, February 1979, pp. 83–90, and in C. T. Taylor and A. R. Threadgold, '"Real" National Saving and Its Sectoral Composition', *Bank of England Discussion Paper*, No. 6, London, October 1979. See also W. H. Buiter and M. Miller, 'The Thatcher Experiment: The First Two Years', *Brookings Papers on Economic Activity*, No. 2, Washington D.C., 1981, pp. 315–67, and W. H. Buiter, 'Money, Deficits, Crowding Out and Inflation: The Economic Foundations of the MTFS', paper presented at the Conference on Monetary Policy, Financial Markets and the Real Economy, International Center for Monetary and Banking Studies, Geneva, June 1982.

[11] See W. H. Buiter, 'Deficits, Crowding Out and Inflation: The Simple Analytics', *Centre for Labour Economics Discussion Paper*, No. 143, London School of Economics, December 1982.

[12] It is assumed that borrowing and money creation *per se* do not affect determinants of the demand for public debt other than expected real rates of return.

[13] This is the *ex post* measure. The *ex ante* real yields are defined in terms of the expected rate of inflation.

[14] Money demand is assumed to be unit elastic in income and wealth.

[15] The accounting framework says nothing about whether or not the real interest rate varies with the inflation rate.

[16] For certain purposes, crowding-out pressure per unit of capacity output or crowding-out pressure per unit of efficiency labour is of interest (see, e.g., T. J. Sargent and N. Wallace, 'Some Unpleasant Monetarist Arithmetic', *Federal Reserve Bank of Minnesota Quarterly Review*, Autumn 1981). This would involve replacing (11) by:

$$\frac{\mathrm{d}}{\mathrm{d}t}\left(\frac{\tilde{B} + B^{H}p^{-1}}{Y} \right) = \frac{G^{C} + G^{I} + \delta K^{G} - \tilde{\tau}}{Y} + (r - \gamma)\left(\frac{B^{H}}{pY} + \frac{\tilde{B}^{H}}{Y} \right) - \frac{r^{G}K^{G}}{Y} - \frac{\dot{H}}{pY}.$$

[17] *Source: Economic Trends*, Government Statistical Service, HMSO, London, March 1982.

[18] *Source:* Commission of the European Communities, *Annual Economic Review*, 1982–3.

[19] We continue to make the further simplifying assumptions about the public-sector accounts made earlier in this section of the chapter.

[20] For a discussion of these issues see J. D. Sachs, 'The Current Account and Macroeconomic Adjustment in the 1970s', *Brookings Papers on Economic Activity*, No. 1, Washington D.C., 1981.

[21] The money stock throughout this chapter refers to the high-powered money stock. Adding a private banking sector will, in general, be required for practical applications, but does not alter significantly the conceptual framework outlined here.

[22] That is, deficits corrected for the reduction due to inflation in the real value of the stock of nominal government bonds.

[23] N. Wallace, 'A Modigliani–Miller Theorem for Open Market Operations', *American Economic Review*, Vol. 71, June 1981, pp. 267–74.

[24] W. H. Buiter, 'Comment on T. J. Sargent and N. Wallace: Some Unpleasant Monetarist Arithmetic', NBER Working Paper No. 867, Cambridge (Mass.), March 1982; and 'Money, Deficits, Crowding Out and Inflation: The Economic Foundations of the MTFS', paper presented at the Conference on Monetary Policy, Financial Markets and the Real Economy, International Center for Monetary and Banking Studies, Geneva, June 1982.

[25] The appropriate discount rate may include a risk premium.

[26] If Table 4.4 represents the balance sheet of those private agents currently alive, the horizons involved in N, T, and L would be finite if operative intergenerational bequest motives are absent. N and T in the private balance sheet would, therefore, be smaller than the corresponding items in the public-sector balance sheet, even if public-sector and private-sector discount rates were identical. If there are operative intergenerational bequest motives, or if the private sector is viewed abstractly as containing both current and future generations, an infinite horizon for T, N, and L in Table 4.4 is appropriate. Even with common horizons, different discount rates as between the public and private sectors could lead to changes in private net worth, resulting from changes in the public-sector balance sheet that leave public-sector net worth unchanged. These issues are discussed further in Section VI.2.

[27] See R. J. Barro, 'Are government bonds net wealth?', *Journal of Political Economy*, Vol. 82, 1974, pp. 1095–117; J. Carmichael, *The Role of Government Financial Policy in Economic Growth*, unpublished Ph.D. thesis, Princeton University, 1979; W. H. Buiter, 'Crowding out of private capital formation by government borrowing in the presence of intergenerational gifts and bequests', *Greek Economic Review*, Vol. 2, August 1980, pp. 111–42; W. H. Buiter and J. Tobin, 'Debt neutrality: A brief review of doctrine and evidence', in G. M. von Furstenberg (ed.), *Social Security versus Private Saving*, Ballinger, Cambridge (Mass.), 1979; and J. Tobin and W. H. Buiter, 'Fiscal and Monetary Policies, Capital Formation and Economic Activity', in G. M. von Furstenberg (ed.), *The Government and Capital Formation*, Ballinger, Cambridge (Mass.), 1980.

[28] The Modigliani–Miller theorem for money financing has been established formally for models in which money serves only as a store of value. Such 'money' has only the name in common with what economists have always meant by money, that is, a means of payment or medium of exchange. See. N. Wallace, 1981.

[29] Debt neutrality, i.e. invariance of the solution trajectories of real economic

variables under changes in the borrowing–taxation mix of the government, also requires the taxes to be lump-sum. With non-lump-sum (distortionary) taxes, transfers, and subsidies, public-sector claims on the private sector and private-sector claims on the public sector still are netted out in the balance sheet. Real behaviour will be altered when the borrowing–taxation mix changes because the familiar allocative effects of non-lump-sum taxes, etc., will alter equilibrium prices and rates of return.

[30] The first-best policy of eliminating capital-market imperfections as far as possible, should of course be pursued to the full. Budgetary policies should aim to neutralize those imperfections that cannot be eliminated.

[31] Because governments have the unique power to impose taxes (unrequited transfers to itself) and because of their ability to declare certain of their liabilities legal tender, the risk of default on government bonds is less than that on private debt. Total current and future natural income is in a sense the collateral for government borrowing. National income tends to be much less variable and uncertain than the incomes of individual private agents. Governments effectively pool individual risks and thus eliminate diversifiable risk. An obvious question is why this risk-sharing cannot be done equally well through private insurance markets. One answer is that even if this were possible, it would be more costly than making minor alterations to a tax structure that is required in any case.

A second answer relies on familiar moral-hazard problems in insurance markets. It may be possible to devise efficient private insurance schemes for 'bad-luck' default. Private insurance markets will operate inefficiently (or may not exist at all) if there is frequent 'voluntary' or 'dishonest' default and if lenders and insurers cannot differentiate between dishonest and honest borrowers. If it is easier and less costly for the government to levy taxes on reluctant taxpayers than it is for private lenders and insurers to comel performance by dishonest borrowers, then governments have a role as financial intermediaries and government debt will not be 'neutral'. (See D. C. Webb, 'The net wealth effects of government bonds when credit markets are imperfect', *Economic Journal*, Vol. 91, 1981, pp. 405–14, and 'Default risk in a model of corporate and government finance', *Journal of Public Economics*, Vol. 17, April 1982, pp. 286–306.)

[32] See J. S. Flemming, 'U.K. Macro-Policy Response to Oil Price Shocks of 1974–75 and 1979–80', *European Economic Review*, Vol. 18, May/June 1982, pp. 651–66.

[33] See S. Brittan and B. Riley, 'A People's Stake in North Sea Oil', The Liberal Publications Department, London, 1980.

[34] D. M. Jaffee and T. Russell, 'Imperfect Information, Uncertainty and Credit Rationing', *Quarterly Journal of Economics*, Vol. 90, 1976, pp. 651–66; D. K. Benjamin, 'The Use of Collateral to Enforce Debt Contracts', *Economic Inquiry*, Vol. 16, 1978, pp. 333–59; D. C. Webb, 1981 and 1982; and J. Stiglitz and A. Weiss, 'Credit-Rationing in Markets with Imperfect Information', *American Economic Review*, Vol. 71, June 1981, pp. 393–410.

[35] 'Spending constrained by current disposable income' means that the effect of current disposable income on spending exceeds that of permanent income multiplied by the share of current disposable income in permanent income (allowing for the effect of changes in current income on expectations about future income streams, and evaluating permanent income using government interest rates).

[36] These higher taxes during the upswing fall on a population which, on average, is likely to be less constrained by current disposable income than it was during the downswing.

[37] The earlier caveat about differences in the efficiency with which the assets are managed applies again here.

5

Monetary Policy and Budget Policy: Blend or Dichotomy?
Some Considerations with Special Reference to Recent Italian Experience

RAINER S. MASERA*

Introduction

This chapter considers the interactions between budgetary policy and monetary policy.

It is argued in this respect that the traditional controversy between Keynesianism and monetarism is now largely sterile. This follows primarily from: (i) the broad acceptance of relatively stable demand functions for monetary assets, which should be viewed as an important component of overall financial wealth, (ii) the recognition of the links between monetary and fiscal policy via the government budget constraint, in nominal as well as in real terms, and (iii) the agreement on the non-neutrality of money in the short run.

The view is also advanced that the traditional IS–LM paradigm cannot recapture the stock-flow interactions between wealth, monetary erosion of government debt, the inflation tax (which should be defined net of interest rate payments), and private disposable income. A more satisfactory approach is presented, which identifies the important effects of policy on the private sector via changes in real wealth.

Data are presented showing the importance of the inflation tax in Italy in the 1970s. This tax on financial wealth acted as a means of reducing real disposable income, and ultimately the total real wage bill, in the presence of wage push and a very high degree of indexation of nominal wages to prices. Attention is drawn to the implications for the effectiveness of exchange-rate depreciation. It is also shown that as inflation has gradually come to be anticipated, the yield from the inflation tax has fallen drastically because of the rise in interest rates required by the household sector.

Significant links do exist between monetary and fiscal action. The

* Banca d'Italia.

chapter warns however against some extreme views which have been advanced in the literature, namely the conclusions that bond financing of the deficit is more expansionary than monetary-base financing and that fiscal parameters determine the long-term growth rate of the monetary base. These arguments depend crucially on the assumption that outlays for interest are not matched by any form of revenue, in contrast with other forms of expenditure. This hypothesis is implicitly made when interest-rate payments are singled out as an expenditure item in the budget restraint. The argument is also developed in the Appendix, which shows how an exogenous monetary policy can, under this assumption, automatically lead to instability even if the public deficit net of interest is a constant ratio of GDP. The suggestion made here is that, in terms of long-run analysis, the original formulation of the budget restraint—where interest-rate payments were treated, as other transfer expenditures, on a net aggregate basis in the taxation function—is more satisfactory.

Finally, it is contended that, if the determination of prices and real variables cannot in reality be dichotomized, restrictive policy measures to eradicate inflation should not be based exclusively on control of monetary aggregates and control of credit to the private sector. The real costs of monetary adjustment would be minimized if coherent policy actions were taken in other fields. The case for this approach is made with specific reference to the Italian situation. But it is argued more generally that attempts to build a zone of monetary stability in Europe should also be developed in this framework: monetary and exchange-rate convergence towards low-inflation countries should be supported by direct action aimed at harmonizing the procedures of budget-deficit formation and of the collective-bargaining process —including notably wage-indexation mechanisms.

I. Are we all monetarists now?

To paraphrase Milton Friedman's famous expression, 'We are all Keynesians now', the opposite could well be said to be true today, i.e. We are all monetarists now. Indeed, the two central characteristics of the monetarist model are now commonly inserted in macroeconomic schemes of analysis. The nominal stock of money is basically determined by supply conditions, which are set by the monetary authorities. The real stock of money, on the other hand, is determined in the first instance by demand conditions.

More specifically, the basic distinction made in macroeconomics between real variables and nominal variables now appears to be universally accepted. Moreover, the two approaches also agree that money should be regarded as a stock in a portfolio of total assets: the yield

on money is partly explicit—in respect of sufficiently wide definitions
—and partly implicit, in terms of productive and consumer services
offered.

In addition, the traditional distinction regarding the mechanisms of
transmission of monetary impulses is blurred. In the cash-balance
mechanism (which is associated with the approach of the Cambridge
school, of Walras, and of the 'monetarist' school), when actual money
balances exceed the desired level owing to monetary expansion, they
directly generate increases in real aggregate demand. In the interest-
rates mechanism, associated with the Keynesian school, the monetary
surplus first affects credit instruments, by reducing their yields and
subsequently causing a switch to investments in real assets.

Beyond these extremely simplified illustrations, both monetarists
and Keynesians now agree that the transmission mechanism is hinged
on relative shifts in the yields on all the assets—monetary, financial,
real—in the overall portfolio.

Lastly, it is to be noted that the monetarist school now commonly
accepts the hypothesis of short-term rigidity of prices. This implies that
the transmission of monetary impulses does not follow the classical
model: monetary policy first affects income and employment and only
in the medium term do the effects spread to prices. More generally,
there is now broad agreement that the short-run Phillips' curve is hardly
exploitable for economic-policy purposes, although it is also recognized
that the economy can depart from the natural rate of unemployment
for protracted periods.[1]

Although acceptance of the monetarists' premises is basically correct, in some respects I believe it has been taken too far. In particular,
exaggerated importance has been attributed to a single intermediate
objective of monetary policy, trusting in the accuracy of the behavioural
relations estimated on the basis of experience. It is logically—as well as
empirically—difficult to define a given monetary aggregate for which it
is possible to determine demand that is stable over long periods yet
'robust' enough to allow the dynamic simulations used for the purposes
of monetary control to be sufficiently accurate.[2]

This is not only true for quasi-money aggregates, in respect of which
the entire financial system tends to collapse in the event of strong
uncertainty and variable, but averagely high, interest rates. The concept
of money in terms of transaction balances (M1) is also changing radically at present, particularly in the more sophisticated markets and
notably in the United States. On one hand this is due to the introduction of NOW interest-bearing accounts, and on the other, to systems of
automatic transferral of balances over a given amount at the end of
each working day from traditional current accounts to other deposits
carrying market interest rates.

The difficulty of measuring and defining liquid assets has been aggravated by the rapid expansion of the Euro-markets, which are often not incorporated coherently in the range of definition of the aggregates within individual countries.

The stability of the economy's demand for the monetary base, on which the IS–LM paradigm is really hinged, is the precondition for ensuring—on the supply side—that the chosen nominal stock of money can be effectively controlled and is crucially dependent on institutional factors and on the existence of compulsory reserve requirements: i.e. elements which are not absolute nor uniformly defined, but which depend on contingent factors that change over time.

Finally, the question arises whether, in addition to the relation between money stock and income, it would also be worth examining the relation between credit flow and income, particularly if the financial surpluses and deficits of the various sectors of the economy open up. This is a well-known problem in Italy, although it is now attracting increasing interest abroad as well.[3]

However, I do not wish to dwell on these aspects. Rather my intention is to concentrate on other limitations which affect both the Keynesian scheme and the monetarist model in a dynamic analysis, within the widely accepted models described by the IS and LM curves. By focusing on some 'missing links' I emphasize that dogmatism should be carefully avoided when using econometric relations of demand and supply of a particular monetary aggregate for the purposes of economic policy. This should help to overcome the traditional, but now sterile, controversy of monetarism *v* Keynesianism.

II. The public sector's budget constraint and the wealth of the economy

Economic—and especially monetary—theory is necessarily based on the stylized representation of the economic reality it is to interpret. One can therefore speak of the relativity of theory, in the sense that the phenomena to be measured and explained can have characteristics that vary over time and in space: their analytical representation bases its premises on simplifying hypotheses that are not necessarily unchangeable.

Two such changes have occurred since the end of the 1960s. The overall importance and particularly the borrowing requirement of the public sector have increased substantially in all the major industrialized countries, albeit to different extents; and the average rate of inflation has risen sharply.

This makes it necessary to re-examine some of the simplifying hypotheses often implicitly introduced in both Keynesian and monetarist models by ignoring certain relations. Specifically, direct consideration must be given to the definition of the wealth of the economy in real terms and to the public sector's budget constraint. It is a question, in other words, of correctly integrating stocks of real and financial assets and flows of income and expenditure.[4]

I shall first consider the equations defining wealth at current and constant prices:

$$V = B_M + B + K \qquad (1)$$

$$v = B_M/P + B/P + K/P \qquad (1')$$

where B_M is the stock of monetary base (external money) held by the private sector and issued by the public sector, which for the present analysis includes the central bank; B is the stock of interest-bearing securities issued by the public sector, and K the stock of physical capital at current prices.

Saving is correspondingly defined as change in wealth:

$$S = \Delta V \simeq P\Delta v + v\Delta P = S' + v\Delta P \qquad (2)$$

If the second-order terms are ignored, the change in nominal wealth can be divided into the real change at current prices (S') and the increase in the current value of the previous stock of wealth. The term S' is of special interest since it represents the part of the private sector's disposable income that is allocated to the accumulation of real wealth.

The private sector's budget constraint is given, with the hypotheses formulated, by:

$$S' = Y^d - C \qquad (3)$$

where Y^d = private nominal disposable income and C = private nominal consumption.

The corresponding budget constraint for the public sector is not explicitly introduced in the traditional IS–LM model. On the other hand, recognition has to be given to the fact that the public-sector deficit must always be financed either through the creation of monetary base or through other forms of interest-bearing debt. It is useful to express the constraint, at current prices, as follows:

$$G - T + iB = D = \Delta B_M + \Delta B \qquad (4)$$

The expenditure on goods and services (G) less taxes (T) net of all transfer expenditures, except those connected with interest payments on the public debt (iB), generates the sector's financial balance (D), which is covered by the private sector's acquisition of new money (ΔB_M) and/or securities (ΔB).

The aggregate taxation function, implicitly introduced by expressing the budget constraint as shown in (4), does not envisage revenues designed to guarantee automatic cover of the debt burden. The implications of this formulation will be considered shortly.

As in the case of saving, the flow of investment at current prices (I) has to be defined as the change in the corresponding component of wealth—physical capital. That is

$$I = \Delta K \simeq p\Delta k + k\Delta P = I' + k\Delta P. \tag{5}$$

The traditional equation describing equilibrium in the output (Y) market should therefore be written in nominal terms as follows

$$Y - C - I' - G = 0. \tag{6}$$

The definition of disposable income that is consistent with this scheme is of course different from the traditional one[5] since equations (1), (2), and (3) introduce a link between stocks and flows. As can be easily shown,[6] disposable income is now given by:

$$Y^d = Y - T + (i - \pi)B - \pi B_M \tag{7}$$

where $\pi = \Delta P/P$ is the rate of inflation.

Aggregating the budget constraints of the public and private sectors, we obtain moreover:

$$S' + \pi B_M + \pi B = I' + (G + iB - T) \tag{8}$$

Equations (7) and (8) are two crucial theoretical relations of macroeconomics which none the less are still often ignored.

Equation (7) shows that, in addition to the explicit traditional taxes, account must be taken of a hidden tax on wealth which is levied on the private sector when the monetary erosion of the government debt exceeds interest-rate payments by the government itself. Equation (8) shows that the accumulation of capital plus the public-sector deficit are financed by the private sector's flow of unconsumed income and the monetary erosion of the public sector's total debt.

The hypothesis that saving (or, alternatively, consumption) depends on disposable income corrected for the change in purchasing power of wealth requires the assumption that economic agents are not influenced by money illusion and the hypothesis of consistency between savings plans and the desired accumulation of total wealth. In reality, Hicks,[7] who proposed the IS-LM interpretative model in *Mr. Keynes and the Classics*, suggested nine years later (in *Value and Capital*) a definition of income that logically incorporates the effects described here.

However, as long as public-sector deficits and rates of inflation remained extremely small in practice, the introduction of the complications outlined above would have been useless or even harmful. But, as has been pointed out, the 'stylized facts' of forty, thirty or even twenty years ago are different from those of the last ten years; and to carry on using the traditional schemes in present conditions would lead to serious analytic and economic policy errors.

III. Monetary erosion and the inflation tax in Italy

It is possible to offer an indication of the empirical importance these problems have taken on in Italy by applying the approach described above retrospectively, i.e. by assessing from a purely accounting point of view the amount of monetary erosion and the inflation tax (the latter measured, as mentioned above, net of the flow of interest paid by the public sector).

It is a question of expressing the public sector's budget constraint at constant prices. If we work with annual data, deflate variables in relation to consumer prices (specifically with an index of the average prices, i.e. $P_m = (P_t + P_{t-1})/2$, for the period), and only consider the creation of monetary base directly attributable to the Treasury (BMT), we obtain the following equation:

$$\frac{G - (T - iB)}{P_m} = \Delta\left(\frac{B_{MT} + B}{P_t}\right) + \pi\left[\frac{(B_{MT} + B)_{t-1}}{P_m}\right]$$

$$+ \frac{P_t - P_m}{P_m}\Delta\left(\frac{B_{MT} + B}{P_t}\right). \qquad (9)$$

If equation (9) is solved for the change in the volume (at constant prices) of the stock of public debt during the year, i.e.

$$\Delta\left(\frac{B_{MT} + B}{P_t}\right),$$

one can check that it is equal to the public-sector deficit at constant prices in the period, corrected for the change in purchasing power that the initial stock and the flow of new assets have undergone during the year.

The government can finance its expenditure on goods and services through fiscal revenues and net borrowing. In real terms, as equation (9) shows, public spending has as counterpart (i) explicit traditional taxes (net of transfer payments), plus (ii) the inflation tax on public debt (which is given by the difference between the monetary erosion, i.e. the loss in purchasing power, that the initial stock of debt and the flow of new debt have undergone during the period under consideration, and the flow of interest-rate payments, at constant prices, paid by the public sector) and (iii) the change in the volume of debt over the period.

There is therefore a clear analogy between the traditional analysis in nominal terms and that at constant prices. In the latter càse, however, *total taxes* are made up of two components; in particular, as indicated in equation (7) above, the inflation tax must be correctly measured by allowing for—as a contra item—interest-rate payments on government debt.

Empirical evaluations of the inflation tax vary according to the precise definition of the public sector. In particular, a decision can be made on whether the central bank should be consolidated within the public sector.[8] From many points of view the consolidation approach is desirable; for simplicity's sake however the estimates presented in this study (see Tables 5.1a and 5.1b) give the results obtained in Italy with reference to total net liabilities of the public sector, starting from 1960. Until 1970 monetary erosion of the debt hovered between 0.2% and 1.5% of GNP. Since interest payments were higher than these values, though still below 2% (2.28% in 1971), in reality the 'inflation tax' represented a net transfer of wealth of an average 0.8% of GNP in

TABLE 5.1a

Loss of purchasing power and inflation tax on the public sector's net financial liabilities: 1960-82
(constant 1970 prices)

	Loss of purchasing power (1)	Interest paid by the public sector (2)	Inflation tax (3) = (1) − (2)
1960	106.2	553.8	−447.6
1961	202.5	565.7	−363.2
1962	479.9	582.6	−102.7
1963	521.3	574.4	−53.1
1964	459.8	559.3	−99.5
1965	235.1	607.2	−372.1
1966	317.0	766.7	−449.7
1967	294.8	921.4	−626.6
1968	132.2	997.8	−865.6
1969	602.4	1,107.1	−504.7
1970	942.6	1,252.3	−309.7
1971	910.7	1,471.3	−560.7
1972	1,696.9	1,689.5	+7.4
1973	3,183.6	1,973.1	+1,210.5
1974	6,297.0	2,324.7	+3,972.4
1975	3,401.4	3,007.0	+394.4
1976	6,980.5	3,662.9	+3,317.5
1977	4,570.9	3,907.2	+663.6
1978	4,357.7	5,038.8	−681.1
1979	7,439.9	5,323.7	+2,116.2
1980	8,505.8	5,896.4	+2,609.4
1981	7,505.5	6,929.7	+575.8
1982	8,063.0	7,937.0	+125.0

Source: F. Cotula and R. Masera, 1980, with updated data.

the period 1960-71. Irrespective of the sign, the very low value of the
variables demonstrates that there was no compelling reason to take into
consideration the analytical complications introduced here in the
macroeconomic scheme.

TABLE 5.1b
*Loss of purchasing power and inflation tax on the public sector's
net financial liabilities: 1960-82*
(% of GNP)

	Loss of purchasing power (1)	Interest paid by the public sector (2)	Inflation tax (3) = (1) − (2)
1960	0.29	1.53	−1.24
1961	0.52	1.45	−0.93
1962	1.16	1.40	−0.25
1963	1.19	1.31	−0.12
1964	1.02	1.24	−0.22
1965	0.51	1.31	−0.80
1966	0.64	1.56	−0.91
1967	0.56	1.74	−1.19
1968	0.23	1.77	−1.54
1969	1.01	1.85	−0.85
1970	1.50	1.99	−0.49
1971	1.41	2.28	−0.87
1972	2.54	2.53	+0.01
1973	4.41	2.73	+1.68
1974	8.43	3.11	+5.32
1975	4.70	4.16	+0.55
1976	9.01	4.73	+4.28
1977	5.69	4.87	+0.83
1978	5.20	6.01	−0.81
1979	8.43	6.03	+2.40
1980	9.2	6.3	+2.8
1981	8.2	7.6	+0.6
1982	8.7	8.6	+0.1

Source: F. Cotula and R. Masera, 1980, with updated data.

From 1972 on the situation changes dramatically: inflation tax
truly becomes an additional hidden tax burdening the economy, and
the various aggregates reach values that it is no longer possible to disregard. Monetary erosion of the net debt rises from 2.5% of GNP in
1972 to an average 8.6% in the four years 1979-82. Inflation tax
reaches its highest level in 1974 and 1976 (5.3% and 4.3%, respectively):
the economy suffers in those years the effects of the peaks reached
by the rate of inflation. As, gradually, monetary erosion is anticipated
—or even over-anticipated—the economy demands interest payments

at least high enough to compensate for it.[9] For instance, in 1982, given a loss of around 41,100 billion lire (8.7% of GNP) in the purchasing power of the public sector's net liabilities, interest payments rose to 40,500 billion (8.6%); inflation tax therefore dropped to about 600 billion (0.1%).

It can be argued that the inflation tax provided a means of partial absorption of the basic disequilibria of the Italian economy in the decade of the two oil crises. It may be of some interest to offer some elaboration of this point, which has implications for the role of exchange rates in the adjustment process.

It is commonly held, notably by Corden,[10] that if a depreciation of the domestic currency is accompanied by offsetting rises in money-wages, the expenditure-switching effects of the depreciation cannot manifest themselves. In particular, according to this approach, high-inflation countries displaying this 'real-wage resistance', either because of frequent wage contracts or because of full indexation clauses, would not encounter significant real costs in locking exchange rates and monetary variables *vis-à-vis* strong currency countries.

This argument should however be integrated by allowing for the inflation tax on the private sector's wealth. Even in the limiting case of full indexation of wage flows and income-tax rates (so as to compensate the fiscal drag), the true real-wage bill is affected by depreciation and inflation in so far as disposable income, as defined by equation (7), is reduced by the inflation tax.

If the explicit real wage that is insisted upon by wage earners exceeds the marginal product of labour at full employment, total real wages can be lowered via exchange-rate depreciation and inflation, output can be shifted from domestic to foreign absorption, and the unemployment costs can be reduced, in so far as a resistance does not develop to the inflation tax.

For an evaluation of these points, reference should also be made to the figures reported in Table 5.2, on comparative wage trends in the seven main industrialized countries. As can be seen, notably in nominal but also in real terms, wage push in Italy was far in excess of that experienced in all other countries. This argument would even be reinforced if adjustments were made for productivity trends, after allowance for the loss in the terms of trade, mainly as a consequence of the changes in relative prices of energy.

Under these circumstances the government sector played an increasing role of short-term shock absorber, albeit at the cost of delaying or even impeding structural adjustment: its 'compensatory' interventions included increased transfers to the enterprise sector and to the unemployed. The structural deficit which built up was lowered in real terms by the inflation tax, which ultimately

TABLE 5.2

Wage trends in the seven main industrial countries: 1973–82

Hourly earnings in manufacturing industry
(% change)

Year	Canada	US	Japan	France	FRG	UK	Italy
1973	8.96	7.61	23.52	14.05	10.59	12.83	28.6
1974	13.48	8.25	32.28	18.66	10.76	17.32	23.9
1975	15.93	8.998	15.72	18.11	8.11	29.94	27.4
1976	13.74	8.00	8.74	14.06	6.50	19.84	19.3
1977	10.76	8.56	8.48	12.91	7.28	4.72	26.4
1978	7.33	9.16	5.27	12.93	5.02	18.24	15.3
1979	8.69	8.39	6.09	12.90	5.63	14.93	19
1980	10.04	8.46	7.97	14.91	6.10	17.19	20.3
1981	12.05	9.96	6.54	14.30	5.39	9.74	24.5
1982*	12.25	6.5	6.75	15.75	4.75	10	16.9
Average yearly rate 1973–82	11.3	8.4	11.8	14.8	7.0	15.3	22.1

Consumer prices
(% change)

Year	Canada	US	Japan	France	FRG	UK	Italy
1973	7.52	6.30	11.82	7.36	6.90	9.11	10.80
1974	10.93	10.89	24.33	13.72	7.02	15.99	19.08
1975	10.74	9.17	11.85	11.73	5.93	24.22	16.95
1976	7.5	5.8	9.3	9.6	4.3	16.5	16.8

	Canada	US	Japan	France	FRG	UK	Italy
1977	8	6.521	8.05	9.39	3.64	15.88	17.03
1978	8.95	7.542	3.81	9.09	2.77	8.29	12.14
1979	9.17	11.304	3.58	10.70	4.05	13.40	14.74
1980	10.13	13.491	8.03	13.32	5.53	17.97	21.20
1981	12.42	10.385	4.88	13.34	5.90	11.86	17.82
1982*	10.25	5.75	3.75	13.5	4.5	9.5	16.5
Average yearly rate 1973–82	9.6	8.7	8.8	11.2	5.0	14.2	16.3

Real hourly earnings
(% change)

Year	Canada	US	Japan	France	FRG	UK	Italy
1973	1.33	1.23	10.47	6.23	3.44	3.40	16.06
1974	2.30	−2.37	6.38	4.34	3.49	1.15	4.04
1975	4.69	−.15	3.46	5.71	2.06	4.60	8.92
1976	5.80	2.08	−.51	4.07	2.11	2.87	2.14
1977	2.55	1.92	.40	3.21	3.51	−9.62	7.99
1978	−1.48	1.51	1.40	3.52	2.19	9.18	2.81
1979	−.43	−2.61	2.41	1.98	1.52	1.34	3.71
1980	−.08	−4.42	−.04	1.39	.53	−.66	−.74
1981	−.32	−.37	1.58	.84	−.47	−1.89	5.66
1982*	1.81	.70	2.89	1.98	.23	.45	.34
Average yearly rate 1973–82	1.5	−0.3	2.7	3.2	1.9	0.9	5.0

* Estimates
Sources: National sources and Banca d'Italia calculations.

reduced the true real-wage bill, since it was borne by the household sector.[11]

After the severe losses experienced in the 1970s, the household sector gradually built up a resistance to the inflation tax, in the sense that it commanded increasingly high nominal rates of interest to match the anticipated rate of inflation. As we have seen, the yield from the inflation tax has decreased to almost nothing. And it would be a serious mistake to believe that inflation need only be increased to reobtain a larger yield. All other considerations aside, since most interest-bearing public debt is short term and in any case at variable interest rates, the wealth effects of inflation would be more than off-set by the substitution effect, with adverse consequences on the total yield. It is evident, however, that a careful analysis of nominal interest payments on the public debt, which have become very important from an empirical point of view, is particularly necessary: they contribute to the formation of the overall deficit, but still do not, on average, represent a real net transfer of wealth to the economy.

The analysis and the data presented here naturally do not imply that the propensity to consume in relation to the flow of disposable income defined traditionally should be considered for any period of time equal to that connected with the change in the purchasing power of wealth. This is an empirical question that has to be answered with suitable econometric studies. These, however, are made difficult by the very fact that the perception of—and the reaction to—the changes in the value of capital at constant prices have probably varied over time.

The theoretical model also shows that it would be wrong to believe that the effects of public-deficit spending are only the impact ones commonly summarized by the so-called deficit multipliers. In all likelihood the 'flow effects' of public expenditure are countered with a lag by the 'wealth effects' connected with the changes in stocks of assets at constant prices.

Some reduced form estimations of GDP at constant prices[12] suggest that recently in Italy the public-sector deficit, as traditionally measured, has not been able to support real demand beyond the short term. Better results are obtained by considering the increase in the public debt at constant prices, which evidently follows a very different path from the traditional measure of the current deficit.

In particular, the importance of public expenditure declines and even becomes of uncertain sign when interest payments are included, which confirms the special nature of this type of outlay. As we have seen, it has tended over the last ten years to be associated with the efforts of the economy to restore the real value of the government debt in its possession.

IV. Monetary and fiscal policy

The analytical models described above have important implications for the assessment of the interactions between monetary and fiscal policy and their respective effectiveness. In the first place the budget constraint means that only $n - 1$ of the n economic policy variables can be fixed independently.

It is also obvious that if inflation (disinflation) has to be accompanied by a given rate of change in the money supply, there will be an interaction—via the consequences of the change in the real stock of public debt—between fiscal policy and monetary policy.

Other reasons for interaction can derive from the influence on the total taxation function of interest payments on the stock of interest-bearing public debt. In fact, when the equation (4) formulation of the constraint is adopted mechanically, financing of the deficit with bonds tends to produce a progressive reduction in the effective taxation of the economy and thus creates a permanent increase in disposable income.

In this way macroeconomic analysis of monetary and fiscal policies has led to two conclusions which upset conventional wisdom. On one hand it has been argued (Blinder and Solow)[13] that deficit spending is, apart from impact effects, *more expansionary when financed with securities than with monetary base*. On the other hand, it has been asserted that monetary policy is not independent of fiscal policy. The reverse is indeed true: *fiscal parameters*—public expenditure and tax revenues—*determine the long-term growth rate of the stock of monetary base* (Sargent and Wallace).[14]

Given the constraint represented by equation (11), the first paradox derives immediately from what was said above about the effects that the relative increase in the stock of interest-bearing public debt has on the economy's disposable income. The second only requires the additional assumption that there is an upper limit to the ratio of public debt to national income.

However these results, which would turn conventional wisdom on its head, depend on the implicit hypothesis that no corrections are made to the flow of public expenditure, or, more importantly, to tax revenues as interest payments vary. This does not appear theoretically satisfactory. In the first place it leads to an analytical mingling of monetary policy and fiscal policy that underlies the paradoxical results described above. In the second place the models can be marked by instability of the stationary state at constant prices for certain configurations of the real parameters and those of public finance (see Appendix). This is because in many cases the ratio of the gross public deficit to national income shows an explosive growth since real outlays for interest are not matched by any form of cover, in contrast with other forms of expenditure.[15]

These models are useful, on the other hand, if, correctly interpreted, they persuade those responsible for economic policy not to overlook the need to provide suitable cover[16] for real interest payments on the public debt.

The considerations made so far help in understanding the complex links between monetary and fiscal policy, but they also show, analytically, how the two policies can be made to act independently.

The intermingling is clearly to be seen in the analysis of recent Italian experience, not only with reference to the implications of inflation tax, but even more directly in connection with the formulation of the objectives of economic and monetary policy. The special empirical importance of these phenomena in Italy also stems of course from the fact that of all the major industrial countries Italy has the highest values of the PSBR to GDP ratio, of the share of public-sector borrowing on the credit markets, and, finally, of the ratio of public debt to the outstanding debt of all the other non-financial sectors (see Table 5.3).

In the 1970s the intermediate objectives of monetary policy in Italy consisted primarily of the quantity of credit and liquid assets. More specifically, from 1974 on an objective for total domestic-credit (C_{TD}) expansion was set regularly.

The logical scheme is based on a current-price total flow-of-funds approach which determines the links between the flow of financial assets and the channels of their creation.

$$\Delta A_F - \Delta A_{FE} = \Delta A_{FI} \tag{10}$$

$$\Delta A_{FI} = [\Delta L_{FI} + (G - T)] + B_P = \Delta C_{TD} + B_P \tag{11}$$

where:

A_F = Total financial assets of the private sector.

A_{FE} = Financial claims of the private sector on non-residents

A_{FI} = Financial claims of the private sector on residents

L_{FI} = Financial liabilities of the private sector *vis-à-vis* residents

B_P = Overall (non-monetary) external accounts balance

With a known stable demand equation for financial claims on residents of the private sector (A_{FI}), which is expressed in real terms and which responds *positively* to nominal and real interest rates (in contrast with what happens in the IS–LM scheme for the quantity of money),

TABLE 5.3

Borrowing and outstanding debt of the public sector
in the six main countries[1]

Countries	General government				
	1973	1975	1979	1980	1981
Financial requirement[2]	% of GNP				
United States	1.2	6.2	2.1	3.7	3.2
Japan	3.6	5.1	7.7	8.0	7.7
FRG	0.1	6.6	3.4	3.8	4.8
France	−0.9	2.2	0.6	−0.4	1.6
United Kingdom	5.0	9.5	6.3	5.7	4.5
Italy	10.3	14.2	11.8	10.9	13.2
Borrowing on credit market[3]	% of borrowing on credit market of all domestic non-financial sectors				
United States	11.4	49.1	14.4	26.9	26.8
Japan	12.8	21.1	38.0	37.4	34.6
FRG	17.2	57.6	23.9	29.6	40.6
France	1.1	26.8	14.2	11.6	18.2
United Kingdom	28.3	63.3	44.2	42.5	28.8
Italy	41.1	55.7	55.5	53.3	60.1
Outstanding debt with credit market[4]	% of outstanding debt with credit market of all domestic non-financial sectors				
United States	26.9	28.3	25.6	25.8	25.8
Japan	10.5	13.0	22.2	24.2	25.4
FRG	18.0	22.7	25.3	25.7	27.1
United Kingdom	46.1	49.5	47.6	49.6	48[5]
Italy	42.2	44.7	51.9	52.1	54[5]

[1] BIS estimates using national data based on different concepts from country to country.

[2] Net change in indebtedness and in liquid balances (including borrowing for granting of credit). In the case of France's general government: net credit (−). Figures based on public finance and financial-flows data.

[3] In principle, borrowing in national currency from other sectors, in the form of securities issues and credit from financial institutions. Data based mainly on financial flows.

[4] Excluding shares. For United States, FRG, and Japan, excluding outstanding liabilities otherwise corresponding to credit flows. For the other countries, data partly based on other sources.

[5] Preliminary estimates.

Source: BIS, Annual Report, Basle 1982.

and an objective set in terms of B_P, it is possible to determine a consistent objective in terms of ΔC_{TD}.[17] The domestic-credit approach is thus more directly amenable to *ex-ante* policy co-ordination among countries, with respect to a money-targeting approach.[18] It should be noted that equation (11) has to be seen as simultaneously the condition for equilibrium in both the financial and the real market.[19] In reality, therefore, C_{TD} represents the reference point of overall economic-policy action in an open economy with problems of external equilibrium.

Coherence and rigour are thus needed in setting and respecting the objectives for the two components of C_{TD}: i.e. credit to the economy and the borrowing requirement of the public sector. When—as experienced recently in Italy—the government nominal debt grows at rates of between 25 and 30%, the ratio of public debt to GDP approaches 70%, and the state borrowing requirement comes to represent two-thirds of the expansion in C_{TD}, the stabilization role that the central bank can play encounters serious limitations.

Mutatis mutandis, this is the lesson which can also be drawn from the recent experience in the United Kingdom and the United States. If the Treasury borrowing requirement generates financial assets of the economy at a rate of growth and in a volume which are far larger than those compatible with a non-inflationary growth of money aggregates, an inescapable dilemma is faced. Either portfolio equilibrium is seconded with a monetary growth which feeds inflation or portfolio composition is forced by sufficiently contracting the creation of monetary base. In the latter case, however, private real investment is crowded out, with negative impacts on growth and adjustment. For determinate values of the parameters it is even possible to have situations of unstable equilibrium, as indicated in the Appendix.

V. Further observations concerning the aggregate supply curve

In traditional macroeconomic models the equilibrium level of prices and the unemployment rate derive from the intersection of an aggregate demand curve, summarizing the IS and LM curves, and from a supply equation, which in turn depends on the aggregation of the production function and labour market.

Only in the classical model—or in the context of schemes of rational expectations—can the processes of determination of prices and real variables be separated. Instead it is generally necessary to integrate the analyses in the various markets in order to explain the single variables.

Specifically, whereas inflation is sometimes related only to the relation between the monetary trend and the trend of output or, at the other extreme, is considered exclusively in terms of the interaction between wages and prices, in reality it is necessary to examine simultaneously the process whereby equilibrium is reached in all markets summarizing the economy.

This is the core of present economic theory, around which various conflicting schemes revolve.[20] Without attempting to provide a detailed analysis of this issue, it is important to recognize that modern industrial economies are characterized by different velocities of adjustment in the main markets. Specifically, the reaction in the wages and prices markets is much slower than in the credit and money markets.

These rigidities are aggravated, moreover, by the fact that the areas of adjustment to market mechanisms have been reduced by the very method of operation of the public sector, which has often overstepped its role as a simple buffer against real imbalances. Frequently its shock-absorber effect has been protracted and acquired a structural character that has finally precluded the pursuit of real adjustment, as has been indicated above in the case of Italy.

In this model it is not lack of faith in monetary management but awareness of its limitations in promoting the restoration of basic equilibrium in the entire economy that advises that restrictive measures to eradicate inflation cannot be based *exclusively* on control of money and credit.

As the Governor of the Banca d'Italia concluded in the 1979 Annual Report:[21]

Management of the money stock aimed exclusively at stabilizing its value used to set off a process of adjustment that would last a known time and spread throughout the economy as a vast number of individual adjustments were made; in this process the temporary costs of stabilization were economically, socially, and politically acceptable because they were very widely distributed. Today they would be concentrated in those parts of the economy whose resistance had finally been overcome, perhaps for ever, bringing unemployment to vast areas and broad sections of society and causing the disruption of whole industries, including banking; the economic inequalities would become intolerable.

Theoretical schemes aside, some important links between the evolution of incomes, structural problems of the budget, and conduct of monetary policy are easily observable. For given objectives regarding the containment of inflation and evolution of the monetary base, the level of real interest rates and volume of financing to be allocated to investment will depend on the trend of labour costs and on a reduction of the imbalances in public finances. Virtuous interactions do, in fact, exist between the two components, if the importance of wage expenditures in the public adminstration is taken into account. The real costs of monetary adjustment thus depend on the adoption of coherent actions in the other 'markets'.

These considerations refer specifically to the present Italian situation, but I believe that they are also valid in a larger context.

I am, for instance, convinced that the attempts towards monetary integration and low inflation in the European Community will not succeed until the member states intervene directly in order to harmonize—towards the 'virtuous' end—the procedures of public budget formation and the forms of collective bargaining, including notably wage-indexation mechanisms, as a support to the process of monetary and exchange-rate convergence. Steps in this direction have indeed been recently taken in many EC countries. They are however belated and may not be sufficient.

Appendix*

Budget constraint of the monetary authorities: a simplified dynamic analysis

The purpose of this Appendix is to examine in terms of a simplified model the conditions under which an exogenous monetary policy aimed at ensuring price stability (with money growing at the same rate as real income) can lead to instances of instability via the workings of the government budget constraint. This is formulated, according to current practice, on the assumption that outlays for interest are not matched by any direct form of cover, in contrast to other forms of expenditure. The government deficit, net of interest-rate payments, is assumed to be a constant ratio of GDP.

As is intuitively clear, in this framework the issue of instability is essentially related to the relationship between the rate of growth and the real rate of interest. However, as has been argued in the text, these results depend crucially on the specific formalization of the budget restraint. It is the difference in treatment between interest-rate payments and other transfer payments which leads to the conclusion that bond financing of the deficit is ultimately more expansionary than money financing, and, more generally, to the difficulty of a separate analysis of monetary and fiscal policy. To the present writer these considerations militate in favour of reinstating *for purposes of long-run analysis* the original formulation of the budget restraint, as presented by Ott and Ott and Christ,[22] namely $G - T(Y) = \dot{B}_M + \dot{B}$.

1. Let us rewrite equation (4) in continuous form as follows:

$$G - T + iB = D = \dot{B}_M + \dot{B}. \tag{A1}$$

---

* The author wishes to acknowledge the contributions made to this Appendix by Dr Salvatore Rossi of the Banca d'Italia.

Now let us suppose, for simplicity, that income and the stock of money grow at the same constant rate (n):

$$\dot{Y}/Y = \dot{B}_M/B_M = n \qquad (A2)$$

starting from initial (arbitrary) levels equal to 1.

Let us also assume that the public deficit *net* of interest-rate payments is a constant share of income

$$D_N = G - T = fY \qquad (A3)$$

On these assumptions, the stock of interest-bearing debt would evolve according to the following differential equation:

$$\dot{B} - iB = e^{nt}(f - n) \qquad (A4)$$

where $B_0 > 0$.

2. Let it be noted that equation (4) can also be derived from the model presented in Sargent and Wallace[23] (the formulation with 'quantity theory' demand for money, hereinafter called the S & W model), provided that some simplifying assumptions are made and a constraint is imposed on the (given) initial stock of real public debt.

The S & W model can be presented in the following way, with lower-case characters denoting real variables. If $t \geqslant 1$:

$$B_{Mt}/P_t = h(1 + n)^t, \qquad (A5)$$

$$b_t + k_t = a(1 + n)^t, \qquad (A6)$$

$$\bar{t} = \max\left\{ t \geqslant 2 \mid \forall s \in [2, t] : \tau(s) \leqslant \frac{\theta}{1 + \theta} \right\}, \qquad (A7)$$

$$B_{Mt} = \begin{cases} B_{M1}(1 + \theta)^{t-1} & \text{if } t \leqslant \bar{t}, \\ B_{M1}(1 + \theta)^{t-1} + f \sum_{s=\bar{t}+1}^{t} P_t(1 + n)^s + b_\theta(i - n) \sum_{s=\bar{t}}^{t-1} (1 + n)^s \end{cases}$$

$$\text{if } t > \bar{t}, \qquad (A8)$$

$$dn_t = f(1 + n)^t, \qquad (A9)$$

$$dn_t + ib_{t-1} = (B_{Mt} - B_{Mt-1})/P_t + b_t - b_{t-1}, \qquad (A10)$$

where:

$$dn_t = (G_t - T_t)/P_t, \qquad (A11)$$

$$\tau(t) = \frac{f}{h} + \frac{i-n}{1+n} \frac{\left(\dfrac{f}{h} - A_0\right)(1+i)^{t-1} - \dfrac{a}{h}(1+n)^{t-1}}{(1+i)^{t-1} - (1+n)^{t-1}}, \quad \text{(A12)}$$

$$b_\theta = \left(f - h\frac{\theta}{1+\theta}\right) \sum_{s=0}^{\bar{t}-2} \left(\frac{1+i}{1+n}\right)^s + (f - hA_0)\left(\frac{1+i}{1+n}\right)^{\bar{t}-1}, \quad \text{(A13)}$$

and

$$A_0 = 1 - \frac{B_0 + B_{M0}}{B_{M1}}. \quad \text{(A14)}$$

$B_{Mt}, P_t, b_t, k_t, dn_t, \bar{t}$ are the endogenous variables; $\theta > 0$ is an instrumental variable; and the parameters are subject to the following constraints:

$$h, a > 0; i > n > -1. \quad \text{(A15)}$$

The initial values B_{M0}, B_{M1}, B_0 are supposed to be positive. It is further assumed that:

$$b_0 = h \frac{B_0}{B_{M1}}\left(\frac{1+n}{1+i}\right) \quad \text{(A16)}$$

and

$$1 + i > P_t/P_{t-1}, t \geq 1. \quad \text{(A17)}$$

We note next that (A7) is equivalent to:

$$\bar{t} = \max\{t \geq 2 \mid \forall s \in [2, t] : k_t \geq 0\} \quad \text{(A7')}$$

in fact, $k(t)$ must be non-negative to be economically significant. In turn (A7') can be written as:

$$\bar{t} = \max\left\{t \geq 2 \mid \forall s \in [2, t] : \frac{b_t}{(1+n)^t} \leq a\right\} \quad \text{(A7'')}$$

It is important to note that (A7) requires the following expression to hold for any given θ.

$$\exists t \geq 2 \text{ s.t. } \forall s \in [2, t] : \tau(t) \leq \frac{\theta}{1+\theta}. \quad \text{(A18)}$$

From (A8) and (A13) it follows that:

$$\forall t \geq \bar{t} : \frac{b_t}{(1+n)^t} = \frac{b_{\bar{t}}}{(1+n)^{\bar{t}}} = b_\theta. \quad \text{(A19)}$$

It can be further demonstrated that, if the following inequality holds:

$$A_0 \geqslant \max\left\{\frac{f}{h}\left(\frac{1+i}{i-n}\right), \frac{f-a}{h}\left(\frac{1+n}{1+i}\right) + \frac{f}{h}\right\} \tag{A20}$$

then: $\bar{t} = \infty$.

Let us assume now that (A20) is verified; (A8) becomes simply:

$$B_{Mt} = B_{M1}(1+\theta)^{t-1}, t \geqslant 1. \tag{A8'}$$

We assume next that the monetary authority choose a stationary growth path for money: $\theta = n$, and posit, for simplicity's sake, that:

$$B_{M0} = 1; B_{M1} = 1+n; P_1 = 1. \tag{A21}$$

From (A5) and (A8) we get:

$$P_t = 1/h, t \geqslant 1. \tag{A22}$$

which implies, given (A21), that $h = 1$. Prices now being constant, the model can now be written in continuous form as follows:

$$\forall t \geqslant 0 \begin{cases} B_{Mt} = e^{nt}, \\ fe^{nt} + iB_t = \dot{B}_{Mt} + \dot{B}_t, \\ K_t = ae^{nt} - B_t, \end{cases} \tag{A23}$$

where:

$$B_0 \leqslant \min\left\{n - f(1+n)\left(\frac{1+i}{i-n}\right), n - f(1+n)\left(1 + \frac{1+n}{1+i}\right)\right.$$

$$\left. - a(1+n)\left(\frac{1+n}{1+i}\right)\right\}, \tag{A24}$$

and

$$i > n > 0. \tag{A25}$$

Finally, it is easy to obtain equation (A4) from (A23). The former equation can thus be regarded as a special case of the S & W model.

3. If we denote q the ratio of the gross public deficit to income: $q = (D_N + iB)/Y$, we have:

$$q = f + (i/e^{nt})B \tag{A26}$$

The solution of equations (A4) and (A26) is dependent, in general, upon the value of the parameters i, n, f, as well as B_0.

We obtain, for $n \neq i$:

$$q = f + i\alpha + i(B_0 - \alpha)e^{(i-n)t} \tag{A27}$$

$$B = (B_0 - \alpha)e^{it} + \alpha e^{nt} \qquad \alpha = \frac{f-n}{n-i} \tag{A28}$$

If, on the other hand, $n = i$, we have:

$$q = f + nB_0 + n(f-n)t \tag{A29}$$

$$B = [B_0 + (f-n)t]\,e^{nt} \tag{A30}$$

The possible solutions can be grouped in three categories, as shown in paragraphs 4, 5, and 6 below.

4. All (and the only) cases when the gross public deficit/income ratio shows an *explosive* trend, i.e.:

$$\lim_{t \to \infty} q = +\infty,$$

are the following:

$$i = n < f \tag{a}$$

$$f = n < i \tag{b}$$

$$n < f, i \tag{c}$$

$$f < n < i; B_0 > \alpha \tag{d}$$

It should be noted that, under (c), the dynamics of the stock of debt is described by Figure 5.1. The interest-bearing debt declines in the short run, to take next an 'explosive' path.

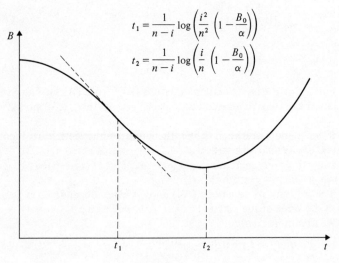

$$t_1 = \frac{1}{n-i} \log\left(\frac{i^2}{n^2}\left(1 - \frac{B_0}{\alpha}\right)\right)$$

$$t_2 = \frac{1}{n-i} \log\left(\frac{i}{n}\left(1 - \frac{B_0}{\alpha}\right)\right)$$

Fig. 5.1

5. The system is instead *stable*, i.e.:

$$\lim_{t \to \infty} q = \bar{q} \, (\bar{q} \in \mathbb{R})$$

when:

$$i = f = n, \tag{e}$$

$$i < f = n, \tag{f}$$

$$i \leqslant f < n, \tag{g}$$

or

$$i < n < f. \tag{h}$$

In case (g), the stock of public debt tends to decline only after a certain period, and vanishes at $t_3 = 1/(n - i)[\log(1 - B_0/\alpha)]$. In this case, if $B_0 > (n - f)/i$, B starts to decrease only after a phase of temporary growth. (See Figure 5.2.)

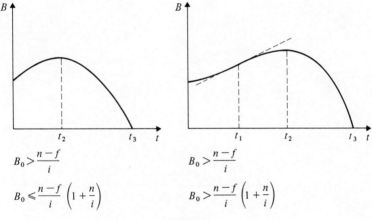

Fig. 5.2

6. Finally, the cases when the public debt outstanding tends to become a net credit *and* the gross deficit tends to *assume negative values* (because of the increasing interest receipts of the public sector), i.e. when $\lim_{t \to \infty} q = -\infty$ are the following:

$$f < i = n, \tag{i}$$

$$f < i < n, \tag{j}$$

and

$$f < n < i; B_0 \leqslant \alpha. \tag{k}$$

Note that in case (k), when $B_0 = \alpha$, q remains constantly equal to $f + i\alpha$.

In the case (i), B becomes equal to zero at $t_4 = B_0/(n - f)$ and q becomes equal to zero at

$$t_5 = \frac{f/n + B_0}{n - f}.$$

In the remaining two cases, B vanishes at t_3 and q at the subsequent point

$$t_6 = \frac{1}{i - n} \log\left(\frac{i\alpha + f}{i\alpha - iB_0}\right).$$

Even in this case there are particular instances when the stock of public debt tends initially to grow. They are described by Figures 5.2 (cases j, k) and 5.3 (case i).

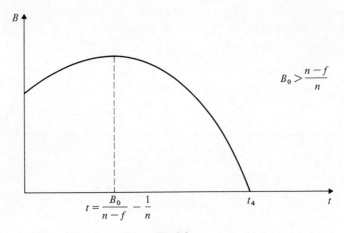

$$B_0 > \frac{n - f}{n}$$

$$t = \frac{B_0}{n - f} - \frac{1}{n}$$

Fig. 5.3

List of symbols

A_F Total financial assets of the private sector

A_{FE} Financial claims of the private sector on non-residents

A_{FI} Financial claims of the private sector on residents

B Private sector's holdings of government bonds, assumed to be (variable-interest rate) bills, in nominal terms

B_M Private sector's holdings of monetary base in nominal terms

B_{MT} Treasury component of total monetary base

B_P Overall (non-monetary) external accounts balance

C Consumption expenditure by the private sector in nominal terms

C_{TD} Stock of total domestic credit

D_N Public deficit net of interest rate payments

f Public deficit net of interest rate payments as share of output

G Nominal government expenditure on goods and services

i Nominal rate of interest on government debt

I Flow of investment (change in physical capital) at current prices

k Real quantity of physical capital

K Stock of physical capital valued at current prices, assuming that the unit value of capital in terms of currently produced goods is unity

L_{FI} Financial liabilities of the private sector *vis-à-vis* residents

n Rate of growth of output

P Price level (end of period)

P_m Average price level (during period)

S Saving defined as change in nominal wealth

S' Variation in the stock of real wealth valued at current prices

t Time

T Nominal government taxes net of transfer payments from the government to the private sector, excluding interest payments on outstanding (interest-bearing) government debt

v Real wealth of the private sector

V Nominal wealth of the private sector

Y Nominal output of the economy

Y^d Private nominal disposable income (defined by adopting the Hicksian correction)

π $\Delta P/P$ = rate of inflation

Notes and sources

[1] Naturally, a hiatus remains between 'monetarists' and 'Keynesians' regarding the assessment of the velocity of adjustment of prices in the various markets,

and notably in the labour market. See, for example, J. R. Hicks, *Economic Perspectives*, Clarendon Press, Oxford, 1977. But the short-term neutrality and the irrelevance of economic policy are results that are now associated with R. E. Lucas's New Classical Approach (*Studies in Business-Cycle Theory*, Blackwell, Oxford, 1981), which starts from the assumption of markets in continuous equilibrium, and not with the traditional monetarist school.

² The continual redefinition of monetary aggregates in the United States is an instance of the reasons for my concern. The question has become particularly important at present, although it is certainly not a new one. M. Friedman and A. J. Schwartz felt it necessary in their latest book (*Monetary Trends in the United States and the United Kingdom*, University of Chicago Press, 1982) to correct the statistics on the stock of money prior to 1903 to take account of the increasing financial sophistication of the economy.

³ Cf., for example, F. Modigliani and J. Papademos, 'Money, Debt and the Monetary Mechanism' an essay presented at the Conference on 'Monetary Theory and Economic Institutions' organized by the European University Institute, Florence, 6–11 September 1982, and the *Bank for International Settlements Annual Report*, 1982, pp. 63–97.

⁴ For a more detailed examination of these points with special reference to Italian experience, see R. Masera, *Disavanzo pubblico e vincolo del bilancio* (Presentazione di P. Baffi), Saggi brevi di economia a cura della Banca Commerciale Italiana, Comunità, Milano, 1979; F. Cotula and R. Masera, 'Private savings, public deficits and the inflation tax', *Review of Economic Conditions in Italy*, No. 3, 1980, pp. 513–45; and. F. Cotula, R. Masera, and G. Morcaldo, 'Il bilancio del settore pubblico e gli effetti di spiazzamento: un esame dell'esperienza italiana' in *Spesa pubblica e Sviluppo dell'Economia*, Saggi brevi di economia a cura della Banca Commerciale Italiana, Comunità, Milano, 1983, pp. 201–93.

⁵ Given the taxation function considered here, the traditional approach would give us:

$$Y^d = Y + iB - T(Y + iB).$$

⁶ By substituting into equation (3), in order, equations (2), (1′), (6), (1), and lastly (4).

⁷ See J. R. Hicks, *Value and Capital*, Clarendon Press, Oxford, 1946, and 'Mr Keynes and the "Classics"; A Suggested Interpretation', *Econometrica*, Vol. 5, 1937, pp. 147–59.

⁸ For an analysis of this argument and an empirical assessment of the relevance of the different approaches with reference to the Italian context, see Cotula, Masera, and Morcaldo, 1983.

⁹ Let it be noted in this respect that the overall government debt is made up of various components, some of which only bear the market rate of interest. Postal savings and monetary-base assets, for instance, pay low or zero rates.

¹⁰ W. M. Corden, *Inflation, Exchange Rates, and the World Economy*, University of Chicago Press, 1981, p. 31.

¹¹ It is not possible to expand on these problems here. The interested reader may refer to R. Masera, 'The Operation of the EMS: a European View', *Economia Internazionale*, Vol. XXXII, No. 4, 1979.

¹² Cf. Cotula, Masera, and Morcaldo, 1983.

¹³ A. Blinder and R. Solow, 'Does Fiscal Policy Matter?', *Journal of Public Economics*, No. 2, 1973, pp. 319–37.

¹⁴ T. Sargent and N. Wallace, 'Some Unpleasant Monetarist Arithmetic', *Federal Reserve Bank of Minneapolis Quarterly Review*, 1981.

[15] Specifically, for the system to be explosive, the real interest rate and the share of income absorbed by the *net* public deficit (excluding interest payments, that is) need not both be lower (and at least one strictly higher) than the rate of growth of the economy. Also in the case in which the ratio to income of the net deficit is lower than the rate of growth of the economy, the system can be explosive if the interest rate is higher than the rate of growth and the initial stock of interest-bearing public securities exceeds a given critical value (see Appendix). For these reasons, theoretically, I think the budget constraint expressed by equation (4) should not be included in the stationary analysis, and prefer the original formulation (*à la* Christ). Cf. R. Masera, *Disavanzo pubblico*, 1979, pp. 54-7.

[16] Coverage need not necessarily be complete, since the equilibrium demand of the economy for public bonds must be taken into account. The fiscal burden of the levy of resources is basically related to the difference between the rate of growth of the economy and the real yield from the debt.

[17] It is clearly sufficient to have stable functions of demand for the different components of AFI in order to do so. On the C_{TD} approach, see F. Cotula, 'Gli obiettivi intermedi della politica monetaria' in *La politica monetaria in Italia: istituti e strumenti*, F. Cotula and P. De Stefani (a cura di), Il Mulino, Bologna, 1979, pp. 465-83, and A. Fazio and S. Lo Faso, 'Il controllo del credito e l'intermediazione finanziaria in Italia', *Economia Italiana*, No. 3, 1981, pp. 457-78.

[18] See R. Masera, *L'Unificazione monetaria e lo SME*, Il Mulino, Bologna, 1980, chapter 1.

[19] F. Cotula, 1979.

[20] Cf., for example, R. E. Lucas, 1981, and J. R. Hicks, 1977.

[21] The Governor's Concluding Remarks, *Annual Report for 1978 of the Banca d'Italia*, Rome, 1979.

[22] D. Ott and A. Ott, 'Budget Balance and Equilibrium Income', *Journal of Finance*, Vol. 20, 1965, pp. 71-7, and C. Christ, 'A Short Run Aggregate Demand Model of the Interdependence and Effects of Monetary and Fiscal Policy with Keynesian and Classical Interest Elasticities', *American Economic Review*, Papers and Proceedings, Vol. 57, 1967.

[23] T. Sargent and N. Wallace, 'Some Unpleasant Monetarist Arithmetic', Section 1.

THE EMS IN PRACTICE

6

Domestic Monetary Control in EC Countries under Different Exchange Rate Regimes: National Concerns and Community Options

HERMANN-JOSEF DUDLER*

Introduction

The last decade and the early 1980s saw a marked revival of the general public's appreciation of the economic importance of money, the political potential of independent central banks, and the internal and external stabilization functions of monetary management. The priority accorded to the fight against inflation throughout the industrialized world and the experience of international monetary disorder seemed to call for powerful corrections which only the monetary authorities could provide.

This secular tendency to enhance the stabilizing role of central banks and monetary management had a characteristic European dimension. 'Bloc' formations of stability-oriented central European countries, notably those linked together through the Common Market, developed exchange-rate mechanisms, such as the 'snake' margin arrangements of 1972 and 1973, which prevented intra-European exchange-rate relationships from disintegrating and provided participant currencies with some measure of protection against external shocks. This more or less spontaneous trend towards European monetary cohesion was greatly reinforced by political efforts and initiatives undertaken under the auspices of the European Communities to provide the Common Market with its own monetary organization and foster European monetary integration. The latest and most important Community move in the direction of a European 'zone of monetary stability' was the launching of the European Monetary System (EMS) in March 1979.

With the EMS now operating for more than five years under the preliminary arrangements of its 'initial phase', a reassessment of the chances and advantages of European monetary integration may be

* Deutsche Bundesbank.

overdue—in particular since a world-wide re-evaluation of the benefits and side-effects of monetary stabilization procedures seems to have come under way. Advocates of progressive European economic and political integration have held out the hope that the EMS could pave the way towards a European exchange-rate and monetary union which, in turn, should strengthen the political cohesion of the European Community. Central banks and monetary officials from European treasuries, on the other hand, have tended to exhibit a somewhat more sceptical and reserved attitude and generally profess the view that monetary mechanisms—seen in isolation—might not be very efficient in promoting the European unification process.

In this chapter an attempt will be made to discuss the long-standing issue of European monetary integration, juxtaposing individual countries' national interests and the basic attitudes of their central bankers and monetary officials on the one hand, and Community initiatives and concerns on the other. The author thus adopts what might be labelled a 'political economy' approach, and places some emphasis on technical and institutional problems associated with the transformation of integration manifestos and political blueprints into monetary operating practice. This analysis would, of course, have to be supplemented by the formal application of the theory of 'optimal currency areas' and political processes and institutions to form a balanced judgment on the prospects and implications of European monetary integration.

Part I succinctly describes the historical evolution of the European monetary integration debate and tentatively assesses to what extent country and Community interests in the field of exchange-rate and domestic monetary management can be reconciled. In this context an attempt is made to identify the more lasting attitudes and preferences of larger and smaller EC countries, which in some respects still appear to be distinctly different.

In Part II concrete monetary co-ordination and integration issues are brought into focus as they present themselves to the eye of the national monetary specialist. This discussion inevitably reflects underlying country concerns and positions, but by viewing them from a narrower technical perspective it can easily be demonstrated that unsettled political conflicts are unlikely to be resolved if they are passed down to the expert level.

I. Domestic monetary policy and exchange-rate management: country and community concerns

Evolution of the monetary integration debate

Co-ordination of domestic monetary policies, the search for a common institutional framework for exchange-rate management, and political initiatives aiming at closer European monetary integration evolved as major Community issues only at an advanced stage of the formation of the European Common Market. The Treaty of Rome does not require member states to provide the Community with its own monetary identity or organization. Moreover, during the first ten years of the Common Market, intra-Community exchange rates derived a high degree of stability from the fairly smooth functioning of the Bretton Woods system, the world-wide defence of the dollar standard, and the progressive strengthening of European countries' external payments positions. Early efforts to promote the idea of a European monetary union or regional monetary bloc[1] gained little serious political support. Information and consultation procedures covering the responsibilities of European central banks were established as early as 1958 and 1964, when the Monetary Committee and the Committee of Central Bank Governors were set up. These rather loose arrangements hardly left any marked imprint on the conduct of member states' financial policies.

More substantive steps in the direction of closer European monetary co-operation were undertaken in the wake of intra-Community exchange-rate disturbances in the late 1960s, the incubation of the dollar devaluation crisis, and the incipient collapse of the Bretton Woods regime. The Barre Plan (1969), the Hague Summit (1969), the Werner Report, and the European Council of Ministers' resolution on the realization by stages of an Economic and Monetary Union (1971) paved the way for embryonic Community undertakings to accord the EC an independent monetary organization. Concrete measures included the agreement between EC central banks on a short-term monetary support system (1970), the introduction of a medium-term financial assistance scheme financed by central banks (1972), the narrowing of margins between European currencies—which was backed up by a very short-term financing facility in EC currencies ('snake in the tunnel', April 1972 to February 1973)—and the joint floating of European currencies ('snake outside the tunnel', March 1973 to March 1979). Fundamental differences dividing polar integrationist schools of thinking among member states, the economic and financial upheavals of the past decade, and the desire of larger EC countries to pursue independent monetary and fiscal policies under flexible exchange-rate arrangements, however, prevented these tentative steps towards a European Monetary Union from reaching an advanced stage.

Following two carefully engineered, but rather unsuccessful, attempts to keep the idea of a European Monetary Union politically alive at the Community level (Tindemans Report 1976, Jenkins initiative 1977), the preparation and launching of the European Monetary System in 1978/9 constituted the most important single step to date towards institutionalizing a process of progressive European monetary integration. The main financial elements of the EMS in its present, prolonged initial phase—the ECU, the exchange-rate arrangements, and the credit mechanisms—could be regarded as the nucleus of a European currency union. In its envisaged final phase, the system would undoubtedly severely limit the freedom of participating countries' central banks and treasuries to manage independently their domestic and external monetary affairs.

After more than five years of operation the EMS seems to have lost much of its original political appeal and momentum. Monetary authorities in most member states—while strictly observing the exchange-rate commitments undertaken under the EMS—apparently still view and define their policy principles and priorities according to national preferences which, on balance, may not have fundamentally changed since the inception of the EMS. In essence, member states still have to choose whether decisive moves towards a currency-area type of European financial integration should finally be undertaken, or whether much less ambitious consultation and technical co-ordination arrangements among national monetary authorities satisfy the needs of the Community. Judging from positions taken by individual member countries on the one hand and Community bodies on the other, the prospects for integration remain rather uncertain.

Community options: instrumental vs. complementary functions of exchange-rate and monetary management

The long-standing debate and controversy over dynamic mechanisms designed to promote European monetary and exchange-rate union and the desire of integrationist political groupings to persuade the Community to develop a distinctive financial personality of its own are rooted in a specific perception of the possible role of firm and irrevocable monetary arrangements in the European unification process. At the lowest level of ambition, intra-European exchange-rate and monetary stability are looked upon as a precondition for preserving the European customs and agricultural union. At the highest level of vision, early steps in the direction of complete monetary integration are envisaged as a potential driving force towards the ultimate formation of a European economic and political union.

These rather optimistic contentions have been seriously questioned by academic and political sceptics who have doubted the integrating power of monetary mechanisms. Adherents of the latter school of thought draw attention to the still existing differences in labour productivity, inflation-proneness, and socio-political cohesion among member states and regard these rifts as serious obstacles to the successful launching of a monetary union. They accordingly perceive monetary integration commitments as merely supplementary or complementary steps which should move in unison with the desired convergence in economic performance and general policy co-ordination. According to this view, the creation of a currency union should be seen as a far distant 'crowning act' accompanying the final stages of economic integration.

While Community organs and bodies, notably the European Parliament and the European Commission, have traditionally tended to lean towards a monetary-integration strategy, public opinion, government administrations, central banks, and politicians in a number of member states have sympathized with the sceptics' view. The EMS arguably includes elements of both strands of thought: its financial characteristics include, albeit in a nutshell, key technical features of a future currency union, while its built-in flexibility with respect to parity realignments, the scope left for the pursuit of national monetary objectives, and the gradual implementation of the system's definitive phase prevent the EMS, for the time being, from passing the 'pseudo-union' stage.[2]

Given the embryonic nature of the EMS, it is not surprising that the European Commission has urged member governments to develop the system beyond its initial phase. Commission interpretations, pronouncements, and initiatives accompanying the first years of the EMS[3] have emphasized the dual role of the exchange-rate and monetary arrangements of the scheme. While increasing convergence of economic performance is regarded as an indispensable precondition for the successful operation of the EMS, intra-European exchange-rate stability is, at the same time, accorded a catalyst function. Since firm exchange-rate arrangements can be expected to impose constraints on the conduct of national economic policies, it is hoped that such commitments would ultimately also serve to facilitate a reduction of differences in economic fundamentals among EC countries.

Moreover it is asserted that stable intra-European exchange-rate relationships safeguard commercial and financial interdependence in the Community and prevent exchange markets from over-reacting to short-term divergencies in member countries' economic policies and performances. There seems to be a mainstream view, widely held among the Commission's economic and financial experts, that the preservation of stable exchange rates primarily rests with national monetary policies. Central banks are therefore more or less continuously urged to closely co-ordinate their actions and policy approaches in the light of EMS exchange-rate commitments and to agree on common intervention and interest-rate strategies with respect to third currencies, notably the US dollar.

Country positions and preferences

It is no secret that EC central banks and treasuries have viewed these suggestions to develop tighter forms of co-operation with scepticism. They have, in effect, shown little inclination to compromise vital aspects of their national monetary sovereignty. The apparent reluctance of the national monetary authorities to breathe life into present EMS arrangements seems to reflect a perception of national interests in which the potential welfare benefits and political gains which might be derived from irreversible monetary integration are not rated very highly compared to the perceived costs.

It is, of course, difficult to identify the positions taken by individual countries. Changes in economic and political conditions, possible differences of view between ministries and central banks, and the almost continuous evolution in economic thinking may prevent countries' attitudes from being completely homogeneous and constant over time. Nevertheless, an attempt is made below to characterize EC member states' more durable preferences with respect to exchange-rate stability and national monetary autonomy, based on official statements, policy actions, and national institutional arrangements since the transition to a world-wide floating exchange-rate regime.

Smaller EC countries

Smaller open economies, such as Belgium, Denmark, Ireland, and the Netherlands,[4] would at first sight appear to be the most likely political candidates to accept the obligations and responsibilities associated with the transition of the EMS to a complete exchange-rate union. These countries have traditionally given high priority to external policy considerations and used the main instruments of monetary policy together with exchange-market intervention to maintain fairly stable exchange-rate relationships with neighbouring countries. The main considerations which lie behind these attitudes seem to be the following:

High trade integration. Intra-European flows of tradable commodities account for a high share of smaller countries' total foreign trade and claim high weights in their GDP. (See Table 6.1.) Against this background, smaller countries emphasize the advantages deriving for their exporters and importers from trading in a stable exchange-rate environment and are anxious to avoid the disruptive changes in economic activity and prices which could result from erratic exchange-rate movements.

Narrow foreign exchange markets. Active trading of smaller currencies is often rather thin. Foreign exchange markets may therefore tend to react excessively to unanticipated 'news' on economic and political

TABLE 6.1
Intra-EC commodity trade in smaller EC countries (at 1980 prices)

Country	Exports to EC		Imports from EC	
	% of Total	GDP	% of Total	GDP
Belgium/Luxembourg	72	39	63	38
Denmark	51	13	49	15
Ireland	75	37	75	48
Netherlands	72	34	54	26

Source: Commission of the European Communities, *European Economy*, No. 12, July 1982.

developments in smaller countries. The authorities in these countries are thus ready to give market participants firm guidance with respect to future exchange-rate developments.

'Strong currency' option. Given the traditional commitment of the Federal Republic of Germany to use monetary policy to preserve a high degree of domestic price stability, smaller EC countries see a particular advantage in linking their currencies closely to the Deutschmark. It is hoped that the 'disciplinary effects' resulting from such commitments will perform an educative role comparable to the persuasive influence on expectations which can be associated with publicly announced money-supply targets in larger economies.

The typical monetary instrument used by smaller central banks for influencing the exchange rate in the short run is the manipulation of short-term money-market rates. In addition, these countries use gross and net credit ceilings or guidelines to limit the growth of domestic bank lending.

It would be rash to conclude from this brief description that the monetary authorities in smaller EC countries already comply *de facto* with typical rules required to establish a complete exchange-rate and monetary union. With the possible exception of Ireland,[5] smaller EC countries tend to block the full integration of their financial asset markets with those abroad and direct their monetary policies —within the constraints imposed on them by their exposed external position—to the pursuit of purely domestic objectives. To this end, undesired liquidity effects from exchange-market intervention are sterilized, capital movements are subjected to restrictions or blocked with the help of a dual exchange-rate system (Belgium), and domestic credit controls are occasionally handled in a selective manner.

Larger EC countries

Larger EC countries gear their monetary policies predominantly to
internal economic goals. Since the second half of the 1970s highest
priority has been given to winding down domestic rates of inflation
with the help of publicly announced intermediate monetary objectives.
France, the Federal Republic, and the United Kingdom have used
broader definitions of the money stock for targeting purposes. The
specific intermediate monetary variables used by these countries are
neither statistically nor economically fully comparable, and they are
implemented through widely differing procedures.

Italy has, at least in principle, also preferred wider monetary
aggregates (such as the monetary base M3 or total financial assets).
However, the authorities' prevalent concern has been the correction of
current-account disequilibria and compliance with conditions attached
to multilateral balance-of-payments assistance granted to Italy during
the 1970s. Total domestic credit has thus become the most important
intermediate target variable in Italy since the middle of the past decade.

Intra-European exchange-rate relationships are closely watched by
the larger EC countries, since extreme movements in bilateral rates
might entail undesired shifts in international trade competitiveness.
However in the event of potential conflict, countries are hardly willing
to allow EC exchange-rate commitments to compromise their longer-
run domestic monetary objectives and ultimate policy goals. Moreover,
larger central banks have shown a strong tendency to offset the
monetary impact of massive exchange-market intervention. The dis-
connection of the pound sterling (1972) and the Italian lira (1973)
from the 'snake in the tunnel', the abstention of these two currencies
from joining the 'snake outside the tunnel' after 1973, and the two
departures of the French franc from the European 'joint float' (in
1974 and 1976) provided good examples of the way in which larger
countries typically responded to perceived conflicts between internal
and external policy requirements during the 1970s.

Among the larger EC countries, *France* may, in principle, have the
strongest preference for stable exchange-rate arrangements—as long as
these seem to be reconcilable with the pursuit of domestic growth and
inflation objectives. However, in the field of domestic monetary
management a high degree of freedom from external constraints is
being sought, and the French authorities use a sophisticated array of
measures and regulatory devices for this purpose. These include large-
scale official and semi-official foreign borrowings, restrictions on international capital movements, administrative control of bank lending and
deposit rates, and selective application of *encadrement du crédit*
instructions.

Following the breakdown of the IMF parity system, *the Federal Republic* showed some willingness to provide a 'hard currency' standard for stability-oriented neighbours (notably the Benelux countries and Austria) and to accept the responsibilities of a 'dominant economy' in the European context, especially when this was felt to be consistent with international trade concerns and wider foreign policy considerations. The independent Bundesbank, on the other hand, has tended to advise against far-reaching exchange-rate and external-credit commitments which could erode its ability to exercise full control over domestic monetary conditions and the rate of inflation. This cautious attitude —which is strongly supported by public and academic opinion in the Federal Republic—was corroborated by the fact that the European 'snake' arrangements occasionally involved the central bank in large-scale exchange-market interventions (see Table 6.2).

TABLE 6.2

Changes in the net external position of the Bundesbank, 1973–8 (DM billion)

Period	Changes in total position	Interventions under 'snake' arrangements*
1973 (Apr.–Dec.)	+6.6	+8.3
1974	−1.6	+0.2
1975	−2.2	−1.8
1976	+8.9	+17.1
1977	+10.5	+1.5
1978	+20.1	+7.9

* Figures are not netted against settlements.
Source: Deutsche Bundesbank.

All larger EC economies are sensitive to excessive variations in third currencies, e.g. interest-rate induced fluctuations of the US dollar, because dollar-denominated world trade prices claim a disproportionately large share in their import bills. Links between larger European currencies provide some degree of fortuitous redistribution (or 'communitarization') of such external price shocks if an individual EC currency is exposed to extreme pressures *vis-à-vis* the dollar. Despite such shared interests and concerns, a common EC dollar strategy has failed to evolve. The Federal Republic, in particular, was hesitant to give its consent to a Community dollar policy, since such an approach was difficult to reconcile with its perceived national interests.

Key obstacles to integration

The foregoing assessment of the policy concerns and preferences which EC countries developed in the course of the past decade and, at least partly, still exhibit at present has revealed powerful constraints on the European integration process. Predominance of domestic monetary objectives and a predilection for a relatively high degree of exchange-rate flexibility or autonomy in the larger EC economies tend to prevent these countries from accepting strongly binding exchange-rate obligations.

The apparent reluctance of the monetary authorities in the Federal Republic to incur high inflation risks by providing a 'hard currency' standard to inflation-prone member states is likely to limit the extent to which stable exchange rates can be used to promote convergence in EC countries' price performance. The application of exchange restrictions, dual exchange rates, and selective credit controls hampers the integration of European financial markets, and cross-country differences in monetary instruments and control procedures could entail destabilizing pressures on intra-Community exchange-rate relationships and interest-rate differentials. Finally, the Deutschmark's exposed position as an international currency (as well as the petro-currency role of sterling) complicates the formation of a uniform Community identity *vis-à-vis* third currencies.

Many of these impediments are bound to block or retard progress towards a European exchange-rate and monetary union in the immediate future. They also tend to militate against closer forms of co-ordination and harmonization of domestic monetary policies in EC member states at the purely technical level. The following sections discuss these institutional aspects of the integration issue in somewhat greater detail.

II. Co-ordination and harmonization of monetary management in EC countries

Institutional infrastructure

The Treaty of Rome requires member states to organize co-operation between their central banks and set up an advisory monetary committee (Article 105). Two committees were established which provide the basic institutional framework for co-ordinating monetary and exchange-rate policies among EC countries: the Committee of Governors of the Central Banks of the Member States of the EC and the Monetary Committee.

The *Committee of Governors*, which was set up in 1964, usually meets monthly, in conjunction with meetings of the Group of Ten Central Bank Governors, held at the Basel headquarters of the Bank for International Settlements. It enjoys a high degree of independence from Community organs and admits representatives of the European Commission only as observers. Its tasks and functions cover monetary issues which typically lie within the responsibility of central bankers.

The *Monetary Committee* was set up in 1958 and is composed of senior officials from EC finance ministries, members of the governing boards of EC central banks, and two Commission representatives. This 'mixed' EC committee also meets monthly to examine monetary and financial developments and payments conditions in member states and in the Community. It reports to the European Council and the Commission and advises Community organs on financial matters, especially exchange-rates and external monetary affairs.

Macroeconomic aspects of monetary co-operation and co-ordination are also considered by the *Economic Policy Committee* of the EC. This committee assists the Commission, among others, in the preparation of Community guidelines for general economic and budgetary policies (Annual Reports and Medium-term Economic Policy Programmes).

The work of the Monetary Committee and the Committee of Governors is assisted by two expert groups. The *Working Party on Harmonization of Monetary Policy Instruments*, which was set up in 1974 as a 'mixed' group consisting of delegates from treasuries and central banks, covers those technical aspects of monetary policy which relate to the interaction of the financial and real sectors of the economy and the choice of instruments, control procedures, and indicators for carrying out national policy objectives. The Harmonization Group is expected to study, in particular, the adequacy and compatibility of existing techniques of monetary control in member states and the possible scope for their harmonization.

A central bank *Group of Experts on Monetary Policy* advises the Committee of Governors on current issues of domestic monetary management and, more recently, the co-ordination of monetary policies in EC countries with special regard to the functioning of the EMS.[6] Since 1978, the Group of Experts has reported twice a year on the compatibility of monetary measures taken by individual EC countries and their conformity with commonly-defined objectives. These reports, which are supplemented by special studies on selected financial topics, are also made available to the Monetary Committee.

The Monetary Committee and the Committee of Governors, which work closely together, perform important technical functions with respect to the current monitoring and management of European exchange rates, the creation and administration of EC credit mechanisms, realignments of EC parities, and the possible identification of common EC positions on international monetary issues.

In the field of domestic monetary control, the work of both committees and their expert groups has undoubtedly contributed greatly to a smooth exchange of information among national monetary officials, facilitated 'demonstration effects' across national borders, and created

a better mutual understanding of national monetary operating procedures and policy constraints. Since the late 1970s, and notably after
the launching of the EMS, the interdependence of national monetary
policies has become a central topic of the discussions held in the two
committees and their expert groups. The institutional setting for
monetary co-operation among EC member states thus appears to be
sufficiently well developed.

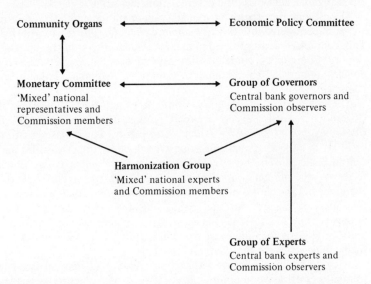

Fig. 6.1. Co-ordination of monetary management in EC countries: institutional
infrastructure

The effective degree of 'hard' co-ordination[7] (in the sense of
domestic monetary actions linked closely to Community mechanisms,
decisions, or directives) which has been achieved through the existing
institutional infrastructure is, nevertheless, still rather low. The European Commission has repeatedly undertaken comprehensive initiatives
to re-invigorate the process of monetary policy co-ordination. In some
cases this has elicited positive reactions from the European Council
(Resolution on European Monetary Union and related Decision on
closer central bank co-operation, 1971; 'Convergence Decision', 1974;
'Stability Directive', 1974; EMS Resolution, 1978). This did not,
however, enable the competent committees to propose or establish
close monetary co-ordinating procedures.

According to Commission proposals and initiatives, national monetary
authorities would ideally consider the following steps:

- prior consultation or 'concertation' of national monetary policy objectives and of major short-run policy adjustments;
- presumption of, among other things, monetary action when an EC currency crosses the EMS 'divergence threshold';
- harmonization of national instruments and techniques of monetary control;
- reconciliation or unification of national monetary-policy bases (preferably using 'domestic credit' as a common indicator) and of domestic intermediate objectives;
- synchronized adoption of common quantitative monetary guidelines.

Such Commission proposals appear logical in the light of an integration philosophy which accords monetary and exchange-rate management an instrumental role in promoting convergence in member states' economic performance. But they clearly run ahead of member countries' present willingness to sacrifice elements of their national monetary independence.

Apart from these fundamental constraints, 'hard' co-ordination proposals also run up against technical and institutional obstacles. These have their origin, in particular, in the inherited differences that exist between member states' economic and financial systems. This impression is corroborated if one looks more closely at the way in which the Harmonization and Monetary Expert Groups and their parent committees considered concrete policy co-ordination and harmonization issues which were brought to the EC monetary infrastructure's attention.

Co-ordination and harmonizaton efforts[8]

In accordance with mainstream economic thinking during the early 1970s and the spirit of the 1974 'Convergence Decision', a Council Directive in 1974 required member states to build up a comprehensive array of monetary instruments with a view to enabling EC central banks to pursue commonly adopted short-run stabilization goals efficiently. (See Appendix B.) With the emphasis shifting away from 'fine tuning' to medium-term policy considerations, co-ordination and harmonization of intermediate monetary objectives became a prominent analytical and statistical Community issue in the second half of the 1970s.

The reconciliation of short-run national operating procedures remained a Community concern in the context of day-to-day monetary and exchange-rate management. With the advent of the EMS, technical conflicts resulting from the co-existence of domestic monetary objectives and exchange-rate commitments evolved as a topical issue in the current work of EC monetary committees and expert groups. Neglecting the time sequence in which the actual technical discussions took

place, the main topics of this debate will be dealt with systematically
—in the framework of the familiar instrument-target methodology—
on the following pages.[9]

Community concerns at the instrument level

In implementing their short-run objectives, EC central banks either rely
primarily on instruments which operate directly on intermediate monetary variables, such as gross or net credit ceilings, or prefer instruments
influencing domestic money-market conditions, such as changes in
official lending rates and measures affecting commercial banks' reserve
positions. (See Table 6.3.) The co-existence of two types of monetary
control procedures—with virtually all smaller countries preferring
direct implementation methods in combination with capital controls—
has at times given rise to conflicts among member central banks.

Smaller EC countries in particular gained the impression that major
policy shifts engineered by a larger central bank, which operates exclusively through the money market, tended to generate avoidable
exchange-rate pressures or destabilizing capital flows. An outstanding
example is the monetary linkages observed between the Netherlands
and the Federal Republic. The former has by tradition closely tied its
currency to the Deutschmark. It was therefore forced to adjust its own
money-market rates whenever FRG short-term interest rates moved or
when the DM/guilder rate came under pressure. (See Figure 6.2.)

Attempts to solve such apparent conflicts through the uniform
introduction of direct credit controls in the Community have not been
successful. On the one hand, it was difficult to prove that—as proclaimed by some countries—direct control procedures produce less
powerful external repercussions than do money market strategies. On
the other hand, the preference given to particular implementation
procedures in individual member states are closely related to specific
financial structures, the division of power between central banks and
treasuries, the relative size and openness of the economy, competition
and allocational effects accompanying the use of particular instruments,
and the typical way in which the monetary authorities react to external
disturbances. Differences in these respects between EC economies help
to explain why member states have shown hardly any inclination to
change and harmonize their monetary control methods in the interest
of the Community.

Reconciliation of intermediate objectives

Technical investigations into the scope for unifying the disparate intermediate monetary objectives used by member central banks have met
with broadly the same institutional obstacles which prevent member
states from adopting fully identical national sets of policy instruments.

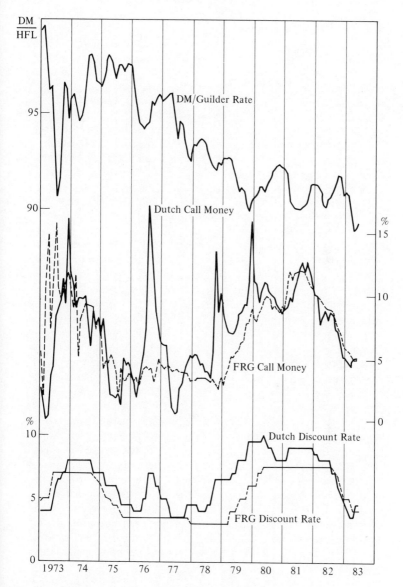

Fig. 6.2. DM/Dutch guilder rate and FRG and Dutch short-term interest rates
(monthly averages)
Source: Deutsche Bundesbank.

TABLE 6.3
The instruments of monetary policy in EC member countries

	Belgium	Denmark	Federal Republic of Germany	Greece	France	Ireland	Italy	Netherlands	United Kingdom
(i) Instrument through which authorities supply the markets with central bank money									
Open market operations: on short-term securities	–	–	in use	–	in use	–	in use	not since 1971	in use
on long-term securities	–	in use[7]	–	–	–	–	in use	–[2]	in use
Rediscounting: rediscount rate	in use	–	in use	in use[6]	in use	not since 1980	in use	in use	–
rediscount quotas	in use	–	in use	in use[6]	not since 1971	–	–	in use	–
Advances	in use	in use[8]	in use	in use	in use	in use	in use	in use	in use
Swaps	–	–	in use	–	in use	in use	not since 1968	in use	–[4]
(ii) Reserve requirements									
Compulsory reserves[1] on deposits	not since 1974	not since 1971	in use	in use	in use	in use	in use	not since 1963	–
on credits	not since 1974	–	–	in use	in use	–	–	–	–
Liquidity ratios as monetary instruments	–	–	–	–	–	in use	–	not since 1979	–

(iii) Measures directly affecting bank assets or liabilities

Gross credit ceilings	not since 1971	not since 1972	in use	–	–	–	not since 1978	in use[9]
Net credit ceilings	–	not since 1982	–	in use	in use	–	–	–
Corset	–	–	in use	–	–	in use	–	–
Minimum holdings of securities	–	–	in use	in use	in use	in use	–	–

(iv) Control of external operations

Special compulsory reserves on non-bank foreign borrowing	–	–	–	–	–	–	not since 1974	not since 1974
Temporary deposits with the central bank on purchase of foreign currency by non-bank residents	–	–	not since 1982	–	–	–	–	–
Regulation of payment of interest on non-resident deposits	not since 1971	not since 1976	–	–	not since 1973	in use	not since 1974	not since 1973
Two-tier market	–	–	not since 1973	–	not since 1974	–	–	in use
Two-tier market for special capital transactions	–	not since 1974	[2]	–	–	–	–	–
Regulation of the external position of banks	in use[5]	not since 1980	in use	in use	in use	in use	[3]	in use

[1] Excluding supplementary reserves to be placed with the central bank if norms under (iii) are not respected.

[2] Not in use.

[3] In the Federal Republic a number of measures have been taken to ward off capital inflows through the banking sector:
— licensing of transactions with non-residents in domestic money-market paper, of repurchase agreements, and of bonds: not in use since 1981;
— special reserve requirements on non-residents' deposits: not in use since 1978;
— withholding tax on non-residents' income from domestic bonds: in use.

[4] But repurchasing of bills, gilts.

[5] Only prudential, not an instrument of monetary policy.

[6] Of limited use for indicative purposes.

[7] Tap sales of government securities.

[8] Subject to quotas.

[9] Credit guidelines since 1980.

Broadly speaking, the financial variables selected in member countries
for targeting or projection purposes relate to either the assets or the
liabilities side of the domestic financial sector or banking system
(see Table 6.4). Credit aggregates, which are preferred by most smaller
countries, comprise at one extreme a large part of total credit outstanding in the economy (Belgium, Italy), or at the other extreme
merely a segment of domestic bank credit (Ireland). The money-stock
measures chosen by larger central banks account for a large share
(France, United Kingdom) or only a small proportion (Germany,
Netherlands) of total bank liabilities.

TABLE 6.4

Intermediate monetary variables used in EC member countries

Country	Variable
Belgium	Total domestic credit expansion
Denmark	Domestic credit expansion
FRG	Central bank money stock*
France	M2*
Ireland	Domestic credit expansion to private sector*
Italy	Total domestic credit expansion*
Netherlands	Money creation from domestic sources*
UK	£M3 (plus M1 and PSL2)*

* Policy objectives. Variables shown for Belgium and
Denmark are forecast or projected.
Source: Commission of the European Communities.

Apart from purely institutional factors, these widely divergent
national choices can at least partly be attributed to the fact that
member countries perceive the monetary transmission process in
opposing conceptual settings. Central bank and government economists from smaller countries (notably Belgium) tend to interpret their
policies in a traditional eclectic framework, while larger central banks
are to some extent influenced by recent monetary thinking. Moreover,
empirical studies undertaken by national experts seem to indicate
that statistically similar money and credit aggregates do not necessarily
perform identical intermediary roles in the different economies.

In Belgium and Italy, for example, the supply of total credit is
believed to stand in a closer relation to expenditures than does the
money stock, especially in the short run. For these reasons, harmonization or reconciliation of national monetary objectives is not thought to
be feasible, at least not for the time being.[10] A large majority of EC
monetary experts seem to agree, however, that quantitative intermediate objectives should be accorded a central role in the co-ordination

of monetary policies as part of an overall economic policy effort to improve convergence.

Technical implications of the EMS for domestic monetary management

The co-existence of firm exchange-rate commitments and national monetary objectives within the EMS has served to deepen member countries' perceptions of potential contradictions between the external and domestic concerns of monetary management. Technically speaking, conflicts of a more durable nature originating from unresolved fundamental differences in economic performance are not necessarily embodied in the system's operating modes, since such tensions can be offset through parity realignments. Monetary experts from EC member countries recognized at an early stage, however, that parity adjustments could easily be delayed owing to political and economic considerations (e.g. concerns over the strength of foreign demand or 'imported' inflation). Some burden of adjustment would therefore always fall on domestic monetary management, especially if other policy instruments could not be geared promptly to external stabilization requirements.

It has so far proved virtually impossible to work out any novel technical rules or procedures which could mitigate such strains or evenly distribute the corresponding monetary adjustment burdens among member countries. Apart from the operational intricacies and analytical complexities involved, perceived conflicts between national interests provide an obvious stumbling-block over which ambitious co-ordination schemes are bound to falter.

Community efforts to build up an 'early warning system' on the basis of economic and monetary performance indicators mostly failed because stability-oriented member countries were reluctant to accept 'Community benchmarks' which seemed to imply that member states' monetary, inflation, and cyclical performances would be gauged against EC 'averages'. There are no firm procedures triggering automatic and symmetrical monetary adjustments if a currency crosses its 'threshold of divergence' under the ECU-basket formula, or if it has to be kept within the permissible fluctuating margins through exchange-market interventions.

There seems to be general agreement that such compulsory interventions hamper the conduct of monetary policy and, in extreme cases, the achievement of intermediate monetary objectives. Most monetary experts seem to be convinced, however, that the 'rules of the game' in the EMS prevent neither deficit nor surplus countries from sterilizing the liquidity impact of intervention through offsetting monetary action. Finally, the transition to commonly agreed domestic bank credit objectives with a view to controlling the 'EC money stock' —an idea which has repeatedly been under discussion—is repudiated by larger countries which still see themselves as being in a position to control the national money supply independently and to keep its expansion consistent with domestic inflation objectives.

Unsolved technical and analytical issues

The foregoing succinct description of expert concerns and deliberations suggests that future progress towards closer forms of monetary policy co-ordination and harmonization could depend, among other things, on the removal of technical and analytical impediments which appear to contribute to the evolution of Community 'deadlock' positions.

It still seems to be unclear among central-bank economists whether more than transitory exchange-market disturbances could result from the use of different monetary operating procedures by larger and smaller member central banks. Unanticipated changes in economic fundamentals, as perceived by market participants, may represent the dominant influence operating on intra-European exchange rates. This could still leave room for the consultation and 'concertation' on important shifts in money-market management initiated by larger central banks to enable smaller countries to cope smoothly with the resulting irritations in their domestic money markets.

The case for developing monetary mechanisms which entail reciprocity or symmetry in the monetary adjustment burdens carried by stronger and weaker EC currencies could be made technically more convincing if it could be proved empirically that financial market integration within Europe has by now become so close that EC central banks should concentrate on credit-supply policies with a view to jointly controlling the aggregate 'EC money stock'. It seems to be obvious—not least from an analytical perspective—that some smaller EC countries may be unable to control their national money stock due to their exposed external position. On the other hand, larger countries—in particular the United Kingdom and the Federal Republic, which issue important international reserve and investment currencies —may interact more closely (through financial asset substitution) with third countries and the Euro-currency market than with other EC economies, all the more so since the latter obstruct international capital flows through regulatory restraints. Against this factual background it may be premature to conclude that all European central banks participating in the EMS should, on purely technical grounds, collectively regulate the EMS area's aggregate money stock through the consistent control of national bank lending activities, while efficient control of the domestic money stock was no longer feasible. For the same reason, measuring and monitoring the 'EC money stock' may, at present, not be analytically meaningful, and amount to no more than a notional exercise cast in suggestive 'Community prose'.

It is also unclear how much the joint pursuit of 'harmonized' money-stock targets could strengthen policy co-ordination among EC central banks. In principle, Community policies directed towards convergence might best be framed in terms of intermediate monetary variables which can be related most consistently to countries' ultimate domestic policy goals and controlled most efficiently by the national monetary authorities. Uniform monetary targets may neither meet these criteria nor enable central banks to pursue co-ordinated stabilization objectives without creating undesirable exchange-market pressures as a possible short-run side-effect. The available econometric evidence[11] points to the existence of significant discrepancies in the short-run interest rate and income elasticities, speeds of adjustment, and stability properties of comparable national money-stock measures. (See Table 6.5.) This would tend to corroborate the view that broadly similar monetary aggregates may represent different types of linkages in the transmission process in individual EC economies. But further empirical studies may be needed before a final judgment can be formed on the useful-ness of Community harmonization efforts in the field of monetary aggregates.

A most difficult analytical problem, for which no acceptable solu-tion may be found at the technical expert level, is the operational reconciliation of national inflation and exchange-rate objectives within the EMS. Inflation-prone economies might be willing to agree to a fairly high degree of exchange-rate stability and reciprocity in monetary policy adjustments. These countries use the EMS exchange-rate con-straint to reinforce their domestic stabilization efforts; they must therefore be opposed to early and frequent parity realignments. Smooth parity changes in the sense of a 'crawling peg' system would obviously imply that divergencies in inflation performance readily become embodied in the EMS parity structure, and that attempts to reverse these discrepancies through the 'disciplinary effects' of stable exchange rates are frustrated.

Economies with the highest stability standards, on the other hand, may tend to aim at maximum flexibility of the system in order to avoid any loss of control over their domestic inflation rate.[12] National infla-tion targets, which member central banks associate with domestic monetary growth objectives, would therefore have to include consistent assumptions on stability 'gains' and 'sacrifices', heeding the Com-munity's collective desire to lower the overall inflation rate. It is not easy to see how the resulting co-ordination problems could be tackled, particularly since a trade-off between inflation and real output objectives may no longer exist. Operating under the 'Pareto principle', the monetary authorities may only be able to bypass such apparent inner contradictions in the EMS if non-monetary Community

TABLE 6.5
*Short-term interest elasticities in money demand functions**

M1

Study	France	FRG	Italy[2]	UK
OECD (1979)[1] (Boughton)	−0.031	−0.014 −0.023 (SD) −0.009 (ED) ————— −0.046	−0.028	−0.045
Own estimates[3]				
(a) Period 1971–81	−0.023	−0.043	−0.10	–
(b) Period 1973–81	−0.022	−0.042	−0.11	−0.057

M2/M3

Study	France (M2)	FRG (M3)	Italy (M3)	UK (M3)
OECD (1979)[1] (Boughton)	−0,024 (SR) +0,026 (SD) ————— +0.002	−0,023	−0.016[4]	−0.102 +0.040 (SD) ————— −0.062
den Butter/Fase (1981)	−0.14[4]	−0.18[4]	−0.27[4]	−0.13[4]
Own estimates[3]				
(a) Period 1971–81	−0.020	−0.024	−0,039	
(b) Period 1975–81	−0,026	−0.017	−0,014	+0,004

* M1: short-term rates (SR), M2/M3: long-term rates (SD = savings deposit rate) (ED = Euro-dollar deposit rate).
[1] Real money demand (uniform lags).
[2] Long-term rate.
[3] See Appendix C.
[4] For M2 nominal (variable lag in den Butter/Fase study).

objectives, which would permit the compensation of potential stability 'losers', could be taken into account.

European monetary co-operation at the crossroads?

Following an initial two-year period, during which the EMS functioned more smoothly than even many optimists had expected, the more recent history of the system seems to have provided ample evidence that the sceptical attitudes which monetary technocrats have exhibited with respect to the integration potential embodied in the EMS are still well founded. The size and frequency of parity realignments have increased during the last three years, and political agreements on new exchange-rate 'grids' have met with growing obstacles.[13]

In the new, less favourable environment, monetary authorities in EC countries could find it increasingly difficult to reconcile domestic and external policy orientations if recently observed strains and tensions within the EMS exchange-rate mechanism were to persist. Pressures within the system may have reached a point at which the integration-promoting 'catalyst' role of stable exchange rates and supportive monetary policies is in danger of being overburdened. In order to preserve the viability of the system, it may be necessary to realistically assess the consistency of member countries' budgetary and incomes policies, their relative cyclical and competitive positions, and EC member states' political readiness and socio-economic capacity for aiming at higher degrees of convergence.

A reassessment of the functioning of the EMS might also have to include a critical look at the future potential of the system for acting as a vehicle for European economic and political unification. As shown in the preceding parts of this chapter, little substantive progress has been made towards European monetary integration since the late 1970s. Inherited differences in monetary policy instruments and approaches persist, and the interdependence of European financial markets has hardly increased. Consultation and co-ordination procedures among EC central banks remain rather 'soft' on the whole, and country interests and concerns regarding longer-term stabilization goals have apparently not been transformed into generally recognized Community objectives.

The inherent flexibility of the EMS exchange-rate mechanism permitted very sizeable adjustments in European central rates during the first four years of its operation and was invoked more frequently following the system's second anniversary. EC countries tend to pursue national exchange-rate objectives, inside and outside the EMS, which entail significantly different degrees of desired exchange-rate stability (as during most of the 1970s). The United Kingdom remains reluctant to accept the ±2.25% EMS margin commitments, while Italy still observes only a wide ±6% maximum spread. Smaller EC countries continue to show a high 'natural' preference for a stable exchange-rate environment. But the large 8½% devaluation of the Belgian franc in early 1982 seemed to indicate that even the traditional 'hard core' of central European currencies gravitating towards the Deutschmark has begun to dissolve.

On the other hand, the experience of destabilizing 'random walks' of larger countries' real dollar exchange rates around their warranted medium-term trend and the widespread disappointment with the functioning of the floating-rate regime suggest that EC countries could hardly be persuaded to leave the determination of intra-European exchange rates entirely to the market mechanism. Exchange-rate adjustments within the EMS were initially effected fairly smoothly and went consistently in one direction. Moreover, during crisis periods larger currencies, in particular the Deutschmark and the French franc, were at least to some extent protected from drastic overadjustments in relation to third currencies. The EMS exchange-rate mechanism provided a certain measure of *ad hoc* 'communitarization' of abnormal exchange-rate shocks originating from shifts in US monetary policy or transitory political disturbances.

A majority of EC countries may therefore be prepared to continue to avail themselves pragmatically of the stabilization chances and flexibility properties embodied in the operational features of the initial phase of the EMS. Following a period of accelerating inflation, during which the system may have served to prevent a self-defeating struggle for competitive currency appreciations, it may protect member countries from the fallacies of excessive monetary expansion and competitive devaluation in the near future. Such a sobering prospect is, admittedly, a far cry from imaginative hopes and expectations that the EMS might quickly be transmuted into a monetary and exchange-rate union. But have not visions of a European monetary identity, which first emerged twenty-five years ago and were preserved during the last two decades, always proved elusive?

Appendix A

Domestic monetary managment during the initial phase of the EMS

The making and inauguration of the EMS (late 1978–March 1979)

In view of the deep-rooted impediments to European monetary integration and the technical and institutional complications which have tended to retard or frustrate the practical implementation of ambitious EC policy co-ordination, harmonization, and convergence schemes for more than a decade, the making and launching of the EMS in 1978/9 may be regarded as a singular political event. It is indeed arguable that the creation of the EMS owed much to a unique economic and geopolitical constellation which was not very likely to persist.[14]

Towards the end of the past decade, several economic factors contributed to strengthening even larger countries' willingness[15] to tie their currencies more closely together: the shared shock experience of the excessively depreciating dollar, the 'atypical' current-account configurations in which notably France, the Federal Republic, and Italy found themselves (see Table 6.6), and a fairly widespread desire to bring inflation rates under control through firm fiscal and monetary

TABLE 6.6
Current account balances of EC countries, 1978–82
($ US billions)

Country	1978	1979	1980	1981	1982
Belgium/Lux.	−0.8	−3.1	−4.9	−4.0	−3.1
Denmark	−1.5	−2.9	−2.5	−1.8	−2.6
France	7.0	5.2	−4.2	−4.7	−12.0
FRG	9.0	−6.1	−15.7	−6.5	3.3
Ireland	−0.5	−1.7	−1.8	−2.2	−1.3
Italy	6.2	5.5	−9.7	−8.1	−5.5
Netherlands	−1.5	−2.1	−2.7	2.9	3.3
UK	2.0	−1.8	6.8	12.0	6.9

Source: OECD, *Economic Outlook*, December 1983.

policies. On the political plane, weaker countries were attracted by the prospect that more generous credit facilities and resource transfers could become available under the new scheme, smaller 'snake' participants were interested in seeing the existing exchange-rate arrangements consolidated in the EMS, and Ireland regarded its participation in the system as a convenient opportunity to cut off its traditional currency link with the United Kingdom. The Federal Republic's desire to strengthen the Atlantic Community, ward off international pressures to accept an economic 'locomotive' role, and foster European political cohesion, together with the strong sense of joint leadership exhibited by the FRG Chancellor and the French President, may have been the decisive political influences that finally tipped the scales in favour of the EMS.

Many of the factors which supported the successful launching of the system were apparently of a highly transient nature. It is therefore not surprising that the underlying, more durable obstacles which stand in the way of progressive European monetary unification quickly came to the surface again once the scheme had to be put into practical operation. Central banks and monetary experts from EC treasuries, who had not been fully consulted when the EMS was politically forged, inevitably injected a sense of hard day-to-day reality, scepticism, and traditional national interest into the scheme when the system began to take shape and entered its initial phase. Recognition of the constraints on countries' monetary independence and the likely reduction of national administrative powers associated with the envisaged evolution of the system may have strengthened the hesitant attitudes shown by many treasuries and central banks, which exhibited little inclination to develop the EMS rapidly beyond the 'pseudo-union' stage.

The 'period of grace' for monetary policies (March 1979–early 1981)

The monetary authorities' delicate task of acquainting themselves with the new system turned out to be easier than expected, since the EMS worked surprisingly smoothly during the first two years of its existence. Italy joined the system under fairly flexible exchange-rate arrangements (it observed a wide ±6% margin around its bilateral central rates) in order to maintain a 'defensible' position, while sterling was not attached to the margin commitments. This may have shortened the period of 'settling-in', since most of the participants had already co-operated closely under the preceding 'snake' arrangements.

Although the new system was exposed to severe external strains (the second oil shock, the volatility and abnormal strength of the dollar, and geopolitical events that placed European currencies at a disadvantage), its internal cohesion was hardly tested seriously during the initial two years. Among the factors contributing to this favourable tendency were the strong competitive and external payments positions with which traditionally weaker currencies entered the EMS, the pronounced weakening of the Deutschmark (which was heavily affected by the Federal Republic's huge current-account deficit), and a shift in monetary authorities' attitudes, which commonly gave highest priority to fighting inflation. The four parity realignments which took place between September 1979 and October 1981 were separated by fairly long periods of exchange-rate stability lasting up to sixteen months, and only two of them were general (see Table 6.7).

Given these relatively favourable overall conditions, domestic monetary management in member states participating in the EMS exchange-rate mechanism was hardly hampered significantly in a technical sense. National monetary targets were met with a fair degree of precision and monetary policy measures taken in defence of exchange rates could be readily unwound or turned out to be compatible with domestic policy considerations.

Speculative capital movements provoked by realignment rumours (upward pressure on the Deutschmark in the summer of 1979, downward pressure on the Deutschmark during the autumn of 1980 and early 1981, downward pressure on the French franc in May 1981) temporarily necessitated large-scale exchange-market intervention, but central banks generally managed to neutralize the resulting liquidity impact smoothly. Similarly, countries facing undesirable capital inflows induced by domestically motivated interest-rate adjustments (Denmark and Italy in 1979, France and Ireland in 1980) managed to cope with these disturbances without sacrificing internal objectives. Major and lasting conflicts between short-run domestic monetary management and

TABLE 6.7
Parity realignments within the EMS

Date	Central rate adjustments
1. 24 Sept. 1979	Deutschmark revalued by 5% against Danish krone and by 2% against other EMS participants
2. 30 Nov. 1979	Danish krone devalued by 5%
3. 22 Mar. 1981	Italian lira devalued by 6%
4. 4 Oct. 1981	Deutschmark and Dutch guilder revalued by 5.5% against Danish krone, Belgian franc, Luxembourg franc, and Irish pound; French franc and Italian lira devalued by 3% against these same currencies
5. 21 Feb. 1982	Belgian franc and Luxembourg franc devalued by 8.5% and Danish krone by 3% against other EMS participants
6. 12 June 1982	Deutschmark and Dutch guilder revalued by 4.25% against Belgian franc, Luxembourg franc, Danish krone, and Irish pound; French franc and Italian lira devalued by 5.75% and 2.75% respectively against the same currencies
7. 21 Mar. 1983	General realignment including revaluations of the Deutschmark (5.5%), the Dutch guilder (3.5%), the Danish krone (2.5%), the Belgian and Luxembourg franc (1.5%), and devaluations of the French franc (2.5%), the Italian lira (2.5%), and the Irish pound (3.5%)

Source: Commission of the European Communities.

EMS exchange-rate commitments were thus hardly in evidence during the first two years of the EMS.

Growing fundamental tensions (early 1981 to date)

Beginning in the first few months of 1981, when the Deutschmark regained its familiar underlying strong position in the European exchange-rate structure, fundamental strains began to build up from within the EMS. With the favourable starting conditions of the system gradually wearing off, inherited discrepancies in EC member countries' economic performances made themselves progressively felt. Although the 'monetary stability' and 'discipline' imparted by the EMS supported member countries' stabilization efforts, inflation and external-payments patterns among EMS participants failed to converge in a durable manner. The United Kingdom, on the other hand, was able to achieve impressive stabilization gains without participating in the exchange-rate mechanism of the EMS (see Tables 6.6 and 6.8).

Three major parity realignments in 1982 and 1983 (see Table 6.7) served to absorb part of the pressure developing in the European exchange market. But the size and frequency of these adjustments and the strained conditions under which they took place tended to erode the confidence of financial markets in the viability of the exchange-rate

TABLE 6.8

Increase in consumer prices in EC countries (%)

Country	1978	1979	1980	1981	1982
Belgium	4.5	4.5	6.6	7.6	8.7
Denmark	10.0	9.6	12.3	11.7	10.1
France	9.1	10.8	13.6	13.4	11.8
FRG	2.7	4.1	5.5	5.9	5.3
Ireland	7.6	13.3	18.2	20.4	17.1
Italy	12.1	14.8	21.2	19.5	16.6
Netherlands	4.1	4.2	6.5	6.7	5.9
UK	8.3	13.4	18.0	11.9	8.6

Source: OECD, *Economic Outlook*, December 1983.

structure. Market suspicions were aggravated by fears that changes in government in France and the Federal Republic could weaken the political consensus and commitment to converging policies on which the EMS had initially been built.

With the general economic environment deteriorating, monetary policies in member countries have increasingly come under strain. Heavy downward pressure on weaker EMS currencies forced central banks in Belgium, France, and Ireland to counter such pressures through large-scale intervention and upward adjustments in short-term interest rates. These actions have tended to unsettle the stance of domestic monetary management. Since intervention funds were to a large extent procured through officially 'organized' foreign borrowing, liquidity management in stronger countries, notably the Federal Republic and the Netherlands, was initially hardly affected by the growing tensions in the system. However, the large-scale official interventions preceding the EMS realignment of March 1983 caused a massive increase in bank liquidity in the Federal Republic, which threatened to erode the Bundesbank's control over domestic monetary conditions. To reduce the increasing adjustment pressure which weaker countries had to accept, exchange restrictions were reinforced in France and Ireland. Nevertheless, interest-rate differentials in the EMS have increased substantially since about the middle of 1981, mirroring the persistent strains to which the system's exchange-rate mechanism has been exposed (see Table 6.9).

TABLE 6.9
EC interest-rate differentials vis-à-vis *the Deutschmark*
(Euro-currency rates, in % p.a.)*

Month	BF	DKR	FF	LIT	HFL	£
1981						
January	3.25	4.90	1.97	8.20	0.25	4.96
February	1.93	2.52	0.33	7.33	−1.18	1.97
March	1.10	1.08	0.20	5.64	−2.06	0.28
April	4.71	2.11	0.84	6.30	−2.03	0.23
May	4.06	2.19	5.17	8.17	−1.11	0.53
June	2.96	3.89	9.49	10.73	−0.74	−0.01
July	3.56	5.40	9.23	14.68	−0.20	1.22
August	3.09	5.40	11.45	18.99	0.92	1.54
September	3.49	6.43	12.28	17.90	0.86	2.60
October	4.15	5.13	7.44	11.52	1.18	4.87
November	4.18	3.42	5.89	9.99	1.02	4.35
December	4.62	3.11	6.26	11.91	0.31	4.66
1982						
January	4.80	3.85	5.75	11.68	0.16	4.83
February	4.56	5.53	5.13	11.38	−0.17	4.27
March	4.58	6.00	9.77	12.95	−0.55	4.08
April	5.78	9.27	13.54	15.36	−0.82	4.61
May	6.08	9.74	15.59	15.00	0.01	4.69
June	6.30	7.68	12.67	12.89	−0.14	4.05
July	5.98	5.30	6.75	11.13	−0.07	3.39
August	5.30	4.63	8.88	11.23	0.03	2.46
September	5.10	9.73	11.37	12.55	0.05	3.04
October	5.53	10.90	11.58	12.23	−0.06	2.50
November	5.39	9.72	11.34	16.13	−0.66	2.20
December	5.88	9.59	16.13	18.38	−0.69	4.19
1983						
January	6.69	10.66	15.53	17.23	−0.57	5.55
February	6.59	9.46	16.34	16.03	−0.81	5.65
March	8.73	8.30	19.41	15.91	−0.69	5.93

* Monthly averages of three-month bid rates at opening of market.
(Euro-currency rates may differ substantially from corresponding
domestic money-market rates for countries which restrict short-term
capital movements.)
Source: Bank for International Settlements.

Appendix B

Council directive (74/121/EEC) of 18 February 1974, on stability, growth, and full employment in the Community

Article 9

Member States shall take the measures necessary to enable them to take prompt action on the various elements covered by the policy of the monetary authorities, particularly money supply, bank liquidity, credit, and interest rates.

For this purpose, Member States shall confer upon their monetary authorities, in so far as the latter do not already have them, at least the instruments and powers to enable them to apply, where necessary, the following measures:

— imposition or modification of reserve ratios applying to the liabilities of monetary institutions;
— imposition or modification of reserve ratios applying to the credit granted by monetary institutions;
— recourse to an open market policy with wide scope for action, including the use, as necessary, of short-, medium- and long-term securities;
— modification of the rediscount ceilings with the central bank;
— modification of the various intervention rates practised by the monetary authorities.

In addition, the monetary authorities shall, as far as possible, be invested with the instruments and powers enabling them to implement the following measures:

— modification of the borrowing and lending interest rates paid or charged by public credit agencies;
— imposition or modification of conditions for consumer credit, hire-purchase sales and mortgage credit;
— quantitative or qualitative credit control.

Appendix C

TABLE 6.10a
Nominal money demand functions for larger EC countries[1]
(a) Narrow definition (M1)

Country	Constant	Money market rate	GNP	Lagged M1	R^2	DW
Period: 1973-81						
France	4.395 (2.00)	−0.022 (3.40)	−0.160 (0.75)	0.807 (6.66)	0.695	1.50
FRG	1.198 (1.37)	−0.042 (6.59)	0.097 (0.68)	0.739 (11.55)	0.914	1.35
Italy	0.051 (0.03)	−0.114[2] (4.02)	0.308 (2.02)	0.720 (6.45)	0.814	1.68
UK	0.407 (0.28)	−0.057 (5.79)	0.122 (1.29)	0.845 (12.77)	0.864	1.68
Period 1971-81						
France	3.593 (1.79)	−0.023 (3.73)	−0.034 (0.19)	0.727 (7.27)	0.686	1.53
FRG	0.648 (0.91)	−0.043 (7.96)	0.183 (1.63)	0.744 (12.71)	0.923	1.29
Italy	0.584 (0.42)	−0.109[2] (4.42)	0.256 (2.96)	0.744 (9.54)	0.815	1.70

[1] Log-linear regressions based on year-on-year changes for quarterly data, ordinary-least-squares estimates (*t*-statistics in brackets).
[2] Bond rate.

Note: A uniform standard specification has been applied for all countries, irrespective of the results achieved, since the main purpose of these estimations was to test for the proposition that comparable money stock concepts represent more or less identical linkages in the monetary transmission process in larger EC countries.

TABLE 6.10b
Nominal money demand functions for larger EC countries[1]
(b) Broad definition (M3/France M2)

Country	Constant	Bond rate	GNP	Lagged M2/M3	R^2	DW
Period:1975–81						
France	4.490 (2.84)	−0.026 (1.68)	−0.340 (1.93)	0.985 (7.02)	0.777	1.43
FRG	1.15 (1.26)	−0.018 (1.59)	−0.043 (0.30)	0.884 (6.10)	0.725	1.59
Italy	1.874 (1.45)	−0.014 (0.63)	−0.172 (2.04)	1.068 (11.90)	0.910	1.89
UK	3.802 (1.03)	0.005 (0.10)	−0.089 (0.60)	0.823 (4.87)	0.651	1.91
Period: 1971–81						
France	4.306 (2.54)	−0.020 (1.27)	−0.192 (1.43)	0.866 (9.57)	0.747	1.61
FRG	0.726 (1.10)	−0.024 (2.21)	0.022 (0.17)	0.893 (7.17)	0.795	1.91
Italy	1.249 (1.33)	−0.039 (2.97)	−0.044 (0.89)	0.986 (15.11)	0.894	1.50

[1] Log-linear regressions based on year-on-year changes for quarterly data, ordinary-least-squares estimates (*t*-statistics in brackets).
[2] Bond rate.

Notes and sources

[1] The most prominent examples were the Triffin proposals [R. Triffin, *Europe and the Money Muddle*, Yale University Press, New Haven (Conn.), 1957, and 'The Return to Convertibility: 1926–1931 and 1958–?, or Convertibility and the Morning After', *Banca Nazionale del Lavoro, Quarterly Review*, No. 48, 1958, pp. 3–57] and the European Commission's *Action Programme of 1962*.

[2] For a theoretical discussion of wider and narrower concepts of a monetary union see W. M. Corden, *Inflation, Exchange Rates and the World Economy*, Clarendon Press, Oxford, 1977, Chapter 10, R. J. McKinnon, *Money in International Exchange*, Oxford University Press, 1979, Chapter 10, and V. Argy, *The Postwar International Monetary Crisis—an Analysis*, Allen & Unwin, London, 1981, Chapter 27.

[3] See in particular 'Documents relating to the European Monetary System', in: Commission of the European Communities, *European Economy*, No. 12, July 1982.

[4] Greece, which joined the EC only recently, will not be covered in this chapter. Given the wide differences in economic performance between Greece and other Community members, Greece is unlikely to undertake firm intra-European exchange-rate commitments in the near future. Moreover, monetary management in Greece is used for domestic allocational purposes and could not be predominantly assigned to external stabilization tasks at the present stage.

[5] Before joining the EMS in 1979, the Irish authorities had for fifty years kept a stable one-for-one currency link with the pound sterling. Control of bank lending is therefore traditionally geared to maintaining a target level of foreign exchange reserves.

[6] This group was initially established in 1973 to prepare quarterly reports on the evolution of the money supply in EC countries, but it lost this function when the monetary guide-lines adopted by the European Council in the early 1970s ceased to be operative.

[7] On this point see M. Emerson, 'European Dimensions in the Adjustment Problems', *Commission of the European Communities, Economic Papers*, No. 5, Brussels, August 1981, pp. 1–4.

[8] In accordance with Community language 'co-ordination' is used to signify the process whereby countries discuss their policy approaches and objectives and adjust them to be compatible. 'Harmonization' is taken to mean that a uniform instrument or concept, such as the broad money stock, is used to define the activity or stance of monetary policy.

[9] The following description is largely based on personal insights gained by the author, who has participated in many expert discussions. The analysis does not, however, include confidential details relating to any country's views and positions.

[10] Despite the sceptical attitudes shown by national experts, Commission analyses are partly based on roughly comparable or 'harmonized' M2/M3 concepts which are used uniformly for all member countries. A composite 'GDP-weighted' money stock variable ('EC M2/M3') has also been constructed. Moreover, the Commission has begun to project key monetary indicator values for individual countries ahead of national targets in an apparent effort to accelerate the policy co-ordination process.

[11] See the studies by J. Boughton, 'Demand for Money in Major OECD Countries', *OECD Occasional Studies*, January 1979, pp. 35–57, F. A. G. den Butter and M. M. G. Fase, 'The Demand for Money in EEC Countries', *Journal of Monetary Economics*, Vol. 8, 1981, pp. 201–30, and the money demand

functions presented in Appendix C. (The results shown in Table 6.5 suggest that measured elasticities can be quite heavily affected by changes in specifications and observation periods.)

   [12] 'The harmonization of inflation rates at a "midway level" would be quite unacceptable to the Federal Republic of Germany; moreover, it would be conducive to a further rise in the average inflation rate in the Communities.—Under the new system . . . necessary changes in central rates must be made in good time and without impediments. The existing differences between Community countries as regards price increase rates and balance of payments trends will in all probability prevent this means of adjusting to highly divergent underlying conditions from being dispensed with for quite a long time to come.' Deutsche Bundesbank, 'The European Monetary System—Structure and Operation', *Monthly Reports of the Deutsche Bundesbank*, March 1979, p. 18.

   [13] A brief description of monetary policy experience under the EMS since 1979 is given in Appendix A.

   [14] This interpretation clearly emerges from the careful examination of the political origins of the EMS by P. Ludlow, *The Making of the European Monetary System*, Butterworths, London, 1982.

   [15] Britain found itself in a peculiar position with sterling emerging as a major petro-currency and domestic monetary policies providing the corner-stone of an ambitious medium-term financial strategy. The British government therefore decided to 'opt out' of the exchange-rate arrangements of the EMS at an early stage.

Additional sources

Borchert, M., 'On the Efficiency of Monetary Policy in the EMS', *Zeitschrift für Wirtschafts- und Sozialwissenschaften*, Vol. 101, 1981, pp. 417-28.

Cohen, B. J., 'The European Monetary System: An Outsider's View', *Princeton Essays in International Finance*, No. 142, International Finance Section, Department of Economics, Princeton University, Princeton (NJ), June 1981.

Dooley, M. and Isard, P., 'A Portfolio-Balance Rational-Expectations Model of the Dollar-Mark Exchange Rate', *Journal of International Economics*, Vol. 12, 1982, pp. 257-76.

Dornbusch, R., 'Exchange Rate Economics: Where Do We Stand?', *Brookings Papers on Economic Activity*, Vol. 1, 1980, pp. 143-85.

Dornbusch, R., 'Equilibrium and Disequilibrium Exchange Rates', paper presented at the *Conference on Monetary Policy, Financial Markets and the Real Economy*, International Center for Monetary and Banking Studies, Geneva, 14-16 June 1982.

Fratianni, M., 'The European Monetary System: A Return to an Adjustable-Peg Arrangement', in K. Brunner and A. H. Meltzer, *Monetary Institutions and the Policy Process*, Vol. 13, North Holland, Amsterdam, 1980, pp. 139-72.

Goodhart, Charles, *Money, Information and Uncertainty*, Macmillan Press, London, 1975.

Hiss, D., 'Zur Stellung des Europäischen Währungssystems in Rahmen des Weltwährungssystems', *Kredit und Kapital*, Vol. 12, 1979, pp. 354-62.

Judd, J. P. and Scadding, J. L., 'The Search for a Stable Money Demand Function: A Survey of the Post-1973 Literature', *Journal of Economic Literature*, Vol. 20, pp. 993-1023.

Kloten, N. 'Zur "Endphase" des Europäischen Währungssystems', in A. Woll, *Internationale Anpassungsprozesse*, Berlin, 1981, pp. 161-93.

Korteweg, P., Position Paper on the EMS, prepared for the *Third Meeting of the Shadow European Economic Policy Committee* (SEEPEC), Paris, 26-8 May 1979.

Laidler, D., 'Concerning Currency Unions', *Zeitschrift für Wirtschafts- und Sozialwissenschaften*, Vol. 99, 1979, pp. 147-62.

Masera, R. S., 'The First Two Years of the EMS: The Exchange-Rate Experience', *Banca Nazionale del Lavoro, Quarterly Review*, No. 138, 1981, pp. 271-89.

McKinnon, R. J., 'Optimum Currency Areas and Natural Variability in Exchange Rates', *Zeitschrift für Wirtschafts- und Sozialwissenschaften*, Vol. 99, 1979, pp. 177-99.

Mussa, M., 'A Model of Exchange Rate Dynamics', *Journal of Political Economy*, Vol. 90, 1982, pp. 74-104.

Padoa-Schioppa, T., 'Problems of Interdependence in a Multipolar World', *Commission of the European Communities, Economic Papers*, No. 4, August 1981.

Rieke, W., 'Die ECU als Bezugsgrösse und Reserveinstrument im EWS', *Kredit und Kapital*, Vol. 12, 1979, pp. 341-53.

Salin, P., *European Monetary Unity: For Whose Benefit?*, Ipswich Press, Ipswich (Mass.), 1980.

Thygesen, N., 'Exchange-Rate Experiences and Policies of Small Countries: Some European Examples of the 1970's', *Princeton Essays in International Finance*, No. 136, December 1979.

Thygesen, N., 'Are Monetary Policies and Performances Converging?', *Banca Nazionale del Lavoro, Quarterly Review*, No..138, 1981, pp. 297-322.

Triffin, R. (ed.), *EMS: The Emerging European Monetary System*, The National Bank of Belgium, Brussels, 1979.

Tsoukalis, L., *The Politics and Economics of European Monetary Integration*, Allen & Unwin, London, 1977.

Vaubel, R., 'The Return to the New European Monetary System: Objectives, Incentives, Perspectives', in K. Brunner and A. H. Meltzer, *Monetary Institutions and the Policy Process*, Vol. 13, North Holland, Amsterdam, 1980, pp. 173-221.

Vaubel, R., 'Logische Implikationen und Anreizwirkungen des europäischen Währungsystems', *Zeitschrift für Wirtschafts- und Sozialwissenschaften*, Vol. 101, 1981, pp. 1-23.

7

Exchange-Rate Policies and Monetary Targets in the EMS Countries

NIELS THYGESEN*

Introduction

The Economist recently introduced a survey of the European Monetary System (EMS) by the following statement:

Europe's visionaries have long wanted the EEC to add monetary union to the customs union it built in the 1960s. So far Europe's politicians have managed something much more modest: a voluntary system of semi-fixed exchange rates, held together by limited central bank co-operation.[1]

While the qualitative difference between a full monetary union and the present state of the EMS is, indeed, enormous, the rest of the statement may make the EMS look a more modest achievement than it really is. There can, of course, be little quarrel with the description of the EMS as 'a voluntary system of semi-fixed exchange rates' in view of the facts that (i) two of the EC member countries—Greece and the United Kingdom—have chosen to remain outside and (ii) seven realignments of EMS central rates have taken place over the five-year period since the system was launched in March 1979. But the relevant standard of comparison for assessing the performance of the EMS is not full monetary union in the sense viewed by the Werner Report of 1970 or other visionaries. Rather it is the likely scenario of events had the EMS not existed, leaving member countries to manage their currencies individually over the past four years.

The turbulent 1979–82 period saw larger divergences for the major individually floating currencies (the dollar, yen, and sterling) from any notion of equilibrium exchange rates than any earlier period of the post-Bretton Woods era. Understandably economists today are reluctant to make precise judgments about what constitutes an equilibrium structure of exchange rates. This contrasts sharply with the confidence with which such a structure was calculated as a basis for the

*University of Copenhagen and Senior Research Fellow, CEPS.

Smithsonian Agreement of 1971. Equilibrium rates were then perceived to be those required to attain a sustainable, mutually acceptable pattern of cyclically-adjusted current-account balances for the main industrial countries over a medium-term horizon, i.e. after changes in relative prices had been given sufficient time, say two to three years, to bring about adjustments of trade flows.

Over the past decade the confidence which inspired these calculations has been eroded by a number of factors: the observed interaction between changes in nominal exchange rates and changes in relative price trends measured in national currencies, the importance of supply shocks with a differential impact on individual economies, the differences between national resource endowments, and the divergences among national objectives for both domestic and external targets. In particular, the observed dependence of equilibrium exchange rates on the constellation of domestic policies and on the policy-mix adopted in each of the countries concerned has taught us that there is a rather wide range of indeterminacy in the notion of equilibrium exchange rates.[2]

With this experience in mind one has to ask how the members of the EMS would have fared if left to manage their currencies individually. It appears overwhelmingly likely that they would have experienced larger movements and greater instability both in their intra-European and their effective exchange rates. To be more specific, the major EMS currency, the Deutschmark, would have taken a deeper plunge in 1980-1 and recovered more sharply than has actually been observed. The weaker, relatively high-inflation currencies of Belgium, Denmark, and Ireland would have been pushed down earlier and more sharply by the political uncertainties surrounding their efforts to reduce their current-account and domestic-budget deficits without the external underpinning provided by membership in the EMS.

This underpinning may usefully be divided into three elements: (i) the credibility of the exchange-rate strategy, (ii) the constraining impact on the domestic policy debate, and (iii) the limitation of the use of the exchange rate as an adjustment mechanism. Since only the third of these elements will be discussed in detail in the following section, a summary of the first two may be appropriate to remind the reader of some of the more obvious and broader implications of EMS membership for the weaker currencies.

The credibility of an exchange-rate commitment is obviously greatly increased by the EMS central banks' mutual obligations to intervene and the automatic credit facilities available over the very short term. No EMS country can easily be pushed off its exchange rate by short-term pressures in the exchange markets. Awareness among potential speculators of this fact, and of the related fact that EMS-membership bolsters the creditworthiness of weak-currency countries in private international markets, and thereby their ability to replenish their foreign-exchange reserves as the need arises, is in itself a strong deterrent to speculation. Though there are examples of successful individual management of pegged currencies in Europe, the EMS countries are less prone to the dangers of having adjustments forced upon them by the market.

The other side to this coin is that to preserve this benefit the context of the domestic debate on economic policy has changed. Policies that depart aggressively from the pattern followed in other EMS countries are more easily discarded, because they are seen to be obviously incompatible with the degree of stability for intra-EMS exchange rates which is aimed for or permitted by the partners. This argument would seem to apply particularly to incomes policies; wage settlements far out of line with those in partner countries become less likely because they would be assumed to lead to a real overvaluation of the exchange rate. But the argument also applies to monetary and fiscal policy; the range of feasible policies is narrowed, and certain adjustments that would have been impossible in the absence of an exchange-rate constraint become possible. This line of reasoning is, it will be easily recognized, that of the so-called 'monetarists' in the debate on Economic and Monetary Union in Europe in the early 1970s. It applies most directly to a Monetary Union, less so to the more permissive system which has evolved with the EMS. But it still changes the context of the domestic political debate, and most observers would, in the light of experience with floating or individually managed currencies, regard the removal of some illusions about policy autonomy as beneficial both to the country itself and to its partners.

The third element is the constructive use of exchange-rate changes, if and when they become necessary. The greater sluggishness of exchange rates has put more of the burden of adjustment on output and employment levels and the instruments of domestic stabilization. Whether this is a net benefit or not has to be assessed carefully in each specific case, with special emphasis on elements of the domestic economic structure which determine the nature of the trade-off between output and inflation stabilization that might have been available to the individual economies.[3]

The only point I wish to make here is that the performances of the EMS economies are likely to have been affected in an important way by the environment offered by the system. The influence has been of far more than the marginal significance suggested by statements such as that quoted initially.

In the following sections I shall review the constraining impact of the EMS under two main headings: (i) the use of exchange-rate adjustments and (ii) co-ordination of domestic monetary policy and the changing role of monetary targets.

I. The use of exchange-rate adjustments

The essence of the EMS is that participants have undertaken to subject their decision-making on exchange rates to a joint consultation
procedure. On the whole this procedure has worked well in the seven
realignments that have taken place between March 1979 and July
1984, which are indicated for reference in Table 7.1.

The seven realignments permit some general conclusions as to the
direction the EMS is taking. In reviewing them briefly I want to go
beyond the more descriptive features such as size, comprehensive-
ness, and implications for competitiveness to a couple of features that
figured prominently in the EMS debate of 1978, namely the nature of
the exchange constraint in the system, notably the element of joint
decision-making in the realignments, and the stabilizing—or destabilizing—impact on capital flows.[4]

As regards the descriptive features, the adjustments of central rates
have tended to grow in size and, possibly, frequency over time. At the
same time, the joint element in the decisions have become more visible.

The first realignment

The first realignment of September 1979 corresponded with the pattern
anticipated at the start of the EMS. The Bundesbank had been intervening on a large scale to sustain both a depreciating dollar (the realignment took place two weeks before the tightening and redesign of US
monetary policy in October 1979) and two weak EMS currencies, the
Belgian franc and the Danish krone. The realignment was modest and in
the end involved only two countries, the Federal Republic of Germany
and Denmark, in a formal change of their ECU central rates.[5]

There was no easy agreement on this first occasion, and the meeting
lasted nearly to dawn, as if to underline that EMS adjustments were not
going to be unilateral or voluntary acts. The problem related to the
Benelux currencies. Although the Belgian franc had been under pressure
and showed increasingly clear 'symptoms of overvaluation', to use the
term of de Grauwe,[6] the Belgian authorities were anxious to stay at
an unchanged DM rate, i.e. to move up with the DM against most of the
other EMS currencies. This would not, however, have relieved tensions
inside the band, where the Belgian franc had been permanently weak
since March, and the move was therefore resisted by the Federal Republic and others.

The Dutch authorities, who had a stronger case for maintaining an
unchanged DM rate in terms of both position inside the band and more
fundamental indicators (inflation rate and current-account position),
were caught in the middle—between their desire to underline
the quality of the guilder as a close substitute for the DM and their

TABLE 7.1
Adjustments of EMS central rates (%)

	BF	Dkr	DM	FF	IR£	Lit.	Dfl
24 Sept. 79	—	—3	+2	—	—	—	—
30 Nov. 79	—	—5	—	—	—	—	—
22 Mar. 81	—	—	—	—	—	—6	—
5 Oct. 81	—	—	+5.5	—3.5	—	—3.5	+5.5
22 Feb. 82	—8.5	—3	—	—	—	—	—
14 June 82	—	—	+4.25	—5.75	—	—2.75	+4.25
21 Mar. 83	+1.5	+2.5	+5.5	—2.5	—3.5	—2.5	+3.5
Cumulative changes *vis-à-vis* EMS countries (approx.)*	—11	—11	+24	—14	—5	—18	+11

* In terms of effective exchange rates (doubly-weighted by trade shares) as calculated by the author.

reluctance to break up the fixity of rates among the Benelux currencies. The latter considerations prevailed, opening the way for the total realignment compromise. But the course of the negotiations underlined the joint nature of the decisions arrived at, strongly suggesting that a different outcome would have been arrived at in the absence of a formal EMS agreement.

The second realignment

The next two realignments were very different being largely unilateral and surrounded by a minimum of formality. In November 1979 the Danish government asked for a 5% devaluation of the krone, not on the basis of urgent pressures in the exchange market (the krone was comfortably stable near the middle of the EMS band), but with reference to the need for. improving competitiveness. The devaluation was seen as part of a package which also comprised temporary and permanent modifications of indexation mechanisms.

No meeting of the Council of Ministers was held to consider the Danish request; it was approved *de facto* by telephone, though subsequently 'ratified' by the participants in a European Council meeting held two days later. The only concern voiced by other EMS members appears to have been whether the realignment would require changes in the price system of the Common Agricultural Policy, laboriously negotiated earlier in the year.

A linkage had been established during the EMS negotiations; indeed, it was this very issue that delayed the implementation of the agreement by three months. But having satisfied themselves that the cumulative effect of the September realignment and the requested Danish devaluation remained below the threshold at which agricultural prices would have to be changed, there was no effort to assess whether the informality of the procedure and the absence of short-term pressures on the initiating currency created a dangerous precedent. To most participants the case was probably seen as a parallel to the occasions during 1976–8 when the participants in the 'snake', the joint float of the Benelux and Scandinavian currencies with the DM which preceded the EMS, had reached similar decisions with a minimum of formality and essentially unilateral justification.

No further changes in EMS central rates were made over the following sixteen months. This period, by far the longest between realignments in the experience to date, was marked by exceptional features favourable to intra-EMS stability, notably the prolonged weakness of the DM, as the Federal Republic's current account swung into unprecedented deficit. In the course of 1979, the FRG had implemented the expansionary fiscal measures urged on her in successive EC and economic summit meetings, while most other European countries were pursuing cautious policies in view of the boost given to their already high inflation rates by the second oil-price shock. This constellation and, particularly, interest differentials favouring the weaker currencies at a time when an early EMS realignment seemed unlikely, even pushed the DM near the floor of the band for some months around the end of 1980, requiring substantial interventions at times.

This abnormal situation came to an end in February 1981 when the Bundesbank tightened monetary policy considerably. The suspension of the Lombard facilities and the sharp rise in short-term interest rates quickly pushed the DM to the top of the band and into interventions in support of the Belgian franc, while the inherent weakness of most of the other currencies was not yet exposed.

The third realignment

At the end of March 1981 the Italian authorities requested a 6% devaluation. As in the case of the Danish initiative, there was no urgent pressure on the lira, though the volume of intra-marginal interventions to sustain the Italian currency around the middle of the lower half of the wider band accorded to the lira was rising. Italy's request had to be seen as a defensive action to offset some of the wide and growing infla-tion differential above her EMS partners. Italy had found herself unable to check the inflationary impact of the second oil-price shock, due to a mixture of institutional factors—especially the exceptionally high degree of indexation in the labour market—and relatively expansionary fiscal and monetary policies, and was experiencing a sharp deterioration of her current account.

The request was granted informally, confirming the impression that central-rate adjustments in the EMS might be envisaged largely on the basis of unilateral decisions by the participants—with the caveat that the lira was a currency with a special status, underlined by the wider band. The real test remained whether other significant participants could count on a similar attitude.

That has been put to the test several times over the past three years. Following the presidential and parliamentary elections in France in May–June 1981, attention shifted entirely to the ability of the EMS to withstand the increasing divergence of policies and performance between her two largest members. After all, the earlier effort of joint European management of exchange rates, the 'snake', had twice been set back severely by failures of the Federal Republic and France to agree on policy co-ordination, or rather on the exchange-rate implications of not co-ordinating. France left the snake in January 1974 and March 1976; on both occasions because she was pursuing fiscal and monetary policies more expansionary than the FRG's and could, or would, not explore fully with the Federal Republic and the smaller participants the modalities of a comprehensive realignment. Was there any hope that such joint-management efforts would be pursued more successfully within a framework in which the new French government had no stake and was known to be seen as an undesirable constraint on domestic policies by a significant part of the new majority?

The answer on the basis of the first three years of this new phase, must be in the affirmative, though some qualifications have to be added. However, the dominance of Franco–German bilateral concerns have created new tensions, as the record of the four most recent realignments show.

The fourth realignment

The new French government chose not to request a devaluation in the EMS at an early stage, a decision that caused some subsequent soul-searching, as explained by President Mitterand and Finance Minister Delors much later. But in late September 1981 after four months of an unstable French franc, kept well within the EMS band by considerable interventions, a Franco-German compromise realignment was worked out. It involved the largest bilateral change yet seen in the EMS: 8.5% between the initiators.

When presented to the others at a meeting in early October, some objections were unavoidable, in particular from Italy. It had not asked for a devaluation and found unacceptable the Franco–German proposal that the lira follow the French franc in a 3% devaluation. In the end the Italian negotiators were persuaded to request the necessary authorization from Rome. The Netherlands was quite prepared to let her currency follow the DM in a 5.5% revaluation, but showed some resentment at being presented with a *fait accompli* by the two largest members, as did the other participants, for whom the realignment implied devaluations of about 2% in the intra-EMS effective rates.

The fifth realignment

The fifth realignment in February 1982 was interesting primarily as an illustration of the move away from unilateral and informal decisions. The initiative came from Belgium, who could refer both to more or less permanent pressure on her currency and to a manifest lack of competitiveness. Like Denmark in 1979, she argued that devaluation was a vital component in a package of stabilization through incomes policies, which looked like a major new policy departure. While these arguments were not unpersuasive, there was strong objection to the size of the devaluation requested—12%, far more than any previous EMS (or snake) realignment.

There were equally strong objections when Denmark unexpectedly also asked for a devaluation of sizeable proportions (7%). There had been no major pressure on the krone and the scope for improving competitiveness by domestic means were not seen to have been exhausted. The other participants, all concerned with their own competitiveness and rising unemployment, were, in short, only prepared to grant substantially smaller downward adjustments to the Belgian and Danish currencies. After a full day of bargaining a compromise was finally reached to devalue the franc by 8.5% and the krone by 3%.

This was a clear demonstration of the constraints which at least small members could expect to feel, if they had been under the impression that realignments could accommodate them without much difficulty.

A special problem arose for Belgium because of the existence of the Belgium–Luxembourg Economic Union (BLEU). In view of the lower inflation and stronger balance-of-payments outlook for Luxembourg, the authorities of the smaller partner country did not agree with the Belgian request for a large devaluation. However, they were only consulted just prior to the Belgian initiative to request a meeting of the Council of Ministers, and their views had no influence on the final outcome. But the process did make clear that future Belgian initiatives to devalue in any major way were likely to imply the breakup of the BLEU.

In the following months the familiar pattern of a strong DM (and guilder) and a French franc fluctuating in the lower half of the band reappeared. The fact that the bilateral rate between the two currencies had not been adjusted in February 1982, despite increasing divergence between the two economies, increased tension considerably and an increase of 3 percentage points in French money market rates relative to FRG and US rates made little impact on the exchange market.

The sixth realignment

As the franc drifted further towards the floor of the band a realignment was prepared in mid-June 1982, involving a revaluation of the DM and the guilder and a somewhat larger devaluation of the French franc. This brought the total bilateral change in central rates to 10%, the largest realignment so far between any two currencies in the EMS (or in the snake). The lira was also devalued, but by 3 percentage points less than the French franc. The two countries that had pressed for a large realignment in February—Belgium and Denmark—made no move to join in, although at least the Belgian franc continued to be in need of supportive interventions; nor did Ireland. For these three currencies the outcome was very close to *status quo*, in terms of their effective intra-EMS central rates as well. Since all of them rose inside the band following the realignment, their market exchange rates rose slightly.

The seventh realignment

The seventh and latest realignment of March 1983 followed the pattern of the preceding one, except that it was even more comprehensive and involved all participating currencies. The DM/FF adjustment was 8%, bringing the cumulative change in the single most important bilateral rate in the EMS close to 30% over an eighteen-month period. Yet most of the debate centred not on the size of the total adjustment, but on the more cosmetic issue of the composition of upward and downward adjustment. The FRG authorities apparently gave ground by accepting a 5.5% revaluation of the DM, leaving only a 2.5% devaluation for the FF. But these figures are misleading in the sense that they refer to the respective central rates *vis-à-vis* the ECU, and the value of that basket was affected for all currencies participating in the EMS exchange-rate mechanism by the recalculation of the central rate for the non-participating currency, sterling, before the new rates were announced.

Since the UK currency had depreciated considerably since the previous realignment, the ECU central rates of the other currencies were due for nearly 2% revaluation. In reality, therefore, there was less symmetry than appears between the upward and downward movements of the DM and FF. This made it possible for France to claim that the Federal Republic had conceded to being the main cause of tension and for the FRG to claim at the same time that both currencies had moved significantly. As on earlier occasions, there is no evidence that the breakdown between upward and downward adjustments had any relevance for the way in which EMS realignments affect the rates *vis-à-vis* third currencies. The DM remains the pivotal currency for these extra-EMS rates, and only the total size of the bilateral adjustments matters.

Other noteworthy features about the seventh realignment were:

— the separation of the guilder from the DM for the first time since September 1979. While the Dutch authorities had traditionally put great emphasis on strengthening the impression of the guilder as a close substitute for the DM, they allowed their currency to slip by 2% on this occasion. However, this modification of policy does not appear to have changed the close relationship between the currencies of the two lowest-inflation countries in the EMS, and Dutch short-term interest rates have continued to lie close to, though no longer below, comparable FRG ones.
— the Irish punt, long protected against a weakening of the overall competitiveness of Irish industry and by the heavy weight of a strong sterling, was finally devalued after sterling had fallen against the EMS currencies.

— Belgium and Denmark continued their policy of aiming for a stable position near the centre of gravity of the EMS, expressed by the ECU, whereas many observers had expected a resumption of earlier efforts to improve competitiveness through devaluation.

Some tentative conclusions

This brief outline justifies the following tentative conclusions:

(i) The size of realignments tended to grow over time within the first four-year period. The four most recent ones have all been in the 8 to 10% range for a number of bilateral rates, well above what had typically been experienced in the snake and over the first two years of the EMS. Furthermore, realignments have not become less frequent; apart from the sixteen-month break between the second and third realignments, the intervals have typically been six to nine months. Yet a firm conclusion may be premature in view of the extraordinary tension imposed on the system by the apparently temporary divergence in the thrust of French and West German macroeconomic policies over most of the first two years after the 1981 presidential elections in France. That tension subsided in the year following the seventh realignment, which has arguably been the calmest period in the five-year history of the EMS.

(ii) The joint element in decision-making has become increasingly visible without leading to a break-up of the system, as happened with the snake. It is public knowledge that some countries have at times come away from meetings with a different outcome from what they had requested and occasionally had begun to prepare their domestic opinion to expect. It is also evident that the precise shape of several realignments has been hammered out in difficult bargaining sessions among foreign ministers and central bank governors, though attention has sometimes focused on what is from a strictly economic viewpoint a side issue, namely the composition of upward and downward movements within a predetermined total realignment.

These observations demonstrate that the EMS has moved into the largely uncharted waters of discretionary collective management of exchange rates. The EMS has not developed into a permissive framework resembling the final stages of the Bretton Woods system, in which countries could modify their parities in a basically unilateral fashion. Nor has it developed into a crawling-peg system in which countries can count on objective criteria for adjusting parities, as was advocated by some observers at the launching of the EMS. It is *sui generis* in its reliance on the ability of the participants to agree on realignments acceptable to both the initiating country and its partners.

(iii) The total cumulative changes have been large, as indicated in the bottom line of Table 7.1. A system that over a period of four years accommodates a nearly one-fourth upward adjustment of the effective intra-EMS central rate for its strongest currency and a nearly one-fifth downward adjustment of its weakest currency can hardly be labelled rigid. But neither does it qualify the EMS as the decisive first step towards Economic and Monetary Union envisaged by some enthusiasts at the time of the EMS negotiations.

Changes in competitiveness

At this stage it is more revealing to ask whether the realignments have on the whole been furthering desirable changes in the competitive positions of the participants. Table 7.2 provides some of the background for an answer.

If one looks at the intra-EMS relationships, five of the seven participating countries have improved their competitiveness: two significantly (Belgium and Denmark), the other three marginally (Germany, France, and the Netherlands). The improvement is a bit larger in some countries (Benelux, the Federal Republic, and Denmark) when measured by relative unit labour costs than by relative prices expressed by GDP deflators, suggesting a small shift towards non-labour income in these countries. On the opposite side, the two highest-inflation countries (Ireland and Italy) have seen a significant deterioration in their competitive position, as has the United Kingdom which is included for reference despite sterling's absence from the EMS exchange-rate mechanism. At the same time all eight currencies listed have a more favourable (or less unfavourable) competitive position globally than within the EMS because of the large depreciation of the whole EMS band and of sterling *vis-à-vis* the dollar and the currencies linked to it.

On the whole this record cannot be regarded as unsatisfactory. The EMS was set up partly in response to the dollar depreciation of 1977-8, which seemed to undermine the long-run competitiveness of European industry. A major, indeed somewhat excessive, reversal of that situation has occurred as a result of the strengthening of the dollar in 1981-3. The global competitiveness of the EMS countries as a whole has improved by 10 to 15% over the 1979-83 period. The existence of the EMS has increased the cohesiveness of the European currencies, or at least made it possible to avoid a dramatic global realignment—and misalignment—blowing apart the intra-European exchange-rate structure, with very serious potential risks for the functioning of the Common Agricultural Policy and the integrated European market in industrial goods.

The EMS has also permitted a major improvement in competitiveness for two smaller members with particularly exposed external

TABLE 7.2

Changes in competitiveness in the EMS countries, 1979–83

(1979 = 100)

	Belgium	Denmark	FRG	France	Ireland	Italy	Nether-lands	EMS	UK
Relative unit labour costs									
globally[1]	77	82	85	90	104	115	87	90[2]	108
intra-EMS	83	89	93	99	117	132	93	..	121[3]
Gross domestic product deflator									
globally[1]	77	86	87	86	106	110	90	86[2]	110
intra-EMS	83	92	94	98	121	124	97	..	124[3]

[1] Against nineteen industrial countries.
[2] Against UK, Greece, and eleven other industrial countries.
[3] Against other EC countries.

Source: Commission of the European Communities, *Annual Economic Review 1983–84*, Brussels, November 1983, and Commission staff estimates.

positions (Belgium and Denmark), while the two highest-inflation countries (Ireland and Italy) have neither sought, nor been given full accommodation for their excess inflation. France is a borderline case, the cumulative effect of the three devaluations of 1981-3 corresponding roughly to French excess inflation; thus there may still be some doubt as to whether the rules of the system are applied in the same fashion to all participating currencies.

On balance, there is no indication in the experience of the first five years of the EMS that it is evolving into a permissive mechanism for keeping the competitive position of members within a narrow band regardless of their inflationary performance. Unless realignments are typically kept below what inflation differentials could be used to justify, the system cannot contribute to convergence. The EMS has contributed in this sense, though obviously in a modest way.

These are not negligible achievements in a period of major upheaval in the exchange markets marked by major and persistent overshooting of some individually floating rates beyond any sustainable long-term levels. The EMS experience contrasts favourably with the volatility and the cyclical swings which have marked the global system.

(iv) The main remaining concern is that the underlying convergence of the participating economies has been so weak as to require relatively large and frequent realignments. As Williamson[7] has persuasively argued, the Bretton Woods system broke down in the early 1970s because it could not handle the cumulated need for major changes in parities in a world of high capital mobility. Speculative pressures built up as such changes became increasingly predictable and speculators had little to lose except the temporary costs of financing their speculative positions. Is there any evidence that the EMS can survive better under the tensions which inevitably arise as realignments in the 8 to 10% range seem to become the norm? Changes of this magnitude open up possibilities for large gains, even if currencies switch positions in the EMS band following a realignment. To evaluate this important doubt about the future viability of the system it is necessary to look at monetary policy in the participating countries to determine whether the tensions inherent in membership of an adjustable-peg system have proved manageable.

II. The design of monetary policy in light of constraints imposed by membership in the EMS

One of the supposed benefits of the disappearance of the commitment to intervene in the exchange market, inherent in the Bretton Woods system, was the enlargement of domestic monetary autonomy. Some countries, notably the Federal Republic and the United Kingdom, saw the recapture of better control of domestic monetary conditions as the primary benefit. Given the experience of massive dollar interventions in 1970-3, these expectations were understandable.

Following the jump in inflation rates in that period and after the first oil-price shock it became clear that whatever monetary autonomy had been gained could not be used to pursue expansionary or even accommodating policies. Countries which took the latter road risked rapid depreciation and a long transition period to restore moderate inflation and inflationary expectations. All the major European countries therefore opted for the introduction of policies designed to create a stable longer-term monetary framework which could facilitate the anchoring of the longer-term price trend and inflationary expectations. Targets for one or more of the monetary aggregates were seen as suitable for this purpose, and the Federal Republic, France, Italy, and the United Kingdom all gave increasing emphasis to them over the mid-1970s in stating their aims and in implementing short-run policies.[8]

Initially this reorientation did not lead to conflicts with exchange-rate objectives. The French, Italian, and UK currencies were in principle floating individually and had no declared targets for their effective (or bilateral) rates. The DM was tied to the Benelux and Scandinavian currencies through the joint float or snake arrangements, but interventions in support of these weaker currencies were rarely large enough to upset the monetary targets substantially. They contributed to some overshooting in 1976 and again in 1978, but interventions in support of the dollar then were more important.

Targets for the monetary aggregates in the EMS countries

The external constraint changed significantly with the launching of the EMS. The potential intervention obligations of the Bundesbank widened as France and Italy entered into the system; the attainment of monetary targets was complicated in these countries as well. Monetary policy co-ordination and constraints may therefore conveniently be reviewed by looking at objectives and performance for the nationally-chosen monetary-aggregate target. Table 7.3 summarizes the record.

For the EC countries as a whole the growth rate of a broad monetary aggregate (M2/3) had decelerated slightly as intended, though the outcomes in most years have been in excess of objectives or forecasts. But if the UK figures are excluded, with the massive transgression of the £M3 target throughout 1979-81, compliance with the overall objective of moderate and decelerating money growth rates has been good, as have the national performances. The major exceptions here are the large overshooting in France in 1979 and in Italy in 1982. In Germany the target range for the chosen aggregate, the central-bank money stock, was undershot slightly over much of the initial two years,

TABLE 7.3

Main monetary targets, 1979-83

(annual percentage increase at year end)

	Main target	1979 A/O/F	1979 Result	1980 A/O/F	1980 Result	1981 A/O/F	1981 Result	1982 A/O/F	1982 Result	1983 A/O/F
Belgium	TDCE (F)	12	12.9	11	10.0	11.5	9.8	9.0	7.5	..
Denmark	M2H (A)	9	10.8	6	8.1	6.5	9.6	10.3	11.7	6.5
FRG	CBM (O)	6-9	6.3	5-8	4.9	4-7	3.5	4-7	6.0	4-7
France	M2 (O)	11	14.4	11	9.8	10	11.4	12.5-13.5	11.5	9.0
Ireland	PSCE (O)	18	19.3	13	20.9	15	15.6	14	10.4	11.0
Italy	TDCE (O)	18.5	18.4	17.5	18.6	16.0	18.2	15.5	20.8	18.2
Netherlands	DM2 (O)	8.5	10.7	7.5-8	7.8	6.5	2.9	..	5.5	..
UK[1]	£M3 (O)	7-11	13.9	7-11	18.0	6-10	13.8	8-12	9.9	7-11
EC total[2]	M2/3	11	12.3	10.5	11.3	9	10.5	10.5	10.8	10.0
EMS members	M2/3		12		9.2		9.4		10.6	9.8

Notes: TDCE: total domestic credit expansion; M2H: broad money, harmonized def.; CBM: central bank money; PSCE: domestic credit to private sector; DM2: money creation from domestic sources; £M3: sterling broad money; A: Assumption; O: objective; F: forecast.
[1] February to April of following year, at annual rate, except for 1979 figures which are June 1979–April 1980 at annual rate.
[2] Including Greece.
Sources: Commission of the EC, *Annual Economic Review,* 1979-80 to 1983-4.

the period of cyclical weakness in Germany's external accounts or, to
use the terminology of Dudler,[9] the 'period of grace' for the EMS.

Reconciliation of domestic and external objectives by the Bundesbank?

But possibly the most remarkable and surprising feature of the initial
five-year period in the EMS is that it has proved feasible throughout to
reconcile domestic and external objectives in the Federal Republic's
monetary policy. The Bundesbank had feared during the EMS negotiations that hard-won gains in domestic monetary management were
about to be sacrificed, but in fact there is no evidence that the Bundesbank's ability to meet its central-bank money target has been significantly impaired. This applies not only to the 'period of grace', but also
to the following three years in which the DM was strong in the EMS
band more often than not. Although there were fortunate circumstances
in this period which eased the potential conflict (notably when
DM strength in the EMS coincided with dollar appreciation, enabling
the Bundesbank to offset its EMS interventions by sales of dollars)
the ease with which the basic design of FRG monetary policy has been
preserved suggests that at least for the largest EMS country there need
be no conflict between a domestic monetary target and substantial
intervention commitments.

Two factors—beyond temporarily favourable circumstances—
may account for this complacent conclusion. The first is the technical
one of the definition of the Federal Republic's monetary target. The
central-bank money stock is confined to currency and required reserves
(at constant reserve requirements). It excludes excess reserves—
a buffer item on the balance sheet of the banking system, absorbing
a major part of the volatility due to external transactions. Hence the
Federal Republic's monetary target moves much more sluggishly when
the central bank intervenes in the exchange market than alternative
monetary targets such as the monetary base or broader aggregates
(M1 or M2). The Bundesbank does not have to sterilize the impact of
its interventions to maintain carefully the chosen monetary target
within its interval. [In fact, as studies by Obstfeld and Basevi and
Calzolari[10] (which cover only the period up to and including 1981)
suggest, the Bundesbank, like most other central banks, has traditionally
pursued a policy of partial sterilization as well, though with limited
effects, since sterilized interventions have had only a minor impact on
the $/DM exchange rate.]

The second factor is the obvious one that an exchange-rate system is
never symmetrical. The largest country has a greater freedom of action,
provided the other participants either adopt an external orientation of
their monetary policy to defend their exchange rate for the DM, or
modify that exchange rate before it has required very large interventions

in its defence. If either of these conditions is met, the conflict between domestic objectives and external commitments may be resolved for the largest country.

Increasing external orientation of monetary policy in other EMS countries

The main indication of an external orientation of monetary policy in the other EMS countries is the dominance of domestic credit targets over monetary targets in most of them. A domestic credit target implies that external contributions to money creation are not sterilized, but are allowed to exert their stabilizing impact. As shown in Table 7.3 five of the Federal Republic's EMS partners either have a domestic credit target or no aggregate target, implying that they want to keep a maximum of flexibility in the policy responses required to sustain the exchange-rate objective. Belgium and the Netherlands have recently moved in this direction, suspending the domestic credit targets they pursued in the first three years of the EMS; hence the absence of any quantitative target for 1983 in these two countries. Denmark is basically in a similar position, though it does retain objectives for components of domestic credit expansion. Ireland and Italy both rely on more or less comprehensive credit targets.

If these targets were set at a high level or typically overshot, reliance on credit rather than monetary targets would not have protected the Federal Republic against substantial inflows from her partners as their excess money creation leaked abroad. With some temporary exceptions of overshooting of credit targets in Ireland and Italy, compliance has generally been good. The main problem has been in the persistent high rate of credit creation in Italy, running close to 20% annually since the start of the EMS, mainly because of the large and growing public-sector deficit. While the Italian authorities have succeeded in bringing the monetary implications of this large deficit under much better control in recent years through aggressive sales of high-yielding government-debt instruments to absorb excess liquidity, very little progress has been made in containing the overall deficit and the snowballing impact on refinancing needs of growing public-sector indebtedness.[11]

Have monetary targets faded away?

The evidence from the first five years of the EMS does not indicate that the external constraint has made national monetary or credit targets more difficult, not to say impossible, to achieve with the desired degree of precision. This is true for the Federal Republic with her central-bank money target, for the EMS countries with a credit target, and even for France with a broad money target. While in the short run there will often be a conflict between an exchange-rate objective and a monetary (or credit) aggregate target rigidly pursued, the two may, over a medium-term horizon, be more likely to be mutually supportive, provided the domestic objective is selected carefully and with due regard to the external constraint. As they have evolved pragmatically, domestic targets in the EMS countries have not been made uncontrollable by the EMS. They have, intriguingly, proved more difficult to attain in the United States and the United Kingdom in recent years, despite the high degree of flexibility for dollar and sterling exchange rates.

The more critical attitude to monetary targets which has gained ground over the past one or two years in debates in the US and the UK may be explained to some extent by (i) the undesired side-effects on the exchange markets of the pursuit of domestic targets and of private agents' excessive concern over short-run departures from these targets, and (ii) technical issues of controlability.

But there are other reasons as well why monetary targetry is today under more severe criticism than some years ago: (iii) instability of velocity due to financial innovation and/or sensitivity to variations in interest rates and inflation rates; (iv) concern over apparently record-level real interest rates; and (v) perceived difficulties in controlling the long-term inflation rate solely or primarily through monetary targets. These considerations offer a convenient framework for commenting on the monetary experience of the EMS countries over the past five years.

After a period of considerable instability around a slow trend increase during the 1970s, the money-to-income ratio—the most obvious indicator of the degree of liquidity of an economy—stabilized remarkably during the first two years of the EMS in most of the participating countries. Over 1981-3, as recession deepened and monetary targets left increasing room for an expansion of demand, the growth rate of money was gradually allowed to rise above that of income. Excluding the United Kingdom, this build-up of liquidity was very gradual in 1981-2.

There was accordingly little in the experience of the first four years of the EMS to suggest that the erosion of the linkage between the money stock and nominal income had reached such a point that a broad monetary aggregate target had become inappropriate as the basic framework for a medium-term monetary strategy—rather the contrary. This is quite a different picture from that observed in the United States or the United Kingdom, where the relationship between money and income appears to have become distinctly more unstable in recent years—admittedly in conditions of sharper fluctuations of interest rates and inflation rates than in the EMS countries. It is even possible that the impression of greater stability would emerge more clearly, had a narrower monetary aggregate (M1) been chosen for the comparison with non-EMS countries.[12]

In short, the 1979-82 period may be viewed in retrospect as one in which the EMS countries had little difficulty in reconciling approximate observance of their domestic monetary or credit target with their EMS exchange-rate commitment. While few of these countries— primarily the Federal Republic and France—had a monetary aggregate target, in nearly all of them growth rates of money income and the broad money stock were parallel. But the recession dragged on, and fiscal policy was committed to a fairly restrictive stance in view of the initially large deficits. In these circumstances the ambition to provide a stimulus to activity through monetary policy gained ground in several countries and appeared at the Community level.[13] The basic idea was to shift attention from the monetary aggregates to money income as an intermediate policy objective. If money income were then to fall short of target because inflation and/or real growth was slower than expected when formulating the money or credit target, the latter should be allowed to accelerate. The reasoning was accordingly somewhat different from that expressed in the US and UK debate. In the two Anglo-Saxon countries the money/income ratio—or its inverse, velocity—had apparently become so unstable that the danger of monetary policy becoming unintentionally restrictive was also becoming widely perceived among policy-makers. Indeed, the observed increase in the money/income ratio (or decline in velocity) in 1981-2 in the United States was a major reason behind the Federal Reserve's decision to suspend its main monetary target (M1) in October 1982 and allow temporary faster growth in the monetary aggregates for some time thereafter.

The monetary authorities in several European countries moved in a similar direction in 1983, though usually without formally endorsing the view that the past strategy based on money or credit aggregates was in the process of being modified significantly. In moving cautiously the authorities were no doubt motivated both by their wish to retain credibility in the longer run (a suspension of monetary targets might be difficult to reverse and could rekindle inflationary fears) and by the risk that the apparent removal of a domestic reinforcement could complicate the management of their exchange rates inside the EMS and add to the already large depreciation *vis-à-vis* the dollar.

As the Bundesbank allowed the growth rate of the central-bank money stock to rise substantially above the upper limit of the 4 to 7% interval announced for 1983, the monetary authorities of the other EMS countries were encouraged to relax their cautious attitude. Thus the monetary aggregates began to accelerate in several countries in early 1983. Belgium and the Netherlands set no money or credit target for

1983 (see Table 7.3) and these two countries, along with Denmark, allowed money creation from domestic sources to rise considerably faster than originally projected. More modest accelerations were observed in some other EMS countries. Due to the continued weakness of the DM and the somewhat parallel nature of the monetary expansion, the change in strategy has not led to any major pressure on intra-EMS exchange rates. But it has contributed to the further depreciation of the whole EMS band *vis-à-vis* the dollar, 10 to 12% of which occurred between the March 1983 alignment and the end of the year.

TABLE 7.4
Changes in the money/income ratio (% p.a.)[1]

	1970–80 average	1979	1980	1981	1982	1983
Belgium	1.2	1.3	−3.6	1.2	0.8	0.3
Denmark	−0.5	−1.5	1.7	−5.1	−2.9	6.6
FRG	1.5	1.1	−1.0	2.0	2.7	3.5
France	1.5	−0.4	−1.1	−0.2	−3.0	−0.4
Ireland	−0.3	11.5	−2.2	1.4	−4.0	2.5
Italy	1.9	1.1	−4.5	−0.2	−0.3	2.1
Netherlands	0.5	−1.5	1.6	−0.1	3.6	4.4
UK	−1.7	−3.6	−1.7	6.5	1.8	2.9
EC total	1.0	0.3	−0.5	3.0	1.5	3.4

[1] Definition of money is M2 for Belgium, Denmark, France, and the Netherlands; M3 for the Federal Republic, Ireland, and Italy; private-sector liquidity for the United Kingdom. Income is measured as Gross Domestic Product.
Source: Commission of the European Communities, *Annual Economic Review 1983–84*, pp. 125–7.

Any definitive interpretation of the 1983 rise in the money/income ratio in several EMS countries is premature. No doubt it reflects to some extent an adjustment to lower nominal interest rates and inflation, which makes it less costly to hold liquid assets. But it is also a disequilibrium situation which will tend to eliminate itself by pushing up spending and income. Monetary policy in the EMS countries appears to have been more than just accommodating; it has encouraged expansion. This is often overlooked by those observers who focus primarily on real interest rates (i.e. nominal rates deflated by recent measured inflation) because these rates suggest that the stance of monetary policy has remained tight. It is surprising, on the basis of historical experience, that 'real' interest rates have not fallen further in the face of apparent slack in the economies of Western Europe and the rise in liquidity. But this observation should not hide the fact that the monetary authorities of the EMS countries have taken some risks in allowing their past target-oriented policies to be relaxed.

Monetary policy and government deficits

There is a further possible rationalization of the *de facto* suspension of targetry which has become increasingly visible in the EMS countries in 1983; namely the difficulty of controlling the long-term inflation rate by monetary policy alone. At a time of unprecedentedly large public-sector deficits a natural initial reaction is to contain their impact on money creation with its attendant risk of depreciation and inflation by insisting on debt financing, reducing monetary financing to the small share which will typically be consistent with existing monetary targets. But if the deficit persists and comes to be regarded as having a large structural component, a high share of bond financing can only be maintained at rising interest rates which add to the deficit. (Sales of debt to foreigners may not help either, because they are likely to demand an increasing risk premium; and sales to foreigners do not reduce liquidity.) At the same time the maturity of government debt will normally have to decline, creating difficult refinancing problems and constraining monetary policy further. Gradually the perception will spread in the market that the government will be forced to resort to either monetary financing with the associated unavoidable inflation or forced conversion schemes for government debt holders. These speculations will in turn generate switches out of bonds into financial alternatives or goods, hence advancing the pick-up of the inflationary process. It may be possible, when faced with such an acute policy dilemma, to actually delay inflation by allowing the share of monetary financing to rise. This type of reasoning, profoundly disturbing to those who have seen tight control of money creation as a sufficient insurance against an upsurge in inflation, has been advanced in the United States,[14] where the projected Federal government deficits over the medium term are only about half the size of those in several EMS countries. It also appears to have played some role in the design of monetary policy in the EMS countries with the largest deficits such as Italy and Denmark, where the portfolio balance of the private sector was becoming severely lop-sided through the absorption of public debt.

The EMS as a framework for concerted monetary expansion?

Whatever the primary rationale for permitting the monetary aggregates to rise above the upper end of their target ranges—to offset declining velocity, to reduce real interest rates, or to avoid an eventually crushing reliance on debt financing of public-sector deficits—an important further consideration in the more expansionary twist to monetary policy has been the existence of a reasonably stable exchange-rate framework in the form of the EMS. Individually floating countries would have found it more risky to accelerate monetary growth, even if they had known that their main trading partners were acting similarly. The intervention obligations in the EMS have given a greater sense of security in a process of joint expansion.

Since the realignment of March 1983 the EMS has provided a more comfortable framework for monetary expansion than conceivable alternative arrangements. The Federal Republic has contributed by having adjusted sufficiently to make any early further realignment unlikely and by allowing or encouraging a rapid rise in the central-bank money stock. These policies have implied a relatively weak DM near the centre of the EMS band and substantial further depreciation *vis-à-vis* the dollar—of the order of 10 to 12% in the first ten months after the realignment. In contrast to events in early 1981, when the Bundesbank tightened policy sharply to stem the rise in the dollar, there has been no effort to respond to US policies. This in turn has made possible the acceleration in money and credit aggregates and some moderate decline in interest rates. It is implausible that the weaker EMS participants could have taken the calculated risk of this concerted expansion without anchoring their currencies to those of their partners and to the DM in particular. The recent experience may therefore be regarded as a counter-example to the thesis often advanced by critics of the EMS, namely that the system was likely to develop a deflationary bias in putting an asymmetrical part of the external adjustment on the weaker countries. The relevant worry in the recent phase would appear to lie in the opposite direction.

Conclusions

A review of the seven EMS realignments in 1979–83 suggests four tentative conclusions:

(i) Adjustments have become larger and not less infrequent; this creates a risk of destabilizing capital movements, as the scope for speculative gains is perceived to be substantial.

(ii) The joint element in decision-making has become more visible after some initial aberrations, making realignments more complicated than in the Bretton Woods system but also more satisfactory from a systemic point of view.

(iii) The realignments cannot be summarized in a simple, schematic model such as the preservation of competitive positions (a PPP-rule). Some countries in severe structural deficit on current account have been permitted to improve their competitiveness, while the highest-inflation countries have been given less than full accommodation.

(iv) These achievements appear to be broadly satisfactory, given the volatility and overshooting of the individually floating currencies over the initial four-year period.

As regards domestic monetary policy, compliance with targets for monetary aggregates was generally good prior to late 1982. There is little evidence in support of the view that EMS membership has made the chosen aggregates less controllable or less closely linked to nominal income. Using a standardized measure of velocity, the money/income ratio appears to have been more stable since the start of the EMS than in the 1971-9 period. In this light the proposal to move to a money-income target instead of a monetary-aggregate target is unwarranted, but also less radical than implied by its proponents.

Monetary policies in 1983 have been more expansionary and mark a new departure for the EMS countries. They illustrate that the system, far from having a necessarily deflationary bias, may also be used as a framework for concerted expansion. It remains to be seen whether this collective assumption of new risks will pay off through a resumption of economic growth rather than a resumption of inflation.

Acknowledgements

The author is grateful for critical comments made at the inaugural conference of the Centre for European Policy Studies by the two discussants, Dr A. Wellink of Nederlandsche Bank and Dr L. Tsoukalis of St Antony's College, Oxford, and by Lars Kolte of Demark's National Bank, and at a seminar given at the Federal Reserve Board, Washington DC, in March 1983.

Notes and sources

[1] *The Economist*, 20 November 1982.

[2] For a much fuller discussion, see Rudiger Dornbusch, 'Equilibrium and Disequilibrium Exchange Rates', *Zeitschrift für Wirtschafts- und Sozialwissenschaften*, No. 6, 1982.

[3] A suggestive analysis along these lines may be found in John Taylor, 'Policy Choice and Economic Structure, *Occasional Papers*, No. 9, Group of Thirty, New York, 1982. Indexation mechanisms which preserve real-wage rigidity are the most important single such determinant. The higher the degree of indexation, the harder it becomes to achieve lower output variability by accepting higher inflation variability.

[4] See, for example, Niels Thygesen, 'The Emerging European Monetary System: Precursors, First Steps and Policy Options', in Robert Triffin, 'EMS: The Emerging European Monetary System', *Bulletin de la Banque Nationale de Belgique*, Brussels, April 1979.

[5] Obviously a more significant issue for adjustment is how market effective exchange rates moved as a result of the central-rate realignment. The five currencies that did not move formally still devalued by 0.5 to 1% in effective

intra-EMS terms as the DM revalued. The bottom line in Table 7.1 cumulates the
impact of all seven EMS realignments on effective intra-EMS exchange rates.

[6] Paul de Grauwe, 'Symptoms of an Overvalued Currency: The Case of the
Belgian Franc', in Marcello de Cecco (ed.), *International Economic Adjustment:
Small Countries and the European Monetary System*, Oxford, 1983.

[7] John Williamson, *The Failure of World Monetary Reform*, London, 1977.

[8] For a detailed review, see *OECD, Monetary Targets and Inflation Control*,
Monetary Studies Series, Paris, 1979; and John E. Wadsworth and F. Leonard de
Juvigny, *New Approaches to Monetary Policy*, SUERF 1977 Colloquium, Alphen
ann den Rijn, 1979.

[9] H.-J. Dudler, Chapter 6 in this volume.

[10] Maurice Obstfeld, 'Exchange Rates, Inflation and the Sterilization Problem:
Germany 1975–1981' (with comments by H. Bockelman and J. A. Frankel), *Euro-
pean Economic Review*, March/April 1983; and Giorgio Basevi and Michele
Calzolari, 'Monetary Authorities' Reaction Function in a Model of Exchange
Rate Determination for the European Monetary System', in Paul de Grauwe and
Theo Peeters (eds.), *Exchange Rates in Multicountry Econometric Models*, Mac-
millan, London, 1983.

[11] Rainer S. Masera, Chapter 5 in this volume.

[12] A recent study suggests that narrower money and credit aggregates have
out-performed broad money in terms of closeness of relationship to nominal
income in three of the main European countries, cf. Geoffrey E. J. Dennis,
'Monetary Aggregates and Economic Activity: Evidence from Five Industrial
Countries', *BIS Economic Papers*, No. 7, Bank for International Settlements,
Basle, 1983.

[13] See notably Commission of the EC, *Annual Economic Review, 1982–83*,
Brussels. The suggestions of the Commission staff are briefly considered in
Rudiger Dornbusch *et al., Macroeconomic Prospects and Policies for the Euro-
pean Community*, CEPS Papers No. 1, Centre for European Policy Studies,
Brussels, April 1983.

[14] See notably Thomas V. Sargent and Neil Wallace, 'Some Unpleasant
Monetarist Arithmetic', *Federal Reserve Bank of Minneapolis Quarterly Review*,
Fall 1981.

Additional sources

Artis, Michael J., 'From Monetary to Exchange-Rate Targets (with a comment by
    R. Dornbusch), *Banca Nazionale del Lavoro Quarterly Review*, Rome,
    September 1981.
Padoa-Schioppa, Tommaso, 'Rules and Institutions in the Government of Multi-
    country Economies', in Loukas Tsoukalis (ed.), *The Political Economy of
    International Money*, Oxford, 1984.
Ungerer, Horst, *et al.*, 'The European Monetary System: The Experience, 1979–
    82, *IMF Occasional Paper*, No. 19, International Monetary Fund, Washing-
    ton D.C., 1983.
van Ypersele, Jacques and Koeune, Jean-Claude, *The European Monetary System*,
    European Perspectives, Commission of the European Communities, Brussels,
    1983.